~ SOVEREIGNTY ~

Searching for Faith in Treacherous Times

~ SOVEREIGNTY ~

Searching for Faith in Treacherous Times

All content reflects writers' tenants of faith and personal convictions. All information should be taken as an encouragement to seek God for your own faith and should not be misconstrued for legal advice. The contents of this book are informational in nature. Further, the author and publisher are not engaged in the provision of legal advice.

Foreword by Cathryn Rose Robbins, "my Baruch"

As we look back on your life, it has not been a Hollywood rags to riches story. It's been better, it's been a Love Story. The Love of a Father and His Daughter. And what a Love story it is. It has discovery, challenges, witchcraft, betrayal, power, demons, Glory, sleepless nights, Fallen Council, 2nd Heaven, The Garden, success, lots of faith building, humility, school, travel, supernatural, prophecy, pain, sorrow, death, loneliness, shape shifters, marriage, divorce, children, relationships, friendships, courtships, dreams, visions, on and on and Most Important, A Relationship with The Creator of the Universe. The Audible and Ever Sensing Voice of God and His Presence for 34 years of your life.

If it could be a Hollywood movie, it would be a Blockbuster.

Well, this First Book, about God's Sovereignty, is about to make headlines. I mean really, the God, the very God, the mighty God, the infinite (impossible to measure or calculate) God, the one true living God, will be seen in and through this book! He will have His way. He will be heard. The kingdom of darkness will Not Prevail. The Words in this Book will Break Like a Hammer the darkness off of the Captives. Father, we want this Book to Explode on the scene and into the Hearts and Minds of The People! Making the way for the Volumes of Books You have Been Preparing Your Daughter to Write. This is to be just the beginning. The beginning of new life for Your Daughter and the culminating end of captivity for Your Creation.

You have worked very diligently and tirelessly to get this publication out through all the warfare and getting your health back to restoration; you are relentless.

My Forever Friend and Mentor; Thank you for your choices in life that gave me examples of how to be whole. Your examples of kindness to all walks of people. Your example of patience toward me while working against strongholds. Your Purity, Truth, Giving, Counseling, Hope, Long suffering with others. Your consistency,

Your strength, Your Integrity, Your friendship and Your shaking the dust off your feet.

You have changed my life; actually, you have saved my life. I ask how can I ever repay you; but I know you would say… Repent, Obey, Forgive, Serve the Living God with all my heart, soul, mind and strength. Yes, I agree. I love You my Friend, I am God's 'Baruch for His Jeremiah' of these times.

It really is the Supernatural from here on out. Get ready for the Awe. Get Ready for the Signs, Wonders and Miracles, Get Ready for the darkness to fall, Get Ready for His Return! What a Loving and Powerful God we serve.

"Daughter, these are those times that I have been telling you about"

*"At that time Michael, the great prince who stands watch over your people, will rise up. There will be a time of distress, **the likes of which will not have occurred from the beginning of nations until that time**. But at that time your people—**everyone whose name is found written in the book—will be delivered.***

But you, Daniel, shut up these words and seal the book until the time of the end.
*Many will roam to and fro, and **knowledge will increase**.*

*It will be for a time, and times, and half a time. When the **power of the holy people has finally been shattered**, all these things will be completed.*

*Go on your way, Daniel," he replied, "for the words are closed up and sealed **until the time of the end**.*

*Many will be purified, made spotless, and refined, but the wicked will continue to act wickedly. **None of the wicked will understand, but the wise will understand."***
Daniel 12

"Take Heed How You Hear"
Mark 4:24 and Luke 8:18

"It's Everything I say... and Nothing You Think About What I Say"

BOOK DEDICATION

This book is dedicated to **YHVH, YAHUWAH,** the aim of my devotion and dedication to obedience, my Heavenly Father and for the glory of His Son, my Savior, Yahushua.

It is written humbly by His Servant for His Prized Bride, His Church, His Remnant, His Sons and His Daughters, whom He has passionate and unfailing love for.

It is further written for His Leaders. That they will consider. That they will return to their first love. That they will give up anything they have put before Him and learn His conviction by His Spirit again. That you have once heard God is not an excuse. So did Eli. But God raised up Samuel in his stead.

For you all, that you will hear the sound of His Voice. That you will repent from any and all idols of your heart and life, *anything* you put before God. *Anything* and *everything* that stands in His way of reaching you to hear Him.

ACKNOWLEDGEMENTS

First, acknowledging my God, who even brought me this far to make it to the writing of this book. Thank you.

Secondly, to Cathy Robbins, a woman after God's own heart, who spent countless hours listening to me, going through with me, my dark night of the soul, in deep pain and suffering, praying with me and for me and taking endless hours of notes and being patient with me. I humbly thank you.

To Crystal Cleek, a powerful warrioress and intercessor, through whom you could hear the sound of the victory battle cry in the midst of the tribulation. Thank you for never giving up and for always believing God over all else.

Both of these women stood with me, ready at all hours of the day or night for prayer, intercession, any and all alms deeds that they could possibly do, without wavering, standing with and for me for over 10 years.

Without both of you, I would not be here today, to answer His call and mandate, to put in to writing what is on the Lord's heart and mind for His people.

And I cannot and will not ever forget, Crystals husband, Clayton Cleek, who put my life above his own. A man willing to risk all that he had out of love for God. And willing to take a risk, to find His covenant with Yahuwah. I humbly, thank you.

Thank you all, for all that you have done. For your examples of love, humility and service to the Lord. May the Lord repay you for all that you have done for me. I love you all.

*Disclosures to be considered by the Reader

*Enclosed in the pages of this book, you will find notes from personal writings, written at the time of the date recorded. The words and information are prophetic. Some have not yet come to pass. Some have by now, but still others to be unveiled, revealed or manifested.

*From 2014-2016, I was still in a type of cognitive dissonance, if you will, so I would hear the Lord speak to me we would write down what He was saying, but I still was not in full belief. I had to repent of that, as I did over the years. Some information coming from God is just hard to digest.

*The Name of Jesus is written in His given Name, *Yahushua* (deriving from YHVH). Which is a Hebrew Name. Not Greek and not English. You will find more written about this in the book.

*Consideration for the reader: God has instructed me not to take sides politically. In this book you will hear God's view on the matter. Not mine, unless stated. God is not a republican or a democrat. He has a much better and different view than we do.

*If you want to know the ways of God, you must know the Word of God, the Logos and the Rhema. That is to say, the Written Word of the Bible and then to hear God by His Spirit. The two should synchronize. They should bear witness to one another. That is the reason why, in this book, you will see whole scripture, not sound bites of scripture or opinions of man, but the Word of God in this book. This is in order to truly know God and His intention.

*Sometimes I leave the intercession (prayers, conversation, correspondence and interventions) in so that it is taken in context. But the amount of intercessions and conversations with God would require volumes of books written.

*Some Words, Visions, Dreams that I receive from the Lord come to pass faster than others. However, we are in the midst of them now and they will continue to come to pass. If not, by all means, throw the book away, listen to the other prophets who say sweet things to you and I will repent, be happy and keep my day job.

*Visionaries don't always see like everybody else. They are very visual. My gift sees graphically, yet sometimes in non-descript ways. When the prophets of old wrote, they did not always know exactly what they were seeing. We know in part, we prophesy in part. It is God who gives understanding in His time.

*Keep dates in mind when reading.

*The gaps of time are during personal times away or personal Words from the Lord.

*What is written comes from my personal notes or were written by my Baruch (secretary) from the words I spoke. Before 2016 or so, I did not know that any of it would be made public, so, please understand that I am making it the best I can in writing a narrative, in making it palatable for the reader without changing the integrity of what the Lord was saying or His intention. Some things were omitted as they did not have to do with this book or they were personal.

* I did purpose to leave some personal words in, as I know the Lord would like to and is raising up others who will dare to write and to speak what they hear. It is for a witness for them and to encourage them that they can trust God to go further with Him.

*Some things are repeated as the Lord does often when He speaks. In the Bible, if there are more than 2 or 3 mentions, it is Hebrew thought, that it is important to pay attention to. It is for a witness (Matthew 18:16, 2 Corinthians 13:1, 1 Timothy 5:19).
*Throughout this book you will find many "keys". If you pay attention closely, you will find them and be able to use them in your own life to overcome and get to the next level that God has called you to. Or you will be able to see them as a witness in your own life.

*I have been hearing the Lord speak since 1987. Never once did He start using the word, "trump" until 2011. Then it became a theme in His speaking to me. By 2015, He had revealed to me, as you will read, that Donald Trump would be elected President of the United States. There is a caveat on this word that the Lord chose to use, as you will see. It is connected to Sovereignty.

*This is my first published publication, though I have many others. However, I have not written much since the dark night of the soul. I ask in advance for leniency as well as consideration. As this is a work of obedience to Yahuwah.

*Fonts: Italicized font is used when it is either the Written or Spoken Words of Yahuwah or Yahushua. *The Italicized Words in Black are the Written Word of God from the Bible.* *The Italicized Words in Blue are the prophetic Words that I, the writer hear personally from the Lord.* The regular blue font is the mind of the Lord, without hearing the words. *Of course, in Red, they are the Words of the Messiah from the Bible.*

*Special – Other italics, bold or underlined is for emphasis by writer.

*Lastly, I personally edited this book no less than eight times and had friends check it as well. That said, this is my very first self published book. So, if you see editing errors that is the reason why. The information, which is most important in this case, is intact.

*The Writers personal Convictions and Understandings to be taken into consideration when interpreting or understanding

*All Scripture is taken from *all* Translations of the Bible. The Writer is especially drawn to the Berean Study Bible in this Book.

*Interpretation of Scripture taken from the Greek or the Hebrew.

*Interpretation of other Words, taken from multiple dictionary's.

*When something is important, God will repeat it. Hebrew Idiom holds, when something is said in two's or in three's, it means that it is God and to pay attention (Matthew 18:16 and 2 Corinthians 13:1).

*Keep in consideration that there is a time, a purpose and a reason for all things with God. If something does not make sense to you, it is wise to wait on God for a witness from Him and/or for interpretation. There are things in this life that we do not know and are still learning. Especially when it comes to Spiritual things from the Kingdom of Heaven. If you will be patient and prayerful through this book, taking new thoughts and ideas into consideration, allowing the Lord to show you what is for you to know.

Even the Watchers (Fallen Angels) who were first here, were reprimanded by God for telling Heaven's secrets to the people, but God also revealing that the Fallen ones did not know all the secrets of heaven. Only God knows everything. And that should be our #1 lesson in life!

 One of my first trainings with the Lord to hear Him, was to be quiet and not give my own ideas or opinions, but just to hear Him. He told me if I wanted to speak for Him, I had to leave my own ideas and opinions out.

*I truly had trouble not knowing where to put chapters as these entries are in order of date. I have another book started where all revelation is under subject matter. But, this is the format that the Lord has chosen for this book.

*There are also entries where I have written to the reader throughout the book in the journal entries. But none of the Words of God, the revelations or times have been changed. Only certain words to make it palatable or flow better for the reader.

I challenge you to read this book, cover to cover. Especially, if you feel offended at any point. If you believe something different, very strongly, be courageous and let these written words challenge your beliefs.

If your beliefs are valid, they can stand the test of any other theories that do not fit your own. I urge you to consider what I am saying to you prayerfully. After all, God is the only One with all the knowledge, understanding and Truth. By all means, investigate what I say. I can stand to be brought into the light. The end goal is to come to the knowledge of the truth, so you can make appropriate decisions and not miss the end result of your faith, which is to truly know God and spent eternity with Him. You have nothing to lose, only more insight to gain by reading all the way through.

"Consider the things I am saying,
for the Lord will give you understanding
in all things"
2 Timothy 2:7

AUTHORS PRAYER FOR THE READER

That at the trial of your faith, being much more precious than of gold, which perishes, though it be tested and tried by fire, that it be found to result in the praise, honor and glory at the revelation of Yahushua the Christ, the Savior of all whom believe in Him.

That your eyes be opened to the One true living God, YHVH (YAHUWAH) over all and above all and His providential Truth. That your heart and your mind be prepared to read and consider the words of this book. And in consideration, your understanding be enlightened, that you may know the hope to which He has called you to and be prepared in His presence.

May God grant you mercy and grace to acknowledge Him in all you do. And may He grant you the great gift of truly knowing and walking with Him daily, in all of your ways until you see Him face to face.

"It is the mark of an educated mind, to be able to entertain a thought without accepting it"
Aristotle

~ SOVEREIGNTY ~
Searching for Faith in Treacherous Times

CONTENTS

INTRODUCTION

I would like to take the time to introduce myself, but really, I wrote this book at the last minute, while I was working on another work the Lord gave me to do. This book was actually to be first, as I started writing it in 2014, but honestly, I did not have the faith I felt I needed to write it. As God would have it, in the midst of obeying God to write another book, He emboldened and encouraged me to finish this work that you have now before you. I have faith that I will be able to elaborate and to speak publically more about these things in this book, but for now, as the Lord instructs me, I must get to the point.

The main purpose of this book is about His "**Sovereignty**". A subject that most people today do not know the real meaning of. If I were to break it down into plain terms, I would have you read the book of Job for a short lesson on the subject. The real meaning will come with more clarity through reading this book. Succinctly, the word Sovereignty means: Supremacy, Dominion, Power, Jurisdiction, Ascendancy.

In Chapter 1, you will find the defining of God's Sovereignty, the way He showed it to me during My Dark Night of the Soul.

For a brief introduction about me, I will start with, that I was radically saved in 1986, God called me to ministry in 1987. I had a great life and liked the way it was going, but God made it clear that He wanted to show me two things: 1. His Power and 2. His Love. Those two things have been the theme of our relationship and my public work.

As radically as I was saved (and spending much time alone with the Lord) were the functioning of the gifts and the callings of God through me. Many Ministers began to recognize my calling and I was put into and taken through various schools and trainings.

But the Lords personal, One on one training, equipped me for His calling more than any traditional school I went to. Three

Ministry schools, many Ministries, raising up many different works, many roles within those works. But, the beginning and the end of it all, is my relationship with God, the One who called me. And in knowing Him, was the reading and study of His Word and hearing the Word of the Living God daily. As you will see through this book, my life became a living intercession. To seek God and to hear God day and night, was and is my daily life.

I have lived a life of obedience to God for 34 years, no matter what He has had me doing (or not doing that I would have preferred to be doing). Either way, it had me face to face with HIM. Not that I was perfected or did everything perfectly. But this one thing I have always sought after, that my heart is always perfect before Him.

As pertains to this book, God chose me to experience **"The Dark Night of the Soul",** A.K.A. His **Sovereignty,** from 2009 – 2019. While this book is not about my personal Dark Night of the Soul, it is about the Work that God had me to do through listening to Him during this time.

The volumes of experience and the plethora of teachings and writings that have all come from enduring His Sovereignty for those 10 years are immense however, for this cause He has chosen me to write about only certain subjects that He wants me to address, in this book.

I have had many gifts and many callings in life, but the two that the Lord left to function during the **Dark Night of the Soul** were, the ability to hear Him (which without, I would have physically died because the enormous natural and spiritual state of perplexity, that I had no answers for and neither did anyone else that I knew around me) were much to pressure to live through. And He left me the gift of wisdom; by these two gifts, I was able to function still as a counselor and an Intercessor, for the Lord and for others. As well as have my business in Commercial and Residential Real Estate Investment and Management.

The only way I made it through this time was to be in

continual prayer, talking to God day and night. And I had two intercessors that never left my side during that time. And one of them became my note taker (I call her my Baruch), which without, most of these notes would have never been recorded.

It's was no small task getting me to this place of writing. The enemy had oppressed and opposed me for many years on this subject and directly, anything that had to do with creating or expressing what the Lord was saying. Much of my giftings during this time, were extremely oppressed, opposed or were shut down all together.

Numerous times, I thought of Paul saying, *"For we wanted to come to you, indeed I, Paul, tried again and again—but Satan obstructed us"* 1 Thessalonians 2:18. Prior to my dark night, I resisted this scripture. I could not understand how this could happen to Paul! I always thought, "Come hell or high water, I will make Satan bow to my authority in Christ!" I really didn't consider anything else. I did not yet know what God was about to teach me. We just cannot know what we do not know, until it is revealed to us experientially. The Hebrew word for 'know', "yada" carries a Hebrew thought, which is interpreted, "an intimate or experienced knowledge of".

This Spring, there was a quiet calm. My hearing God regarding America and God's people in the way that I had heard Him all the years prior, slowly decreased. It was then, that the Lord spoke to me saying to write this book and to write it just like He spoke it to me.

There are many revelations contained in this book that I cannot take time to explain at this time. Additionally, this book is not about dreams, visions, revelations, gifts, callings or prophecies. This is a book about the Words of God regarding His Sovereignty and about The Dark Night of the Soul. It contains Words that He wants revealed to His Leaders, to His people and to those who will listen to Him, to *know* Him intimately.

For the sake of time and subject matter, I am limiting some

information. I was in the process of writing a book, mandated by Yahuwah. In the midst of writing that book, that is when I was provoked to get the notes together from a book that I started in 2014 to current, to provide information that God wants for you to know.

To 'whom so ever will hear'. To God's people first, His remnant and to and those whom He is calling and will hear His voice in this day of Salvation. As is His heart and mine, evangelistic:

*"**Today**, if you hear His voice, **do not** harden your hearts,*
as you did in the rebellion,
in the day of testing in the wilderness,
where your fathers tested and tried Me,
and for forty years saw My works.
Therefore I was angry with that generation,

and I said, 'Their hearts are always going astray,
*and they have **not known My ways**.'*
So I swore on oath in My anger,
*'They shall **never** enter My rest.'"*

*"See to it, brothers, that **none of you** has a **wicked heart of unbelief***
that turns away from the living God.
*But exhort one another daily, as long as it is called **today**,*
*so that **none of you** may be **hardened by sin's deceitfulness**.*
*We have come to share in Christ, **if** we hold firmly to the end*
the assurance we had at first.

As it has been said:
"Today, if you hear His voice,
do not harden your hearts,
as you did in the rebellion."

For who were the ones who heard and rebelled?
Were they not all those Moses led out of Egypt?
And with whom was God angry for forty years? Was it not with those
who sinned, whose bodies fell in the wilderness?

*And to whom did He swear that they would never enter His rest? Was it not to those who **disobeyed** (Did not do what they heard by faith)?*

*So, we see that it was **because of their unbelief*** (proven by their disobedience) *that they were **unable to enter**."*
Hebrew 3:12-19

Some of the Words that I receive from the Lord are seemingly cryptic, until they are unveiled. Some have already come into being and some have yet to be revealed, to come into being. True servants of YAHUWah will be given parts of the puzzle in order to help others. We are all a part of the whole picture.

There will be a time that I will be able to teach about many of these things that have been revealed. For some of you, what I write on these pages, you are already there. Others are on the precipice. And others, well, it may just make you mad. But keep reading. If you are mature enough in the Lord, you will not only be able to handle it, you will be able to take it to God and test what I say. But if you get angry and throw down the book, that reveals your nature, not mine or Gods.

Throughout this book, I am exposing the enemy's battle tactics (though it would take many books to teach what I have learned in spiritual warfare and in intercession). Otherwise most of what is written, is revelation with the prophetic Word when spoken. All of it is for learning. God has revealed it for our learning and applying His Word in our lives, so that the enemies of our God and our soul do not take us captive at their will.

For many, this book will contend with all of the things you thought you knew. For others, it will mess with their idea of God or their own theology of what they think is in God's Word. I know that there will be those that rise against me and/or the words of this Book. I understand. I came out from where you are at. The Spirit of the Lord bears witness to who I am and my battle wounds speak to all that I have gone through and have overcome. I don't need permission from any man. I serve the living God.

If you do not like some or all of what is written here, to me it makes no difference. I am obedient to God. It is not my business whether you like it or not. It is only my business to listen to God and do and say what He instructs.

The rest is up to you and between you and God. While God is glorified through my obedience, I do hope though at least, that I either inspire or provoke you.

Let me present to you, that if this book does not fit your theology, at least consider and look in the Word of God yourself. God's way of thinking does not fit anyone's way of normal thinking on the earth that I know. Pray and seek the Lord for yourself. The Word of God instructs us to test the Word. That said, the Word's of a prophet can only be tested by other (true and tested) prophets. Don't believe everything you hear from me or from others. Know that information can come from anywhere, but God's wisdom is only found by those who seek for it with their whole heart. It takes time to think like God does.

Some people who are Religious, Christian or Political will be offended at what is contained in this book. Actually, anyone who is not hearing God has the liability to be offended. I won't apologize. Keep reading. Sometimes the Lord has to offend our head to get to our hearts. He does not mind that you are wrong. He already knows that. He wants to make you right. Not as in right-fighting, but as in His right-eousness.

Consider what I say and the Lord give you His understanding. If you can hear, His Words are contingent, based on the mutual agreement of His Covenant:

Yahushua said, *"The kingdom of heaven is like treasure **hidden** in a field. When a man found it, **he hid it again**, and in his joy he went and **sold all he had** and bought that field"* Matthew 13:44.

Wisdom proclaims:

*"**If you** incline your ear to wisdom and **direct** your **heart**
to understanding, if you truly **call out to insight**
and **lift your voice to understanding,**
if you seek it like silver
and search it out like hidden treasure,
then you will discern the fear of the LORD
and **discover**
the knowledge of God."*
Proverbs 2:2-5

And God told the weeping prophet:

*"You will seek Me and find Me **when you** seek Me
with all your heart."*
Jeremiah 29:13

Early on, in learning God and His Ways, it struck me that
people really didn't read their Bibles. I thought, *how can they ever*
know Him then? And that people really weren't taking time to pray,
unless they were in peril, needing something from God or it
pertained to someone they knew that was in desperate need.

In listening, I could hear that their prayers were more of a
past tense hope, instead of a powerful antidote for change from
heaven. That they did not take scripture as if it were meant for today.
It occurred to me, they really don't know what they are doing and
even more, do they want to know? I saw that this was one of the
reasons, that their love had grown cold, like the Bible says.

"And because lawlessness (an increase of sin and wickedness
and a separation from God by it) *will be increased*
and the love of many (toward God and others) *will grow cold*
(spiritual energy blighted or chilled by a malign
or poisonous wind).*"*
Matthew 24:12

To my dismay, I further discovered, that Christians could quote Bible verses of Promise separately (without knowing the intent of the passage in which the promise was given) but they would overlook His instruction. It appears there are very very many books and a lot of promotion over the promises of God. While very few people know that the promises of God are attached to His Covenant agreement (which has instructions for living). The same Covenant that each believer agreed to, in order to have God's Holy Spirit come to live within them.

You may be thinking, "Didn't Jesus die for everyone and now we can do what we want because we are free? What do you mean the instructions and Covenant Agreement? Let me clarify in case no one has told you: the promises of God to you, are NOT valid *without you keeping your part of the agreement*. God's faithfulness is to His Word. If you keep hoping and believing without staying in Covenant agreement with God, you hope and believe in vain. His Bible is not magic. It's Law. Magical sayings, such as: "Once saved, always saved", "We're all sinners saved by grace", will not stand up in God's righteous Court. Look, God loves you and wants for you to know. If you are confused, keep reading.

On the other hand, if you don't want to, you don't have to. That's the liberty of the freedom of choice that God gave to all mankind. Just tell God you made a mistake regarding this Covenant thing, that the relationship should be one sided only and that you only want His benefits. But know this:

"When you make a vow to God, do not delay to fulfill it.
He has no pleasure in fools; fulfill your vow. It is better not to make
a vow than to make one and not fulfill it.

Do not let your mouth lead you into sin. And do not protest
to the temple messenger, "My vow was a mistake."
Why should God be angry at what you say and destroy
the work of your hands? Much dreaming and many words are
meaningless. Therefore fear God"
Ecclesiastes 5:4-7

The whole entire big deal of God sending His Son for us, was for Him to find His true Sons and Daughters (those who will conform to His image), draw them to Himself and bring them home. If you just want the promise and the benefits, without a covenant relationship, just make it easier on yourself and tell the truth. Or repent. Either one. The good news is, God already knows. The bad news is, so does the devil.

> *'He* (Yahushua) *replied, "The knowledge of the mysteries of the kingdom of heaven has been given to you*
> (those that follow the lamb wherever He goes and does what He says)*, but not to them* (those that do not follow Him, nor do what He says).*"'* Matthew 13:11

You can argue if you want, but **faith has proof** (James 2:18-20). And we can go around in circles about your feelings and how much you "feel you love God". As well as we can go around in circles about how much you feel you hate your neighbor and all of the reasons why.

But love is not a feeling. It's a choice and an action. God's Word is true and every person is a liar, as it is written (Romans 3:4). God gave us emotions to benefit us. For us to be in tune with Him and with others. Not "feelings" to lord over us. He gave to us dominion to rule our lives by. Our feelings are not supposed to undermine Him, His Word, others or our own self.

There's only one way to get right with God and that is through the great gift He has given to us of repentance. This was Yahushua's first message to us, a theme throughout the entire Bible and His last message to us.

Honestly, if you love your Bible so much, dust off the leather bound idol and actually read and keep the words written therein. Then God will approve your faith.

The purpose for this book is, God wants for you to know the

Truth and to not be confused about Him, about what is happening in America, in the world today, and in the Church, as well as to you personally.

Though His Words to me regarding Sovereignty, America (some other Countries) and God's people had started early on, **now they are in full effect. We have entered into God's Sovereignty. The Dark night of the Soul. The Time of the End** (of the World as we know it) **as** Daniel and Matthew described it.

I may lose handfuls of you after each revelation. I hope that I don't. But if you will take time to research what I say; Basically, I'm asking you to read your Bible, to take the time to consider carefully as you read and then do more research from there. But every Word God speaks you will find backed up in His Word and confirmed by His Holy Spirit. NOT in sound bites of doctrine (where you can make each scripture make it mean what *you* want for it to mean in order to fit your life), but in the actual original written whole intention of His Word. Not leaning to your own understanding in what you think is truth or right, but asking Him for His Truth and understanding (Proverbs 3:5 and 2 Peter 1:19-21).

"We also have the word of the prophets as confirmed beyond doubt.
And you will do well to pay attention to it,
as to a lamp shining in a dark place, until the day dawns
and the morning star rises in your hearts.

Above all, you must understand that no prophecy
of Scripture comes from one's own interpretation.

For no such prophecy was ever brought forth
by the will of man, but men spoke from God
as they were carried along by the Holy Spirit."

I strongly encourage you to pray before reading further. Repent of believing lies and accepting errors in your life (it's a good daily practice to see clearly). Ask the Lord to bear witness and bring conviction of His Truth to you. I can help you to begin, by telling you to lay down other mind-sets that are in the way and ask God for His Mind.

Do you want the false security of all that you have been taught and believed? Or do you want to know *if* what you have embraced as truth is a lie? The truth of your intention will be revealed in what you do. And will be exposed on judgment day before the Father and everyone else. When He separates His sheep from the goats.

May God prepare His mercy and demonstrate His grace as you open your mind, ears and heart to the Truth of His Word, to prepare you for what is to come. And remember, the first time Messiah came to the earth, He said, *"Take heed how you hear"* (Luke 8:18). Yes and Amen, may we do so.

There's a saying that has circulated the Churches for years. It has it's variations, but it goes something like this: "When the people are happy and celebrating, the prophets are crying. But when the people are sad and lamenting, the prophets rejoice". At first it can sound rather indistinct. The Servant of God's job when it comes to the people, is to make sure they hear God's Word and lead them to Him.

It has further been said, "when the people do not know what to do, God sends a teacher. When the people know what to do, but does not do it, God sends a prophet".

It is now that time. It is up to you whether you want to be taught or you want to be corrected by the Lord. Either way, His Sovereignty is here for it. And if you're looking for where to run, His grace (for enabling you to overcome) will be found in your obedience to Him. There is not one place you can go that He does not know.

At any rate, the Books are now being opened and revelations are being poured out to God's servants. Now is the time that He has warned us of - Daniel 12:9, Revelation 22:10.

"Sometimes people hold a core belief that is very strong.

When they are presented with evidence that works against that belief, the new evidence cannot be accepted.

It would create a feeling that is extremely uncomfortable, called cognitive dissonance.

And because it is so important to protect the core belief, they will rationalize, ignore and even deny anything that doesn't fit in with the core belief."
— Frantz Fanon

****

Our core beliefs manifest in a variety of thoughts and actions, such as: traditions, politics, religion, biases, prejudices, etc. Our thoughts are shaped throughout our childhood and into our adult years by our experiences, our leaders and our peers.

But *if we know* God, He commands to His people, in His Word:

"Do not be conformed
(identified *with,* assuming a similar *outward* form or expression
by following the same *pattern* model, mold) *to this age*
(an age, era, time-span, characterized by a specific quality,
type of existence),
but be transformed
(changing form in keeping with inner reality,
transformed after being with God; transfigured)
by the renewing
(completing a process, which makes fresh,
a new development; a renewal, achieved by God's power)
of the mind,
(the God-given capacity of each person to think, to reason; mental capacity
to exercise reflective thinking. For the believer, the organ of receiving
God's thoughts, through faith)
for you to prove

(to approve by testing, is done to demonstrate what is good,
i.e. passes the necessary test. It does *not* focus on disproving something,
i.e. to show it is bad)
what is the good and well-pleasing and perfect
(mature, consummated from going through the necessary stages
to reach the end-goal, i.e. developed into a consummating completion
by fulfilling the necessary process*)*
will
(a desire, a wish, often referring to God's "preferred-will," i.e.
His "best-offer" to people, which can be accepted or rejected)
of God."
Romans 12:2

CHAPTER 1

THE PROOF OF PROPHECY IS LOSS

God spoke to me years before saying,

"Daughter, It's Everything I Say;
and Nothing you Think About What I Say."

I thought here would be a good place to start. After all, this chapter is about the Title of the Book in part. And it is the single greatest thing you can know if you want to see God face to face.

For those who walk closely with God, it will help you to understand the method of the Lord through this allotted time. For those that may be confused during this dis-order of chaos (or if you know those whose lives are in utter disarray, where normally their lives are in order), it will help you to consider accepting, that God is a Sovereign God. He does not owe you anything. Not even an explanation. He is waiting for you to see things differently. To see things His Way. Why? Because the entire earth *does not know Him* the way He wants them to know Him.

Consider, the whole reason for creating the entire earth and the Garden in it (Genesis 3), was for Relationship. Further, the entire reason for sending His Son, our Salvation to us, was to restore the Relationship back to Him, because it got off track. Well, here we are again. This is the dilemma. That people do not know Him like He wants for them to know Him: In Spirit and in Truth. This is the whole reason He sent His Son, who said this:

"But a time is coming and has now come
when the true worshipers will worship the Father
in spirit and in truth, for the Father is seeking such as these
to worship Him.

God is Spirit, and His worshipers must worship Him
in spirit and in truth."

John 4:23-24

Even if you have esteemed your life perfect or at least pretty good, before God, consider Job: *"There was a man in the land of Uz whose name was Job. And this man was blameless and upright, fearing God and shunning evil"* Job 1:1.

*"See how blessed we consider those who have **persevered.** You have heard of **Job's perseverance** and have seen the outcome from the Lord. The Lord is full of compassion and mercy"* James 5:11.

Yahushua also said, *"I have told you these things so that in Me you may have peace. In the world you will have tribulation. But take courage; I have overcome the world!"* John 16:33.

For greater understanding, if you have not read Job, I suggest you do for even more clarity on the subject. If you have read the book of Job, this may help open your understanding to what the moral of the story is actually about.

Think carefully about what is written here. Your accepting, disregard or rejecting will either help you through the times we are now in or make it harder.

There is a chapter on this. However, it is the theme of this book and it will help to let it sink in. This is the revelation of the Lord to me during my dark night of the soul.

20 CHARACTERISTICS OF SOVEREIGNTY

1. **You Cannot Change SOVEREIGNTY.**

2. **SOVEREIGNTY wipes out your past level of life or experience as you know it.** (i.e. Job, Joseph, David all went through it and came out different on the other side, according to the will and plan of God). It is a total game changer.

3. **SOVEREIGNTY costs a person greater than what they have sufficiency to pay.** Job 13:15 "Though He slay me, yet will I serve Him." Reigning & suffering are synonymous. 2 Timothy 2:12 says, "If we suffer, we shall also reign with *Him*: if we deny *Him*, He also will deny us". Moses, Joseph, David - Their suffering was not for anything they did wrong. **God allows hardship or evil for a greater plan.**

4. **SOVEREIGNTY is for a specific work.** Is it an ordained structure over a person, place or thing, to change everything around it.

5. **SOVEREIGNTY guarantees Satan's arrival.**

6. **SOVEREIGNTY *does not* have to tell you anything.** It rules. You don't.

7. **SOVEREIGNTY seems very dark.**

8. **SOVEREIGNTY seems like a separation from GOD.**

9. **SOVEREIGNTY is lonely.** No one really understands unless they have been through the same things. No one else can do this with you. It's proof of separation from everything and everyone else. Chosen. Sanctified for God's cause and purpose.

10. **SOVEREIGNTY requires you to watch out and pay attention**. Your whole life is being turned upside down and inside out.

11. **SOVEREIGNTY is aligned to a specific cause** (God's trump card).

12. **SOVEREIGNTY will change the course of History *if* you** don't fight it.

13. I hear the Lord say, *"SOVEREIGNTY will shake man to*

their very core. It will set the course of action to bring to divine order."

14. **SOVEREIGNTY looks like chaos.**

15. **SOVEREIGNTY will highly offend you** to the point of turning from God, if you let it.

16. **During SOVEREIGNTY, you understand nothing**.

17. **SOVEREIGNTY sets apart for great change**.

18. **SOVEREIGNTY will change your point of view**, but first it will confuse you, because it will not fit in the small box you have put God in. God is Infinite. You are finite.

19. **During SOVEREIGNTY you will not understand your life.**

20. **Allowing the work of SOVEREIGNTY is trusting God without knowing what it looks like through it.**

You may think that you are no one God would pay attention to, so all of this does not apply to you. But have you read the Bible? If not, you are not qualified to make a decision on these things. And if you have read the Bible and know the stories of all the great heroes of faith, that still does not equip you or make you ready for such things, but at least you have a heads up. *"So then, it does not depend on man's desire or effort, but on God's mercy"* Romans 9:16. Every single thing in life is by or allowed by, the will of God. That is sovereignty.

Reigning (or having true Authority from God) and suffering are synonymous with God. Moses, Joseph, David, Yahushua. Their **suffering was not for anything they did wrong.** God *allows* evil for a greater plan. Further, He promises to turn everything into good for those that love Him (continue with Him) through the process (Romans 8:28).

If you are going through a dark night of the soul, be encouraged, there is a cause from Heaven that God knows, Satan knows and you are going to find out. But first, it will bring you to an ultimate surrender (that feels like annihilation) beyond anything you could have ever realized existed.

If you feel abandoned, stranded, beaten, down trodden, hurt, abused, slandered, betrayed (and even less understand how you got there, much less understanding anything else), know that there is a resurrection and a restoration. But, your life won't be the same as it was before. That is Sovereignty's outcome. On purpose.

Know that the calling on this level is Proof of SOVEREIGNTY. The proof of not only going through it, but then coming under God's power in a whole new way, as someone that has been set apart by Him for a special purpose. By the time Sovereignty has it's way in your life, you won't have to guess if you've ever been through it. It has a special seal of time and longevity that you just can't miss. During sovereignty you can't know God's trump card.

GOD'S RIGHTEOUS JUDGMENT IS NOT A BAD THING

Before God taught me about Sovereignty through experience, He taught me first about His righteous judgment. Many people think that the God of the Old Testament is a mean God, not One of Mercy. But the opposite is true. I contemplate the extraordinary and supernatural work that God had to do, to get His fore-ordained Word (prophecy) about the Messiah (mentioned first in Genesis 3 in the Garden, the seed of the woman to crush the head of the enemy), all the whole 4000 years long, of His rebellious people that were always in danger of the enemy wiping them out before Messiah ever got here! If you've ever seen the historical tribal flow charts and kept it in mind while reading the scriptures, you would have a better understanding of God's righteous judgments and His reasons why.

His righteous judgments are a discipline. God chastens (brings correction to) those whom He loves.

"In your struggle against sin, you have not yet resisted
to the point of shedding your blood.
You have forgotten the exhortation that addresses you as sons:

"My son, do not take lightly the discipline of the Lord,
and do not lose heart when He rebukes you.
For the Lord disciplines the one He loves,
*and He chastises (*God sending severe pain in the
best *eternal interests* of the believer*) every son He*
receives.

Endure suffering as discipline; God is treating you as sons.
For what son is not disciplined by his father?
If you do not experience discipline like everyone else,
then you are illegitimate children and not true sons."
Hebrews 12:4-8

Father is home! Daddy is in the House! To those that fear (highly respect) Him, that is pretty scary. And this verse is taken from the New Testament, for those who like to make distinction of the Old and the New.

Actually, there are Seven Covenants and what we call the "New Testament" is literally, the Seventh Covenant that God has made with His people, through accepting the Messiah. If you are unaware of this, it's just another very important detail that has been left out of the church's teachings. There is a real big reason that the Old Testament is still there and not just the New one. There have been many books removed from the Bible, as well as the changing of the Messiah's Name, Yahushua. God is able to get through to those who are seeking the Truth. Even if we only had a grain of Truth left to find, He would make sure we found it, in order to know Him, as He has first known us (Romans 8:29).

Back to my point about judgment. God remains the same. He

does not change (Numbers 23:19, Psalm 55:19, 1 Samuel 15: 29, Malachi 3:6, James 1:17, Romans 11:29). But He requires change from us (Psalm 7:12, Jeremiah 5:3, 7:5, 15:7, Matthew 21:32, Hebrews 13:8, Revelation 9:20, 16:9). That's why the discipline. The righteous judgment. God has taught me that His judgment it is like putting a period at the end of a sentence. Or like this: *Enough! That's it! Game over!* Like when all of our own shenanigans have come to an end.

Paul wrote: *"Now, if we judged ourselves properly,
we would not come under* (God's) *judgment."*
1 Corinthians 11:31

~ and ~

*"... Let God be true, though every one (else is) a liar, as it is written,
"That you may be justified in your words, and prevail when you are
judged."* Romans 3:4

The Psalmist writes: *"Righteous are You, O LORD, and upright are
Your judgments."*
Psalm 119:137

~ and ~

*"Against you and you alone, have I sinned;
I have done what is evil in your sight.
You will be proved right in what you say and your judgment
against me is just."*
Psalm 51:4

Isaiah said: *"In the night I search for you; in the morning I earnestly
seek you.
For only when you come to judge the earth will people learn what is
right."*
Isaiah 26:9

~ and lastly ~

Ezekiel writes: *'This is what the Sovereign LORD says: "'I am against you, Sidon, and among you I will display my glory.*
You will know that I am the LORD,
when I inflict punishment on you and within you am proved to be holy." Ezekiel 28:22

So judgment is a part of God's Character and His Nature. Just as Mercy, Truth and Salvation are. God could not be Sovereign without Judgment. King Soloman wrote:

"Now all has been heard; here is the conclusion of the matter:
Fear God and keep his commandments,
for this is the duty of all mankind."
Ecclesiastes 12:13

At this point, we should either say, "Selah" (Stop and calmly think of that). Or "Amen" (I agree. God's will be done).

CHAPTER 2

SEEING THROUGH A DARK GLASS DIMLY

You will find that I keep it short throughout the Chapters before 2010, the main idea is in points that are important to the building up of the faith I was to receive, to be able to hear and to accept what was to come.

Early in my relationship with God, as I started to hear Him clearly. It was then that the Lord asked me to speak for Him. He took me from a "Modern American business mindset" and instead, sat me down to train me with a Kingdom of Heaven business mindset.

1986 – 1993

IN THE BEGINNING the Lord would have me spend up to 18 hours a day with Him in hearing, learning and equipping. When the Church doors were not open, I would spend time worshiping the Lord, reading His Word and learning to hear Him speak. It was then, that He began to give me dreams and visions as well and speak to me through Scripture.

Though I read the entire Bible all the time, the Books that He had me focusing on more at that time, was Matthew, Jeremiah, Daniel, Thessalonians and Revelation.

All 66 Books of the Bible are extremely important and I read and had revelation in them all. However, these five books played a key part in my learning and in my training in the years to come, about all that He had foretold in His Written and Prophetic Words (both logos and rhema).

The main points God was instructing me to learn during this time were:

1. America will see it's Zenith and it's fall during my life time.

2. That Anti-Christ Spirit will come to the forefront during my life time.

3. The Church believes that they will be delivered *during* the time of Tribulation; but they err not knowing the Scriptures.

4. That Christian Coalition was inserted early to *influence* the Christian Community to vote all Republican.

5. That there will be another Spirit that is ruling in mainstream Christianity and Christians will barely recognize the Lord that they profess to know. The danger of that, is in falling under the power of the Anti-Christ spirit, who professes to lead you to God but, it is not the God of the Bible.

6. In the midst of the false, that God would raise others up those (myself among them) to sound the alarm to His people.

Over the years, I have had many prophecies from various Pastors, Prophets, Apostles and Servants of the Lord. I have worked for God since 1987. And that's when all the prophetic Words over my life began. I have had ministries I've raised up over the years and many people were with me......until, He separated me through His Sovereignty.

During this designated time, I had to endure without much help in ministry, in business, in my personal life, in every area. My life became slowly, drastically different, than what I had known before. I did not speak of these things I experienced, except to the intercessors that God gave to me or a couple of others close that were to me. And even then, it was in part. No one could know the depths that God was taking me to and through, both naturally and spiritually. I had to depend on Him for absolutely every breath that I took. I was too overwhelmed, with no understanding. No one else I knew or had known was going through any of these things to my knowledge. I had no one to confide in and I was extremely depressed.

However, from 2010 – 2020, the Lord brought to me a secretary. Much as Jeremiah had, my own personal "Baruch", to record what I heard, saw and did. While not everything the Lord has given me is in here, as some is very personal and due to other various complexities, it is enough of the Words of Yahuwah to tell the story and to get the picture for the times we are in and for the times to come.

In the Fall of 2018, the Lord woke me early one morning and said to me, *"Go tell My people".* That very morning He gave to me a Word for the leaders and they continued monthly after that. And so, slowly emerging from this darkness, I have begun to share. This book is only the beginning of a fraction of the tip of the iceberg.

This book will be written in a journal format and in bullet points for brevity and clarity. I have many other books in the works that will reveal more detail of the things spoken of in this book.

Most of the points have the actual dates the Lord was speaking or revealing. Some do not, but it is narrowed down to the same month.

I will be brief in the beginning years and write enough to acclimate you to the reason and the purpose of this book.

Before we move on, I have a question for you to ponder…

THE VALUE OF OFFENSE

What is the assessment of offense to you? What do I mean "the assessment or, *value of, offense*"? Yes, offense has worth and our God uses it all of the time in our lives. He does it in order to get our attention. And at times, to show us our base nature. The parts of us that we have not let God cleanse and deliver from our old nature.

How you react or respond to offense in your life will direct the course of your life, whether you realize it or not. Your decisions, whether knowingly or unknowingly, will create your next action and ultimately set your path.

Do you disregard or deny offense? Conversely, do you argue with it (them) or get mad at it (them)? Maybe a little of both depending on the situation? Either way, you are a participator.

The sin of Omission is as great as the sin of Commission with God. What you do not do, as well as what you do.

The larger question is, what is the cost you will have to pay for *keeping your offense*? The Son of the living God taught us to 'take heed how we hear'. Why? So that you can make appropriate decisions based on truth. Not settling on the lies or stories we tell ourselves, deceiving ourselves in order to 'feel better'. Everything we shove under the carpet, is not out of sight, out of mind. One (or many) will eventually stumble over it.

You will find in this life (and in this book) that God is willing to offend you in order to save you from yourself. That you have an opinion is nothing to God. He is all knowing. Why would your opinion, the thing that causes offense, or you holding your offense be anything to God? Only for one reason, love. Why not find out how wrong you are, to have the opportunity to be made right and altogether quit offending and taking offense?

God places a huge value on choice. The truth is heavy and weighty. Especially in the times we live in currently. People would rather deny it to escape it or argue with it, out of fear or justification. So they have learned to protect themselves by becoming tough or hard hearted. But, it was never meant to be that way. And with God, it certainly does not have to be that way, if we will learn to seek Him and trust Him.

As you read, take these passages into consideration:

*"Blessed is he who is **not** offended because of Me"* Matthew 11:6

*"Great peace have they which love your law: and **nothing shall offend them**"* Psalm 119:165

Both of the words "offended" and "offense" here are also tied to the word, "stumble".

Keeping an offense is a violation with God. He wants (actually commands) for us to deal with the things that offend us, hurt us or make us mad.

*"Therefore each of you **must** put off falsehood and speak truthfully to his neighbor, for we are all members of one another.*

*"Be angry, yet **do not** sin." **Do not** let the sun set upon your anger, and* (in so doing) ***do not** give the devil a foothold."*
Ephesians 4:25-27

All of this said, offense serves a purpose. We can keep it and let it make us prideful. Or we can deal with and face what is offending us and God, (by keeping it) and let it create the humility that is beauty with God.

****

*"Humble yourselves before the Lord,
and he will lift you up in honor"*
James 4:10

."God opposes the proud but shows favor to the humble"
James 4:6b

"He leads the humble in doing right, teaching them his way"
Psalm 25:9

"For those who exalt themselves will be humbled,

and those who humble themselves will be exalted"
Matthew 23:12

*"If my people, who are called by my name, will humble themselves
and pray and seek my face and turn from their wicked ways,
then I will hear from heaven, and I will forgive their sin
and will heal their land"*
2 Chronicles 7:14

*"Finally, all of you, be like-minded, be sympathetic,
love one another, be compassionate and humble"*
1 Peter 3:8

Humility is a fruit of the Holy Spirit that God gave to us when His Spirit came to dwell within. If you don't want it, you may not have God's Spirit residing in you, as it is an **absolute part of God's nature.**

I have broken down the Greek meaning of the Word Humility here for your contemplation:

Greek - *tapeinophrosýnē* ("lowliness, humility") is an inside-out virtue produced by comparing ourselves *to the Lord* (rather than to others). This brings behavior into alignment with this inner revelation to keep one from being *self-exalting* (self-determining, self-inflated). For the believer, *tapeinophrosýnē* ("humility") means living in *complete dependence on the Lord*, i.e. **with no reliance on** *self* **(the flesh).**

CHAPTER 3

GOD, WHAT ARE YOU THINKING?

1986-1989

In 1989, the Lord said to me, *"Daughter, I want for you to open your mouth and speak."* I fell to my knees and pleaded with Him. I told Him I was afraid to do so in the way that He had spoken to me that I would through the prophets. It wasn't that I had fear *to speak* His Word, I only had fear *in case I did it wrong* and led someone in a wrong direction. I stayed there, crying and praying, trying to come up with some way to have tangible faith and in a way that I would never offend God.

As I pleaded, I said, "I never want to be deceived Lord! I never want to deceive another person! I mean, what if I am ever wrong?" At which time, I heard Him say, *"Daughter, **if** your heart is right with Me, **I will always** deliver you."*

At that moment, I felt such a relief! His Words allowed my faith to rise up and I was able with caution, to begin speaking to others on His behalf. I noted He did not say to me that I would never be wrong. Only God is infallible. However, He promised He would deliver me from any deception. My part is to stay pure in heart with Him. As I keep my part, He will keep His part. He is faithful to His Word. It's His Will. In the meantime, I do work on being brought to perfection, in maturity of the work He has called me to do. And to represent Him the way that He has ordained.

He is so kind to accommodate us and help us when we ask. I have, so very many times over the years, gone to Him to grow my faith level when He speaks. He taught me to covenant with Him on His Word, in order to make it to the "other side". He is the One that always can, when we can't. His covenant with us, will help us if we are in agreement with Him.

GOD'S OBSESSION WITH SOULS

I have often said, that if God had an obsession, it would be souls. In my experience, everything He speaks about is in regard to them.

His Church, Souls of Mankind and America. Those three things are continually on Gods mind. To write about all of these things would be a significant volume of books. But regarding this book, He spoke to me about America and gave to me many, many Dreams – too many to count, about a broken and desperate America, rising up in smoke, on fire, people hiding. Natural disasters, injustices, heartless. Not an America that we have known or are familiar with. His desire is to prepare His people.

It was the 1980's and my life was great. It always had been. I was a super positive person and I loved life. Now, the God who saved me by His great power and love was showing me such violence and destruction of the Country I loved. Also showing me that people would *drastically* change. It was very difficult to take it all in. Especially, since my persona, my gifting and calling around the people of God was so positive. I carried a positive message. And I liked that! This other, seeing obscured truth that seemed so negative, in the face of everything having been so wonderful, was another discernment He had to prepare me to train me in.

I often say, delineating that time, that it was the time that God took me from being a super "positive" person, to be a "realist". Between getting experienced in ministry, helping people and hearing God about what is real and true and what is not what I would like for it to be, I was living in an awakening. I won't say a rude awakening….not quite yet at least.

I think also, coming from such a 'positive' place in life, I was naïve to what was truly evil. I genuinely thought that every person had good in them and they just needed to know the Truth in order for them to want change. So naïve. But the Lord had a remedy for that too, by throwing me into the deep end of situations that I had to cry out to Him and learn spiritual warfare to survive it. He taught *"my hands to war and my fingers to fight"* (Psalm 144:1) and as David said, *"with your help I can advance against a troop and leap over a wall" (*Psalm 18:29). I learned the power of agreement with God and with others, *"Two putting ten thousand to flight"* (Deuteronomy 32:30) and having all power and authority over the enemy, nothing by any means shall harm me (Luke 10:19).

I look back at that time and think how easy everything was in the spirit and in the natural to deal with. Back in those days it was, attack the enemy and ask God questions later! As one prophet spoke by the Lord to me, "The Lord says, *that you rush in where Angels fear to tread".* Hearing that made me feel happy and yet scared all at once. So, I embarked on a journey for more much needed wisdom.

1993

Divisions through Spirits

By this time, I had gone to every Church meeting I could, had been involved in evangelistic teams, women's ministry, counseling team, theology schools, deliverance ministry teams.....you name it. I volunteered to help with the children's department, the babies department, cleaning the church kitchen and bathrooms, secretarial help, etc. If they needed help, I was the volunteer. I've been a helper and a leader in every department of the church. Or as God calls it, a servant.

The Lord, by His work in me and through the Church Leaders, made my calling clear. Through testing me as His servant in all things, He was forming me to speak on His behalf. At seven years in, I raised up a ministry school by the Word and Will of God.

Though this book is not about me or all that I do or have done, only to give a glimpse of building from the foundation. An idea of the radical-ness of the calling He called me with, the very school that I raised up, the curriculum of the first two courses was called, "Heart Detox" and "Idols of the Heart".

In my training, as God taught me to speak for Him, one must be pure. Not having their own opinions, ideas or agenda. That is the difference between the false and the true. That said, there is not one on the earth that is perfect. And there is no person that speaks on God's behalf, that is 100% accurate, as they are human and are subject to being finite. God is infinite. And He is the only One 100% accurate all of the time. Falseness isn't as much in being inaccurate, as it is in mis-representing God's Character. Even devils can tell the truth. Nevertheless, if one is being raised up to speak, they should practice their aim to hit their target.

To be formed in His image, to be found in His likeness, we should practice His Truth. Until it is made permanent in and through us. Because Yahushua said, *"Be perfect as your Heavenly Father is Perfect"* (Matthew 5:48). And to undergird His Words and encourage the process, the writers of the Bible continued by writing Romans 12:2, 1 Corinthians 1:10, 14:20, Colossians 4:12, Philippians 3:15, 1 Peter 5:10, James 1:4.

So, back to the story! This is the year that the Lord began to speak that *"Seductions would be rampant on the earth"*. He didn't mean sexual only. He meant anything that would draw us away from Him. *"Spirits of Seduction."*

The Lord had been showing me many falling away from Him and drawn away of their own lusts and desires.

*"But each one is tempted when by his own evil desires he is lured away and enticed. Then after desire has conceived, it gives birth to sin; and sin, when it is full-grown, gives birth to death.
Do not be deceived, my beloved brothers".*
James1:14-16

And others being deceived, but it was because of the things that they believed or were led to believe in their life. Or things they entertained as thoughts. And the lie was never exposed as a lie. The seductions would latch on to whatever untruth or lie that was inside a person to draw their heart away from the Lord. Unwittingly, not even knowing. But other things (affairs of this life, idols of the heart, false pride) would begin to take up residence in their hearts and minds. All the while, they do not notice, their love growing cold.

1998

The Call to be Ready for what is Already the Door

Vision: One day, I was sitting on my couch in prayer and I looked up to see an open vision (a vision with my eyes open); an enormous spider was at my front door. It was the size of a small animal. In the vision, I got up to start trying to kill this huge spider with a rolled up newspaper. I was spending so much energy on making sure it was dead, that when I suddenly looked up from what I was doing, there stood a most intimidating, humongous brown bear blocking the entire door way.

In the vision and in shock, I heard the Lord warn, *"Do not spend all of your energy on the small things, as there are larger things at the door"*.

Relieved it was only an open vision, with my heart pounding, I was taking in the Words that I heard God speak. Don't focus on and wear ourselves out over the small things, because we will need our energy for what is ahead. Something much worse is coming and we need to be ready.

I do believe regarding this particular vision, that the Lord was introducing to me the significance of Russia's appearance in the things of America. Though at that time, I was not as politically aware as the Lord was going to have me be.

1999

"This is the new covenant I will make with my people on that day, says the LORD: I will put my laws in their hearts, and I will write them on their minds."
Hebrews 10:16

Law. The Lord spoke to me saying, *"Daughter, I will exalt My* (the) *Law in the last days"*.

While this Word perplexed me for years, I hid it in my heart until the Lord decided He wanted to talk about it again. And He did. But it was many years later.

God's Word has a way of conveying what needs to be said plainly through His Written Word. So, I will make it plain here:

*If we **deliberately go on sinning after** we have **received the knowledge of the truth**, no further sacrifice for sins remains, but only a fearful expectation of judgment and of raging fire that will consume all adversaries.*

Anyone who rejected the law of Moses died without mercy on the testimony of two or three witnesses.

***How much more worthy** do you think one **deserves to be punished, who has trampled on the Son of God**, profaned the blood of the covenant that sanctified him and **insulted the Spirit of grace**?*

*For we know Him who said, "Vengeance is Mine; I will repay," and again, "**The Lord will judge His people**. "It is a fearful thing to fall into the hands of the living God".*
Hebrews 10:26-31

IF you have accepted Christ, the Messiah, God's Son, through all that He went through and did for you through His death on the cross and making an atoning for your sin, accepting you into His family. *And then* you willfully or purposefully or "accidently continue" to sin, the law that God said that He wrote in your heart is not convicting you anymore. You cannot hear Him and will not do what He says (in His written or spoken Word), then you my friend, need God's Law.

Every person who names the Name of the Messiah as their Savior and accesses through Him, the Father *and then* lives a lifestyle contrary to the Word of God, needs the Law. Laws are for lawless ones. God's Laws are Sovereign. And that is the reason for this book.

Maybe you have never considered your sin to be that bad? Maybe you think you can hide your sin. But God can see you! I am sorry for whoever sold you a "bill of goods" and told you that you can keep your unholy ways and still enter before the King of Kings, the Holy God. God's leaders should not be sales people! No one needs to be talked into doing good. Unless you're a child. And then you are taught through lessons. But if you are an adult and you refuse God's correction, this is what His Word says about that:

"Endure suffering as discipline; God is treating you as sons.
For what son is not disciplined by his father?

If you do not experience discipline like everyone else,
*then you are **illegitimate children** and **not true sons**.*

Furthermore, we have all had earthly fathers
who disciplined us, and we respected them.

Should we not much more submit to the Father
of our spirits and live?"
Hebrews 12:7-9

God is not desperate. He is kind. There's a difference.

Before God's Son was here, before God wrote His laws on

our hearts, the Psalmist said:

"I have hidden Your word in my heart
that I might not sin against You". Psalm 119:11

So, before God wrote His laws on our hearts, how did the Psalmist know to do that? The answer is, that *he wanted* them there. And by his own heart's desire, he knew the secret. The secret of how not to practice sin. The secret of how to stay close to God. It was said, about this Psalmist, that He was a man after God's own heart (1 Samuel 13:14).

If you are deliberate about your sin or you think you can know or serve God and do your own will, your own way, God's Laws are for you! The sacrifice of His Son does not apply to you. I didn't make that up. Who has lied to you that you would not believe the truth?

"All who sin apart from the law, will also perish apart from the law, and all who sin under the law will be judged by the law.

*For it is not the hearers of the law who are righteous before God, but it is the **doers of the law** who will be declared righteous.*

Indeed, when Gentiles (people who do not know God),
who do not have the law,
do by nature *what the law requires,*
they are a law to themselves,
even though they do not have the law,
since they show that the work of the law is written on their hearts,
their consciences also bearing witness and their thoughts
either accusing or excusing them."
Romans 2:12-15

We keep God's laws written on our hearts, not by the external law, but by the internal filling of His Spirit in us, when we ask God's Son to forgive us from our sin and to renew our spirit in Him, becoming born again of a new nature.

It speaks of our own conscience here. But how much more if you say you have the Holy Spirit of God on the inside? Then you are judged by your own (seared) conscience *AND* by God. That's a double whammy worthy of mention. Especially if one's heart is hardened through the deceitfulness of sin and cannot feel the conviction of His Holy Spirit.

If you are reading this and you did not know any of these things, there is good news. You can ask for forgiveness and repent now. This is God's whole entire plan in the first place. God will forgive you and cleanse you of all unrighteousness:

"If we confess our sins, he is faithful and just and will forgive us our sins and purify us from all unrighteousness."
1 John 1:9

If you are reading this and choose your sin over God or still practice sin while serving God, God knows all your secrets. This is a day of opportunity:

"As God's fellow workers, then, we urge you
not to receive God's grace in vain.
For He says: "In the time of favor
I heard you, and in the day of salvation
*I helped you." Behold, **now** is the time of favor;*
***now** is the day of salvation!"*
2 Corinthians 6:1-2

~ and ~

*"Seek the LORD **while He may be found**;*
*call on Him **while He is near**.*

*Let the **wicked man forsake his own way***
*and the **unrighteous man his own thoughts**;*
***let him return** to the LORD,*
that He may have compassion,
and to our God, for He will freely pardon.

*"For My thoughts **are not** your thoughts,*
neither are your ways, My ways."
Isaiah 55:6-8

~ and ~

*"This will come to pass on that day when **God will judge men's**
secrets through Christ Yahushua, as proclaimed by my gospel."*
Romans 2:16

Just where are you going to go, that God won't know? He
knows.

"There is a way that seems right to a man,
but its end is the way of death."
Proverbs 14:12 and 16:25

CHAPTER 4

THE GREAT COST TO RECEIVE

2005

Deception

I was doing ministry work, counseling and reasoning with a woman that came to me for counsel, During the meeting, this person, who claimed to be a leader, started telling me how God had told them some things that were clearly out of line with scripture. And I knew that she knew it was wrong, but she was in denial and used scripture to justify what she was doing. That wasn't unusual, but what came after was. I went to open my mouth and tell this person the Truth of the Word of God, but every time I started to open my mouth, the Lord would stop me.

I was frustrated, so when I finished my session with her, I complained to the Lord about Him not letting me help this person and tell them the truth! I was mad and told the Lord this person was so deceived!

And His reply to me, was: *"So? Everyone is deceived."* I was stunned for a moment and tried reconcile with what I just heard. And then I protested, that at least I had not been deceived!

There was complete silence at my protest and adding myself as innocent. I nervously laughed since He didn't seem to corroborate my enthusiasm. I should have known it was a set up to learn. I nervously inquired of Him, what actually does He mean "everyone"? And so, the greater revealing began and He proceeded to unravel, with much patience over time, to what degree we were all deceived. Stand by. There's more. Much more.

2005

2 Timothy 3 in Full Effect and will get worse as the days converge to the end –

I knew this chapter very well, but in the 80's and 90's I only knew a couple of people or a few people at maximum, that I would say fit this description. By 2005, I was coming out of my marriage and it was as if my eyes were opened to so much that I had not previously noticed. It seemed to me, that humanity appeared to be more on edge. Not as kind. But by 2010 and up through now, these behaviors and indifferences increased exponentially. And it appears there is just no distinction today, between those who do not know God and those who say they love God. What Paul told Timothy was right on the target:

*"But mark this: There will be **terrible** <**chalepoi**> (hard to do or to bear, hard, harsh, fiercely difficult to cope with because so harsh, even injurious, troublesome, fierce, violent, difficult, perilous) times in the **last** <**eschatais**> (finally, till the end, until last cent has been paid, the uttermost farthing, the last state of man, the last group, the last hour) **days** <**hemerais**> (always linked to the specified time).*
*People will be **lovers of themselves** <philautoi> (selfish, preoccupied with their own selfish desires, self interests), **lovers of money** <philargyroi> (covetous, money loving, literally in love with personal gain or having money, avaricious),*

boastful <**alazones**> (one who gives one's self airs in a loud and flaunting way, a wandering vagrant, looking for new listeners, vagabond, empty boasting, vaunting), **proud** <**hyperephanoi**> (disdainful, arrogant, beyond and over, over-shine, trying to be more than what God directs, going beyond the faith that God imparts),

abusive <**blasphemoi**> (evil speakers, revilers, railers, slanderers, blasphemous – reverses spiritual and moral realities) **disobedient to their parents** <**apeitheis**> (unbelieving, disobedient that will not be persuaded, spiritual rebellion, rejecting what God prefers),

ungrateful **<acharistoi>** (ungracious, unpleasing, unthankful), **unholy** **<anosioi>** (profane, regarding nothing as holy, utter disregard of what is sacred, willful disrespect of the things of God, Impious, Wicked), **without love** **<astorgoi>** (devoid of affection, unloving, without natural affection),

unforgiving **<aspondoi>** (implacable, not to be bound by truce, properly unable to please or placate someone, unappeasable, irreconcilable), **slanderous** **<diaboloi>** (ie literally – the devil, false accuser, unjustly criticizing to hurt or malign and condemn to sever a relationship, literally someone who 'casts through' ie making charges that bring down and destroy, slanderers),

without self-control **<akrateis>** (inclined to excess, no discipline, no self restraint, incontinent), **brutal** **<anemeroi>** (not tame, savage, fierce), **not lovers of the good** **<aphilagathoi>** (someone hostile to the things of God, an active opponent or enemy of God's kingdom or good, haters of good, despisers of those that are good),

treacherous **<prodotai>** (betrayers, traitors), *rash* **<propeteis>** (impulsive, rash, reckless, headlong, heady, brought on by unbridled passion, etc.), *conceited* **<tetyphomenoi>** (haughty, to blow smoke, cloud up the air, having a cloudy muddled mind-set, moral blindness resulting from poor judgment with brings loss of spiritual perception, vanity, conceited, foolish, puffed up, proud, high-minded),

lovers of pleasure **<philedonoi>** (hedonistic) *rather than lovers of God— having a* **form** **<morphosin>** (morphosis, form, outline, semblance, shape, formation, appearance, embodiment) *of **godliness** >eusebeias>* (godliness, devotion, inner response to the things of God, reverence to God and what He calls sacred, piety, holiness) *but denying* **<ernemenoi>** (disowned, repudiate, contradict, refuse to affirm or to confess or identify with) *its* **power** **<dynamin>** (miraculous, works, ability, powers, force, energy, efficacy, virtue, strength).

Have nothing to do with them <apotrepou> (turn away from, shun, to deflect, avoid).

They are the kind who worm their way into homes and gain control over weak-willed women, who are loaded down with sins and are swayed (led away, taken captive) *by all kinds of **evil desires** <epithymiais>* (lusts, eagerness for, inordinate desire, passionate desire, passion built on strong feelings, urges, longing, coveting, concupiscence, impulses),

*always **learning** <manthanonta>* (ascertaining, properly learning key facts, learning from experience, come to realize, educated, studied, understanding, receive instruction, have learned), *but never able to **acknowledge** <epignosin>* (discernment, recognition, intuition, contact knowledge, firsthand knowledge, real knowledge, resulting in true knowledge, acknowledgement) *the **truth** <aletheias>* (true to fact, truth of an idea, reality, sincerity, morally, divine truth revealed to man, straightforwardness, universally what is true in any matter under consideration opposed to what is feigned, fictitious and false).

*Just as Jannes and Jambres **opposed** <antestesan>* (withstood, unable to cope with wisdom, resists, contrary position, holding one's ground refusing to be moved, to keep ones possession ardently withstand without giving up or letting go, strongly resist an opponent) *Moses, so also these men oppose the truth—men of **depraved** <katephtharmenoi>* (destroyed, despoil, bringing down to a lower inferior form, utterly corrupt) *minds, who, as far as the faith is concerned, are rejected.*

But they will not get very far because, as in the case of those (kind of) **men** (people), *their **folly** <anoia>* (rage, madness, foolishness) *will be clear to everyone"* 2 Timothy 3:1-9.

(*Author Note: This was from a study and public teaching I taught in 2017).

Does this sound like anyone you know or look like the world we live in today to you?

ABOUT TO BREAK OUT OF THE MATRIX

THE INFORMATION

2005

Christians. The Lord spoke to me one day as I was walking thought my office saying, *"They were first called Christians in Antioch."* I told Him I knew that verse from the Book of Acts and thought it was interesting that He was quoting it. But, I did not follow up until days later, until it began to bother me that He brought it up, but did not say anything else. So, I asked Him what He meant. He simply replied, *"I never called them that".* In wonder, I asked, "You didn't? What did you call them?" He said, *"What I have always called them. Sons and Daughters".*

It was a very moving moment for me, but I had to know. He then led me to Malachi 3 (the last book of the Old Testament written before the New Testament), especially where it reads,

"Then those who feared the LORD spoke with one another.
The LORD paid attention and heard them,
and a book of remembrance was written before him
of those who feared the LORD and esteemed his name.

"They shall be mine, says the LORD of hosts,
in the day when I make up my treasured possession
and I will spare them as a man spares his son
(and daughter) who serves him.
Then once more you shall see the distinction
between the righteous and the wicked,
between one who serves God and one who does not serve him."
Malachi 3:16-18

He further mentioned that *He* never referred to us as "Christians". Rather, it was the custom of the times and it was a name given to the followers of Christ from people who <u>did not know</u> the Messiah. And so this name has been prescribed to those who are supposed to know God, ever since, as it caught on in the early church. Although to be noted: they also had other ways of identifying themselves. "Christianity" today has become it's own Entity.

2005

*"But I will reveal My Name to My people
and they will come to know its power.
Then at last they will recognize that I am the One
who speaks to them".*
Isaiah 52:6

THE NAME

The Name of the Messiah – *Iēsoús – Greek.* "Yehoshua"/*Jehoshua*, contracted to "Joshua") which means "*YHVH* saves" (or "*YHVH* is salvation") or transliterated to "Jesus". So what is the problem here?

Luke 1:31 – *"You will conceive and give birth to a son and you are to call him Iēsoun."* Which literally translated means, **"for He will save".** All of God's Prophets in the Scriptures were given names that <u>were part of God's Name</u>. For example, Elisha – (*'Elishu'a*) meaning "my God is salvation", Jeremiah – (*Yirmiyahu*) – "Yahu will exalt".

Ponder for a moment: Why would God call His own Son, something that is not like His own Name? Especially since His own prophets were named after Him in some way. It's His Son, in His Image. So, when the Angel came and said, *"You are to call Him "He will Save",* I assure you that the angel was not offering to a Hebrew family a Greek name. He was saying that God's Son's Name will be like His own. God's Name in consonants is YHVH. With vowels, it is **YAHUWAH**.

The Messiahs's name is the same as Joshua's (In the book of Joshua, the one that took over in Moses place), but we transliterated his name also. The actual name of both Joshua and the Messiah is: **Yahushua** ie "God will Save". The sound of it was always with the letter 'Yod' in Hebrew. Which had the 'Y' sound – "Ya". *Because* they are Hebrew. Not Greek. Not Latin. Not British, not American. But Hebrew.

The letter "J" did not even exist before the 17th century and even the modern use of the letter "J" as a soft "G" sound is a recent linguistic addition. For further study if you would like to know more, discover how there was not a letter "J" in the English language until the 1600's.

How did God name His Son "Jesus" when there was no letter "J" in Hebrew? And since even English did not have that letter, someone changed the Messiahs name in the 1600's. There is a brief, but important, history lesson for those that want to know the truth. If you search for it like buried treasure, it is there.

To God, that we have called His Son, His Salvation, by a different name all these years? I don't know. Maybe it's like a nickname or something. He's tolerated it. In the Book of Acts, the writer conveys this:

"Although God overlooked the ignorance of earlier times,
He now commands all people everywhere to repent.
For He has set a day when He will judge the world
with justice by the Man He has appointed.
He has given proof of this to everyone
by raising Him from the dead."
Acts 17:30-31.

But, I believe God has been revealing

these important truths to us and He will continue to reveal. Why? Power.

The Church has lacked the power that Yahushua promised we would have, in the time that we need it.

When Yahushua was on the earth, He said, *"I have come in My Father's Name* (Yahuwah) *and you do not accept Me* (Yahushua)*; but if someone else comes in his own name* (Jesus/Christian)*, you will accept him."* John 5:43.

How much can the Truth of the Word of God be changed and we willingly swallow the camel? Do you know the reference? *"You blind guides! You strain out a gnat, but swallow a camel"* Matthew 23:24.

It all started in Genesis. When the serpent said, *"Has God said........?"* Genesis 3:1. Satan twisted God's Words. And so it has been ever since. Why? To divide our relationship with the Father. Satan knows it is the single most important thing to God from the beginning of time. It is the whole reason He sent His Son, to draw many sons and daughters to Himself. Relationship.

All evangelism, all preaching, all teaching, all gifts and all callings, all salvation is for **one purpose**. Just ONE – Relationship. So to change His Name (a name is who you are, it's your reputation), to give the Church the name of "Christian" (instead of a Relational name for Sons and Daughters of God – Relationship), to sow lies and mislead, is what Satan is allowed to do, until his time is up. And it is up to us individually to seek God with our whole heart, to find out the Truth. God's Truth. These are the ones who will *know* the Truth and keep the truth.

Do some research, you will find that a lot of Gods people know about this and have already embraced His Holy Name. I have found that even some Bible Publishers have been restoring His Original Name in the reproduction of the Bible.

LORD HAVE MERCY

2005

Pray to the Father. Not Jesus, not Yahushua. <u>We are to pray to the Father (Yahuwah) in Yahushua's Name.</u> This will surprise many of you. But the Bible *does not* teach us to pray to Jesus or to the Holy Spirit, either. We ask <u>the Father</u> **in the Name of His Son**, Yahushua.

The Holy Spirit is our Advocate, left to us by Yahushua, to help us. But we are not to pray to them, anymore than we are to pray to Michael the Archangel or Aunt Sarah. But now we are getting into a whole new territory. One that is condemned by God, called Necromancy or idol worship. And that is another whole subject. I will say be diligent and search the scriptures and see if what I am telling you is the truth. God gave us all things we need to find out the Truth in His Word. And now with the internet, there is just no excuse for deception if you truly want to know. God would never leave His people without a way.

Yahushua taught His students (disciples):

*"**<u>Pray like this: Our Father in heaven</u>**, may Your Name* (the manifestation or revelation of someone's character, i.e. as distinguishing them from all others*) be kept holy* (to regard as *special;* set apart as holy, sanctify, hallow, purify*)."*
Matthew 6:9

"You did not choose me, but I chose you and appointed you so that you might go and bear fruit. Fruit that will last– *and **so that whatever you <u>ask in My Name</u> <u>the Father</u> will give you*** (when you ask in co-ordination with His Will or Plan for you*)."*
John 15:16

TREADING LIGHTLY, BUT WITH A SWORD

2005

Christian Coalition

Ok look, I am not saying any evil intent was through any singular person who carried this agenda into the Church.

But the Lord spoke to me saying, *"Daughter, My people have been deceived by those who come in this name telling them how to vote. They are to seek Me, not the word of man"*. He further added that, we were to pay attention to the character of the President when we vote and not the issues only. I asked Him if He had ever tried convincing a Christian Republican? And then we laughed and laughed. I'm kidding on that last part, but as you can see from me writing this out loud, publically, sounding the alarm as He has asked me to, He still thinks this is important. Now, more than ever.

Remember, God even said to me, one who is a pursuer of Him and a diligent seeker of truth, that we are all deceived and then He began to reveal just how much! Things we would have never believed were a deception. It's like coming out of the literal matrix; it's very sobering. God's Word tells us:

"Be sober-minded and alert.
Your adversary the devil prowls around like a roaring lion,
seeking whom he may devour."
1 Peter 5:8

Also, Paul told Timothy:

"Remind the believers of these things, charging them before God to avoid quarreling over words, which succeeds only in leading the listeners to ruin.

Make every effort to present yourself approved to God,

*an unashamed workman who accurately handles the word of truth. But avoid irreverent, empty chatter, which will only lead to more ungodliness, and the talk of such men will spread like gangrene. Among them are Hymenaeus and Philetus, who have **deviated from the truth.***

*They say that the resurrection has already occurred, and they **undermine the faith of some*** (Note it can be noticed by irreverent, empty chatter).

*Nevertheless, God's firm foundation stands, bearing this seal: "The Lord knows those who are His, and, "Everyone who calls on the name of the Lord **must turn away from iniquity.**"*
2 Timothy 2:14-19

"But reject foolish and ignorant speculation, for you know that it breeds quarreling.

And a servant of the Lord must not be quarrelsome, but must be kind to everyone, able to teach, and forbearing. He must gently reprove those who oppose him, in the hope that God may grant them repentance leading to a knowledge of the truth.

Then they will come to their senses and escape the snare of the devil, who has taken them captive to his will."
2 Timothy 2:23-26

Father, I bring all these reading this book before You. For the record on earth and in heaven, we declare to You and to the angels and to the demons and to the Fallen Council and everyone today; if any part of our lives, in any shape, form or fashion is deceived, reveal to us the deception and expose it. Do whatever it takes to open our eyes and our hearts. We do not want any lie or deception in our lives; Bring to ruin, anything not of You! We aggressively covenant with You for Your Truth all the days of our lives, in the Name of Your Son, Yahushua.

Moving along......

2007

The Lord spoke to me about restoration
through forgiveness and He said to me:

"...*Every man applauds his neighbor for his accomplishments. But no man says, Brother, seek the Lord. They are all turned aside to their own heroic efforts in an attempt to be "god's' themselves. Standing out. Everyone got lost in this system. But the earth is traveling and ready to give up the system.*

I Am restoring to the chosen ones, My chosen ones, Life. DNA. Restoration of the Life Cells that will cause a diversion and a reversal. I have shown us the two witnesses in the earth. They believe every Word I speak. Not the Serpent, not the world, not the system. They believe Me. Their life is not their own. They have given to Me their life and it is complete in Me. I have worked in them to overcome the evil one. To show them much more than they would have seen otherwise. They see. They understand. The reversal will be through these.

Overwhelming as it may seem, they stand as Adam once did before Me. Oh what a great victory My Son worked in the earth! And if truly Satan had perceived the Truth at all, he would not had received a lie at all. He is shut up in the lie. Leave him there. Come with Me. I have much to show you....."

April 4, 2007

Dream: This dream has several parts, but all were significant for the signs of the times. I will give interpretation at the end.

There was an older female prophet from the Church, with short blonde hair prophesying to me. I wasn't sure if I trusted her or not, as she seemed to have a bit of an attitude toward me in judging me. She was getting some things right, but not all. She prophesied that I would be going to Rome. And I did have plans to go to Rome the next week by the will of the Lord.

The next thing, I was in Rome. And I found myself in a **very old** underground structure, walking through it. A type of Roman Ruin. It was dark, with low ceilings, but large and open with columns. It was very cold, close, musty and it felt claustrophobic and airless. I knew that there were "priests" everywhere, maybe 50 or so. But, I could not see them. They matched the darkness. I knew that they were evil.

I kept walking and at some point, I came across a mirror (like at an amusement park, where they distort your image) and happened to look in it while I passed by. I was shocked at my appearance in the reflection, as it projected back evil onto me. I could see the enemy in the reflection. In the mirror, my nails appeared very long and sharp, my hair was affray, my eyes bulged and my teeth were sharp. I was taken aback, but, I did not stop moving forward. I was not afraid, but I thought, when I leave here, I am going to have to be delivered! And I knew that I could do nothing about it, until I was out of there, lest something worse could happen to me. So, I kept moving forward until I was out of there.

I then found myself on a stage in a park like area, whereby I was to introduce two bands. One's name was R E M and in the dream, I had a knowing that it stood for "**Rest in Him**". And the other's name was, **"Adams Gold".** I was excited about the bands.

Next, I came to a very large structure. I knew that two men were in charge of it. It was many stories high and at the top of the structure, on the marquis outside, was the name **"B & S"**.

I saw the two men who were B & S. "B" was a dark headed man and "S" was a man with blonde hair. They were in charge of everything in that structure. At the top of the building was the business that went on. And at the lower levels, there were all kinds of entertainment going on.

I left there and came into a place with a woman that I know. There, I physically gave birth to three babies, two girls and a boy. I recall the actual birthing and what the children looked like, they were perhaps 6 lbs or so. And I gave them to the woman that I know and to her family. End of dream.

Without going in to all the detail and full interpretation, I felt to put this dream in here as it has to do with the Church and God's people.

Interpretation: The first part of the dream where a woman was prophesying to me, she represented the current charismatic church. I felt she had authority, but I discerned that her heart was not right with God. I did not correct her, but I stayed quiet.

In the second part, I came out from there and went into the Roman ruins, ie. the dark night of the soul. Whereby there, God taught me all the ancient secrets that they have. It was a fight for my life.

The third part, coming out of the dark night of the soul and into a clearing and an elevation, where I could see clearly that the answers were in worshipping God in spirit and in truth (John 4:24). To Rest in Him and a return to the Garden, where there was "Adam's Gold" (Genesis 2:11).

Then in the fourth part, I found myself in a structure, at the systems of the world. Every system was here, including the church that is of the system and not of the Kingdom of Heaven. I saw the men who ran it. Interesting that God thought to call them B&S. I had to find humor in that. But I was able to go through the building and see the structure and how it worked.

Lastly, the fifth part, I came out from all of it, being purified as gold and resting in Him and had been able to conceive seed and quickly gave multiple spiritual births for others and was a blessing to the families of the earth.

The Lord was good to me to give me this dream, along with other words and preparing along the way, as the dark night of the soul was nearing.

CHAPTER 5

THE ASCENT TO GREATER REVELATION

Sovereignty: The Supreme Power or Authority or the Authority of a State to Govern itself or Another State

This is really the beginning of the end, for all things to become new. This was One year before the **Dark Night of the Soul** that God had chosen for me to endure.

Please be patient while reading the rest of this book. There is much revelation to be realized by the reader.

When the Lord speaks, sometimes it is like waiting in anticipation for the next piece of the puzzle. Until all becomes comprehensible. It can happen in a second. Or a day. Or a month. Or a year. Or in many years. One day is as a thousand years and a thousand years, as one day to the Lord, 2 Peter 3:8. Lol, For a fact, God's taught ones need to have patience or they will not win the race they set out to run (Hebrews 12:1, 1 Corinthians 9:24-25, Philippians 3:12-14). Indeed, it is through patience that we win the race and inherit His promises.

*For you have need of patience, that, **after** you have done the will of God, you might receive the promise"*
Hebrews 10:36.

God is really into this longevity and patience thing. As dramatically demonstrated! After all these millenniums', we are all still here!

My endeavor is, by the end of this book, that you will have a clearer understanding of God and His Word, Will and Ways. And if you're
paying attention, you will also have more questions! The more that I know God, the more questions I am patient to have answered. He has

assured with these Words: *"Do not be afraid, little flock, for your Father has been pleased to give you the kingdom"* Luke 12:32. And in this, I am confident, the answers are coming as I seek Him. *"By your patient endurance, you will gain your souls"* Luke 21:19.

Aside from the Words of the Lord here, there were many more Words and many other personal things that happened during this year that shaped me and prepared me, though I did not know, prepared for what.

Among them, my spiritual father passing in May 2008. When my own earthly father died in 2004, it was as if I felt un-whole for the first time in my life. I had never known that feeling until then. But, when my spiritual father died in 2008, I felt for the first time in my life, unprotected. There was no one standing in front of me, facing the battles with me. And little by little, as I entered into the dark night of the soul, those who had encouraged and endorsed me were no longer standing next to me. It was just me and the Lord. And He seemed to be indicating that there was yet more change, great change coming.

THE YEAR OF 2008

The year of 2008 was dichotomous. It was such a good year for so many reasons, but it also was what I came to know as a time of preparation for what was to come, though I did not yet know what was coming. I heard, but did not understand what it was. 2008 was quite a crucial pivotal time.

I had not yet been affected by the Real Estate market in my business being a Commercial and Residential Real Estate Investor and Management Company. I had been successful to this point in my life, ministry and career.

January 21, 2008

- The Lord Spoke to me saying, *"You cannot make it be what time it's not. I'm establishing you in this change. It's a transitional time. From Death to Life. From rule to reign. From freedom to follow through."*

He then spoke to me various words and phrases, as He often does when I am listening. Again, parts of the puzzle.

- Cave of Adullum – David and Saul

- Ziklag – **Definition:** Winding

- Quintessential – State of Quintessence. Fifth element, dark matter. Dark night of the soul

- 4 elements (earth, air, fire, water), the 5th if above them, higher, heavenly, celestial, substance

- Dark Night, Roman Ruins, Nucleus, Dark Matter, Gravity, Expansion, Yahushua on Cross, from death to life

- David went from Sheppard, to Warrior to Vagabond, to King

- God sent a prophetess in 2008 that said to me, *"God is allowing the 'fellowship of His sufferings' to be part of the relationship process that the Charismatic church rejects".*

Though I was not happy about this, I stayed quiet. At the very sound of it, there was nothing in my being that was looking forward to this. I felt that the last 22 years of obedience to the Lord had been good and I was looking forward that same year for the Lord rewarding me for my service. He was. Just not in the way I thought.

- A few weeks later, my Spiritual Father (just before he suddenly passed) gave to me a Word from the Lord, in which he said: "The Lord says that, *He is allowing you to identify with His sufferings on the cross".*

So, I had arrived, through patience and obedience, to the place where I learned to become unmovable and unshakeable in the time of affliction. Not saving myself. Not abandoning those that abandoned me. Not re-acting, but following through to what God's plan is. No matter what the cost. Standing in the face of this, seemed to be everything that He had prepared and equipped me to do.

$$B_{ut} \text{ I came to learn, He didn't want what I had.}$$

He wanted what I did not yet have.
What I would acquire through trusting Him greater than I knew was possible.

And as I found, the cost was very high.
More than I had to pay.

The Cost I Could Not Afford

I thought my relationship and obedience to the Lord over the previous 22 years was intense. But I was about to learn a whole new level, in which I will give a bit of insight by these passages:

Yahushua speaking to Peter: *"Truly, truly, I say to you, when you were young(er), you used to dress yourself and walk wherever you wanted, but when you are old(er), you will stretch out your hands, and another will dress you and carry you where you do not want to go"* John 21:18.

Great. Exactly **not** my plan (that I thought was His plan). I had a destination in mind, all by prophecy and it was one of purpose and success. I knew the Will of God for my life. So, let's Go! But, God seemed to be flipping the script. And it was His script! My greatest goal in life is that I may truly know Him. So, I wasn't going anywhere except for where He was. Though I thought about it many times over the years!

Since I was born again, my life had always been a life intensity with truly knowing God and walking by faith. I was been able to hear God, know His mind and sense Him, but I was about to embark on a journey more meticulous in following the exact direction of the Lord than ever before, as if my life depended on it. And it did depend on it. It is best summarized here by Paul, who's words began to resonate personally and take shape within me.

"That experience is worth boasting about, but I'm not going to do it.
I will boast only about my weaknesses.
If I wanted to boast, I would be no fool in doing so,
because I would be telling the truth.
But I won't do it, because I don't want anyone
to give me credit beyond what they can see in my life
or hear in my message, even though
I have received such wonderful revelations from God.

So to keep me from becoming proud,
I was given a thorn in my flesh, a messenger from Satan
to torment me and keep me from becoming proud.

Three different times I begged the Lord
to take it away. Each time he said,
"My grace is all you need. My power
works best in weakness."

So now I am glad to boast about my weaknesses,
so that the power of Christ can work through me.

That's why I take pleasure in my weaknesses, and in the insults,
hardships, persecutions, and troubles that I suffer for Christ.
For when I am weak, then I am strong."
2 Corinthians 12:5-10

At this level of submission, all one can do is receive from the Lord and give to Him all the glory which is due. Though, it is a process which requires patience.

The more you grow accustomed to Him and His Ways, the less in shock you are at the journey He takes you on, as opposed to the journey you have mapped out in your head.

2008

Prophetic Word I spoke in a Public Prophetic Assembly

The Lord had for me to announce to His people that they were coming into a time of the *"Valley of Division, the Valley of Decision"*. A time of testing. Of making decisions through the things that He allows in division in our personal lives. And that, this is His mercy.

I was as surprised as everyone else. It was the summer 2008 and there was such a sense of new beginnings in the air. This was not the Word that I was expecting to deliver. And the one to hear the Word first, is usually the forerunner to experience it first.

My mind had not caught up to it yet and there is more to say about this. But keep reading, you will find it throughout these pages. It's one of God's themes.

2008

Open Vision: While driving past a large open field, one that I often drove by, I had an open vision. There I saw very many people, beings, taking up space. It was entirely crowded; they were packed in all together. I heard the Lord say, *"There are as many of them, as there are of you."*

As I drove, I looked back again and the field was empty. It

was a spiritual vision, obviously. I knew He was showing me that the battle field is thick with those of the enemy's camp on the earth. He was preparing me to see in the spirit, for what was to come in the spirit and in the natural.

July 23, 2008

Angel of God Visitation – About midnight, I rolled over to see a very illuminated and tall Angel before me. He greeted me and began to speak to me about the end times and that the days were very near.

It was surreal. I have seen Angels before, but none ever spoke to me. I covered my head as He spoke thinking, "The Lord is the only One I listen to!" But as soon as he finished what He had to say, he left. I was so busy wondering why the Lord would send an angel and just not tell me Himself, that some of the visitors words were lost on me.

He left signs behind and carried with him a power to accommodate what was coming. About a week later, in the same place, he showed up again to emphasize and to speak about the last days.

The second time he came, when he left, he did so in mid-sentence, saying something about "the last days" and ending with the word, "And". So, I waited. And waited. I finally uncovered my head and said, "And?" I turned to where he had been standing, but he was gone. I tossed the covers off at that time and said, "AND WHAT?!" Alas, he was gone and so, this is what the next 12 years has been about. My training to help others in the days of God's Sovereignty on the Earth.

I did not know it at this time, though I had several prophetic Words through leadership around me and from the Lord to me personally, but I was getting ready to go into a **Sovereign** time of the Lord's choosing known as, **"The Dark Night of the Soul"**.

I suppose for each person that enters into such a place, it may be a different experience. I tried to write about it over the course of years, but especially in the beginning, I could barely speak about any of it. In the natural, it was a nightmare and it turned my life completely upside down and inside out.

Over these years, I had lost my ability to write and my desire to create. It was so overwhelming that all I could do was cry out to God. I found myself blurring the lines of my life with things that God would have not preferred, just to be able to handle my daily life and the insanity of all that was happening to me.

In the spiritual, it was even a bigger nightmare, as this was a time of spiritual battles and things that I had never experienced before to this level. But God was with me to teach me what it was I was living through and learning.

At this time, I also learned that alot of what was taught in church was not God's conveyance of Truth or impartation from the Kingdom of God. And more importantly, I learned it was becoming a new time on the earth and the same rules that we, the church, had been playing by and applying, God was done with. He had no choice but to get ahold of those whom can and will listen to show the truth about what was happening. I have come to believe that it was as important to God for this time, as it was for during Jobs time. No one truly knew God in Jobs time. And for God, it was worth inconveniencing a righteous person (Job 1:8) in order to save others. As risky as it sounds, God knows the heart of every person. As it was then, so it is now. Souls are on the line.

The amount of the trials of my faith and experiences that I had gone through is not possible to write all here. So, I will write what I can.

When people have asked me how I have learned all of these things or how I know what I know, I often tell them that, I think that God thought I was the only one that was listening!

And while I believe paying attention is of utmost importance,

I also know that God is looking for those in His image with humility, reverence, faith and trust in Him alone.

So, if any of the above bothers you, what you are about to read next, you should really pray about.

The angel of the Lord visitation was undoubtedly an experience, but what was to come was about to be a great sacrifice on my part.

I was about to learn on another whole level, the Prophecy that I had been given in 1993:

"To wield the Sword of the Lord, you must first be cut by the Sword of the Lord."

CHAPTER 6

WHAT IN THE ACTUAL HELL?

The Lord raised me up in Deliverance ministry early in my getting to know Him. He actually has thrown me into the deep end of Every. Single. Thing. that He wanted for me to know. So, for me to have discernment of Angels or Demons had not been anything new.

But in 2009, a whole new dimension and set of evil workers appeared on the scene, along with my new life of living in God's Sovereignty. And so also, a whole new level of warfare that I was not acclimated with. God was about to show me *who* the demons work for and under. Along with another whole world that I never knew existed.

Earlier, the Lord reminding me in His training all the years previously:

"If you have raced with men on foot
and they have worn you out,
how can you compete with horses?

If you stumble in a peaceful land,
how will you do in the thickets
of the Jordan?

Even your brothers,
your own father's household,
even they have betrayed you;
even they have cried aloud against you.
Do not trust them,
though they speak well of you."
Jeremiah 12:5-6

YEAR OF 2009

That year in January, the Dark Night started, January 1, 12:02am, with a phone call. While I do not desire to write the deeply personal things here that have happened throughout the dark night, I will say that the experiences in the natural and in the spiritual, changed me forever. Exactly, the way God wanted it.

September 2009

"The words of the blessing of Enoch, wherewith he blessed the elect and righteous, who will be living in the day of tribulation, when all the wicked and godless are to be removed.

And he took up his parable and said, Enoch a righteous man, whose eyes were opened by God, saw the vision of the Holy One in the heavens, which the angels showed me and from them I heard everything and from them I understood as I saw, *but not for this generation, but for a remote one which is for to come"* The Book of Enoch Chapter 1:1-3.

Nephilim or Watchers (or Giants)

My introduction, to whom I refer to now as, "The Fallen Council" started in September 2009. I have continued to see, hear and be privy to their presence since then, as part of my equipping to help others.

God has a godly council in heaven and on earth. But there are the fallen ones who left their first estate. They were the council of God at one time. They are present (loosed) on the earth now for the end times and are masters at deception and advancement of evil. Again, I can write more about these, but anyone who reads the books of the Bible (should) know about them.

"In the council of the holy ones God is greatly feared;

He is more awesome than all who surround Him".
Psalm 89:7

They are real. The ones that I am referring to are a part of the Fallen Council of God. (I will write another whole book at another time, if the Lord permits). For the short version, they were here in the beginning, in Genesis 6, Numbers, Deuteronomy, Joshua, 1 Samuel and the Book of Enoch and you can read about them again in Revelation 9:14, when they are released. There are other teachers and prophets that have their own experiences with them. I do not teach what I do not know from experience. But there are others who have experience or information about these.

It was September 2009, while on vacation in Newport Beach, CA., when four (approximately) 8-10 ft. tall dark shrouded and hooded beings of stood at the end of my bed while in my hotel room. This was my first encounter with them. I did every kind of warfare over the course of hours, I rebuked with all authority, I demanded and commanded. And they did not yield in any way. They stood there, indomitable. I had never, in all the years I had done warfare, ever seen anything like it. They were formidable, a bit intimidating and very concerning.

The next morning, I called two intercessors and we prayed. The Lord revealed who they were. They were Watchers, whom I came to know, in this case, as Nephilim. They were definitely letting me know who they were. That was not the last time I would see them. This was just the beginning of the darkness and God allowing them into my own personal 'blessed' world, where all of my faith, through fire, would turn to gold.

What the Lord has taught me, is the fallen ones have been released into the Earth to destroy through introduction of new technology, to advance the time (speed up technology) and to stop any kind of advancement of God's Kingdom. To facilitate the darkness and deception until the time of the end. They have the run of things on the earth at this time, per God's permission. And all the while, God's remnant has been without understanding of what is happening. The cares of this life have them distracted in fighting the wrong battles.

So the year of 2009 was my baptism into God's Sovereignty. Like Shadrach, Meshach and Abednego standing in the fire. Like Daniel, in the Lion's Den. Like David, standing before Goliath. Like Esther replacing Vashti and undermining Haman's plan. I wish I could say my learning curve sounded as gracious as the King James Version tells each one of their stories. But it was a contentious struggle over my life and the will of God being done in and through me on the earth. I didn't feel like I was learning. I felt like I was literally dying.

There is so much more on this subject, however, it will have to be another time or place that I am able to tell about it all.

At one point, about five years into this plan of God's, I called Pastor John Sandford (he had been a spiritual overseer at one time in the early part of my ministry. I had the opportunity to re-connect with him during my DNS). John and his wife, Paula had gone through their own dark night of the soul years before.

I told John whole story and I said to him, "John!!! I am going to die!!!!" He said, "Good!! That's exactly the point!" But I thought, "you don't understand! The only thing left for me to do is to physically die, because I am already dead!" (Except I had way too much emotion to be actually dead). So, I knew I still had more to go.

I came to know that was a test, that I was about to pass as well. Or rather, that God would have mercy on me. But, at that time, I still had so much farther to go. It was not looking good....

......And so now comes the year of 2010.

CHAPTER 7

THE KINGDOM MODUS OPERANDI

THE YEAR OF 2010

At this point, for me to even make it to the next day, I lived and breathed prayer. The only way I could make it, was to hear Him, as hearing Him carried His presence. I became an open vessel to Him, in which God poured out revelation about the days ahead. The things that are on His mind: His People, The Church, America and Souls.

2010

God's People are not Good Receivers

- The Lord had been teaching me for years to *"pay attention"*. It's a theme, a practice He has taught me. But one day He said to me, *"Daughter, My people are not good Receivers. They do not slow down to allow Me to speak to them and to convey to them what I mean by what I say. They assume. They love the soundbites of doctrine that they hear and they quote it perfectly, without knowing My heart or mind."*

Let it be known, that every Word that proceeds out of God's mouth, I take into consideration for myself even before it goes out to others.

This Word above, which the Lord spoke, has been a burden on repeat for me to get through to God's people from day one. There is **God's Word.** Then there is **His Will.** And then there is **His Way.** And if one does not listen, to speak God's Word, by His Will, *only* His Way, you will find yourself in a bigger mess or more worn out than if you would just take the time to "pay attention" and be a good "receiver". Take the time, it's worth it.

This may offend many of God's people. But you can ask Him for yourself. I paid the price to hear already.

News Flash!!! God is Not an American. Neither is He a Democrat. Nor is He a Republican. And, He is Not a Christian.

During Intercession, He informed myself and a group of Intercessors, that He is NONE of these persons!

He is THE Sovereign God from the Kingdom of Heaven.

He reminded us that we are "in this world but **Not** of it" (John 17:16). In addition, *Do not love the world or anything in the world. If anyone loves the world, love for the Father is not in them"* *1 John 2:15.* And He had us to renounce having such passions for the things of the world, over the Kingdom of God.

To be certain, there is *some* value in tradition. **But not if you put it above God.** Listen to how Yahushua feels about this:

> *"They worship Me in vain; they teach as doctrine the precepts*
> *of men. 'You have disregarded the commandment of God*
> *to keep the tradition of men. He went on to say, "You*
> *neatly set aside the commandment of God to maintain your*
> *own tradition."*
> Mark 7:7-9

"Do you not know that if you present yourselves to anyone (or anything) *as obedient slaves* (submission – under another), *you are slaves of the one to whom* (or what) *you obey; either of sin, which leads to death, or of obedience, which leads to righteousness?"*

Romans 6:16

He is talking to **us**. His Words are eternal. They are the same yesterday, today and forever. It stands to reason that God does not want for you to bow your knee to any of these ABOVE Him! When you do, you bring yourself under another power and along with it, come corresponding thoughts, ideas and attitudes. It is not the Mind of God.

And if you want a closer relationship and clearer view of God and His Ways, renounce that you have loved these things more than Him. The Kingdom of Heaven and all therein becomes much clearer to one who lives a repentant (renouncing anything that God does not approve of) lifestyle. And you can only truly know by knowing Him and His conviction by His Spirit of Truth.

August 11, 2010

- I heard the Lord speak and say to me: *"You will see great things now. Blind people can't see. You will have sight for the blind. You will say to them, "it's going be this simple". You will say to the blind, what is your prophecy (where is your faith)?*

  You will help them in their darkest hour understand faith like never before. You will know a way like Abraham...."

  God doesn't fix the problem, but He fixes (to fasten something securely in a particular place or position, direct one's eyes, mind, or attention steadily or unwaveringly toward, be directed steadily or unwaveringly toward) His prophecy. God turns around our way of thinking.

September 11, 2010

- The World Trade Center not only stood for Economic growth, it stood for greed.

- The Lord said to me, *"What will they put in the high place?"* (High places in the Bible represented what the people worshipped) *I tried to comfort them and they did not want it".* America, the called out One. *"It is time to call them out. It's a time of separation."* We will recognize who is with God and not with God. And God's love will be the foundation. The enemy is working hard (overtime) at aggravation and offense.

- *"Know those that stand with you. Know them. Greater division will be on the Earth like never before"* Matthew 24. *"You can't afford to be weak* (give in to your weaknesses). *You are going to take this kingdom by force (invasion)"* Matthew 11:12. There will be changes beneath and changes above if you do it *MY* way.

- **Vision:** I see skulls everywhere, territory of damned, ie, those who fell to the wayside; ones who did not do it God's way. *"The enemy will use every one of your words against you! You are not going to like what I have to say, because it will cost you something. There is a cost to the Kingdom being brought to earth. If they want it, they must seek Me for it, not you."*

- *"They are smoke screens what the enemy is throwing out to you. The Messiah walked through the smoke screens that were thrown at him. The enemy is going to show you what he can do, it's going to feel like what he is saying is true."* But, God says, *He* is going to show me what *He* can do.

- **Vision:** *"Changes will come."* I see a thick blanket laying over America.

October 10, 2010

This is Very Important if you want to Make it through the Days Ahead *and* make it to Heaven

- The Lord says, *"Offenses abound on the earth.*

  Forgiveness is rarely demonstrated on the earth today. The only way to release the prisoners, is to forgive their debt.

  Great, great offenses, unbelievable offenses, offenses coming through (our) *government. People are going to be mad and angry. It's standing at the door now like a tsunami and overtaking people. You need patience with people".*

- <u>Vision</u> and I hear the Lord say: *"People are in the water and I need you to be able to reach down and pull them up. They don't understand, they are just grateful to be helped. It's about the many I want to save.*

  On this level, the demons are at an all out warfare".

- *"It is superior information than before and being privy to that information, I will not leave you alone or stranded.*

  That is Satan's domain, the 2nd heaven. It is where wars are fought and won. If you see the captivity on the earth, the battle is already won. You have seen the battles and that is why watchers were sent. They are watching you, they know you know what they know. The sacrifice has been commenced. I believe in you enough to do My work through you".

- *"This year has been a teaching of overcoming. That is why I trust you, because you sought Me to make it through. The press* (like a mind in a sieve) *has been hard, but the revelation was to be much greater. Things aren't as they seem on earth. I will show you something greater, as I see*

93

it."

- *"I know all their secrets and I have every key to set people free. Your sacrifice is complete now. I can do the work. It's the time of restoration of all things and I've called you to restore and you could not restore without going down and getting the keys to set the captive free. You have known the depths and now I will show you the heights."*

- *"Don't bend to people's wills. A taxation of guilt, like you are responsible to make them feel better. It's not about them, don't focus on them when they are affected. James and John wanted to call down fire from heaven. No! Stop reacting. You can be touched by feeling of their infirmity, but it doesn't mean you have to react."*

November 10, 2010

- The Lord says, *"Shame covers this generation living on the earth now,* (they are) *discontented."*
It's not about how they got here, but that they are here. He wants to set them free. Their eyes are closed, they can't see.

- The Lord said, *"The enemy has these people in darkness and in bondage. I want to bring to them revelation, light and Truth."*

- *"There are channels and avenues of opposition, but you will overcome every one of them. I've not sent you in there for defeat. Challenges for your ministry are ahead of you. Challenges to strengthen you; the more you overcome them, the stronger you get.*

  Do not fear these challenges and do not let them take you by surprise, because I have told you beforehand.

  I have invented everything. They are not there to crush you, but for you to overcome. Nothing, by any means, shall destroy you."

November 11, 2010

- David had to learn how to bring the kingdom into existence.

  The Lord said, *"To be a successful King to rule, you must be willing to obey every Word. There is no other way to bring it to the earth. Hear and obey.*

  *Obedience demonstrates a power and authority and solidifies it on the earth. The world **(cosmos)** doesn't know how much they need the Kingdom of Heaven on the Earth. The battle is fierce and rages on earth for the souls of men. Your words calculate and create. My witnesses on earth shall know this (truth)."*

- **Vision:** I saw two witnesses and a missile try to divide them (Revelation 11). The Lord says, *"I give to you knowledge of things the rest of the world does not know. What I plan to do, is to bring it to earth."*

- **Vision:** I saw Armageddon, as the people of earth were fighting against God and the two witnesses (Revelation 11) died and laid in streets for three days and thereafter, their bodies ascended and the people saw and fear came on them and they (the people) gave glory to God.

  But, they only gave to Him the glory due when He accepted the sacrifice (of His two witnesses). The degradation of man has declined deeply to the underworld, as to their knowledge of things. It is the basest, vile, most corrupt of human nature.

  And the Lord said, *'These are the ones you must understand to let go, they have chosen their own way."*

95

"But these, like irrational animals, having been born as creatures
of instinct for capture and destruction, blaspheming in what they are
ignorant of, in their destruction also will be destroyed, suffering
wrong as the wage of unrighteousness;
esteeming carousal in daytime as pleasure;

blots and blemishes, reveling in their deceptions,
feasting with you; having eyes full of adultery, and unceasing from
sin; enticing unestablished souls; having a heart having been
exercised in craving, children of a curse!

Having forsaken the straight way, they have gone astray,
having followed in the way of Balaam son of Bosor,
who loved the wage of unrighteousness."
2 Peter 2:12-15

To be noted, these are the ones who first knew and loved God. Who first did what He said. And *then* they changed their minds.

November 14, 2010

- The Lord instructed me to, *"Come up to that higher level and trust Me. I trust you."*

November 18, 2010

- **Open Vision:** I saw a 4' tall x 2 ½' wide wing span flying over the top of my head at night. I had started calling them "dream weavers".

  By 2014, I came to know this as a (Fallen) Seraphim, part of the Fallen Council. A flying serpent, snake like being.

  The Lord spoke to me regarding it: "This going on everywhere. I've shown you so you would know."

John Paul Jackson said: "What is coming to USA is worse than what we expected. Great difficulty."

Lord, strengthen us!!

- **Vision:** I see the "Accuser of the Brethren" (Revelation 12:10) like never before. They let go of the hand of unity in the covenant and they point. They, the Accuser of the Brethren, will strengthen themselves in our midst, through those that are weak (of heart, understanding and faith).

November 21, 2010

- I heard a word: *"Mount Hermon"* Hermon (or Herman) = person of high rank or Mount Hermon being the place the Watchers swore and bound themselves by mutual imprecations, ie curses.

November 23, 2010

- Dream - There were fires. Fires in areas that looked like they were States, but there were gulfs in-between with no water. The fires were bad and they outlined the States and were in the States, but the gulf in-between was filled with water by people and it quenched some, if not all of the fires.

December 16, 2010

- The Lord said to me, *"Why do you let people into your life and remain, who do not love you? If you know the secret intent of their heart, then why do you let them remain? Christ did not let the Pharisees in. When I knew Judas' intent to betray Me, I sent him out and* (did) *not let him stay. Are you accepting mixture?"*

"What **(who)** *hung me on the cross Dawne?"*

I know, it is the betrayal of those that are close. Those that have other motives. Those who are religious. Those who do not think like Yahuwah. They are enticed by the enemy and taken captive by him at his will.

December 22, 2010

- The Lord spoke to me saying, *"They are all lies, cast them down. They want to distort your reality. You must know and believe who you are. The enemy wants to disgrace and discredit.*

   You want to feel the glory in My presence again, the wholeness and awesomeness in My house. But that is not what is going on in the world. I want you to see them for who they are. They are controlling My church. I am showing you a parallel kingdom; one not of Me, but of the enemy. What you are experiencing is the parallel kingdom. I said, know what you believe."

   Lord, what do I do?

   *"I called you to go in and confront the kingdom of darkness because the people are held prisoner here. You are not who the enemy said you are, you are not that distorted, picture in the mirror, that is **his** reflection. You are not a showgirl of others judgments. You are not who enemy and the people say you are.*

   You are who I say you are. I set your forehead like flint hard against the enemy's schemes to prevail. He will not prevail. You are affected, but not overcome. You are affected so that you will know the enemy and that he is a liar!

   You are affected but the enemy is not able to do anything. I have called you one to see, to know, to hear everything and it is alot.

You see all, you hear all and you know it all. I want you to know the battle on the 2ⁿᵈ Heaven is extreme, it rages. On the 2ⁿᵈ Heaven, this is where you must know who you are."

- **Vision**: I see Yahushua, standing in wilderness and enemy saying certain things to him.

  And the Lord said to him, *"It is written, we overcome by the blood of the lamb, the word of our testimony, not loving our lives unto the death."* Revelation 12:11

- The Lord spoke, *"It is not about the enemy disgracing you or defecating on you, but about YOU NOT RECEIVING IT OR BELIEVING IT! The world has become narcissistic. They are used to polluting others through the words of their mouth.*

  *"Daughter, I want for you to receive My Words only, proclaim My Words only. You have thought, it was anything **you** could do, but it is because of My righteousness and presence in you. You are My elect, My chosen. Because you are chosen to stand and proclaim My Word in the midst of a crooked and perverse generation. I want you to feel the exactness of the perverseness that it is. You and I are One.*

  I have given you **(intimate)** *knowledge of it, exponentially, because you need to know what you are dealing with. The people are used to it, you are not, you are not given into it and do not walk in it.*

  I granted insight and wisdom to them, but to you I grant the Kingdom. The Kingdom is for those who prevail in the battle."

The Opposite of "the tormentor" is the true worship of the living God. And Satan's shame **is** the Son's and Daughters of God who prevail against all of his wiles with God's Word, to bring God's Kingdom to the Earth, in the face of all adversity.

"And then the lawless one (one having disregard for proper authority) *will be revealed* (uncovered, revealing what is hidden, veiled, obstructed, especially its inner make-up; to make plain, manifest, particularly what is invisible), *whom the Lord Yahushua will consume* (slay, make an end of) *with the breath* (Spirit) *of His mouth* (speech, point of the sword) *and will annul* (abolish, sever, bring to nothing*) by the appearing* (epiphany) *of His coming* (be present, arrive to enter into a situation, technical term with reference to the visit of a king or some other official, 'a royal visit').
2 Thessalonians 2:8

CHAPTER 8

THE BUSINESS OF THE KINGDOM

YEAR OF 2011

The Lord spoke to me saying:

"There is no true Kingdom ministry without a Ziklag, because everything worthy has to abide the fire."
1 Samuel 30

*"So that the authenticity of your faith— more precious than gold, which perishes,
even though refined by fire— may result in praise, glory, and honor at the revelation of Yahushua the Christ."*
1 Peter 1:7

January 9, 2011

Yahuwah said, *"You destroyed the enemy's entire camp when you forgave* (all of your accusers and offenders) *offenses. Now you are ready and you can recover all. Now every stone you had cast down, is now in your arsenal to hit the enemy with."*

I have mastery now because I allowed the Lord to do the work in me. This is the test of every great Kingdom rule and authority. David had to seek God for every answer, as to what he should do. This stretched and transformed him into the King he was to be.

January 21, 2011

God's Prophets, Leaders, People Going Astray

- The Word of the Lord came to me saying, *"They went the*

way of Balaam for lucre, power and greed. Evil is one with them. Evil is personified, solidified, intrinsically one with their nature. I said, he (Anti-Christ) *would stand in the place of the holy in the end times."*

- **Vision:** *"It's not done, it's going to run rampant."* I saw it run down through strong leadership (in this world) and surge to all they are connected with. It's going to come through the holy. The Anti-Christ system will call them holy, but they are not.

*"Daughter, did you know it would ever get this evil? It's at the door. Their throne **will not** be exalted above Mine, but they think it will be. They do think to **trump** the King of Kings and Lord of Lords, all the while they* (look like they) *worship Me. Freedoms are being taken away from the people."*

Many times the Lord will give me just single Words as you see below. Included are the meanings accommodating each one.

- I heard the *Word: "Remnition"*- creating balance out of chaos. (Evidentially, it was a race born from the cosmos during the chaotic periods of time on earth).

The Lord spoke saying, *"Remember I told you it was done in the heavenlies first, where battles are fought and won. There are others that will not understand you.* (But) *They never got what I was saying.*

You are not addressing them, but the principalities and they know what you mean and you will shake them to their core level."

I am hearing the following Words:

- *"Remedial"* - relating to special teaching for backward or slow learners.

"The religious people of my day got what I was saying." And

yet, they still did not want to believe, nor would they repent to be able to see that He was who He said He was. They were stubborn, which I guess, makes one remedial, as noted.

- *Connectivity"* - graph theory. Closely relating to network flow. Molecular equations.

- *"Collectivity"* - quality or state of being collective.

- "Aggregate" - Formed by the collection of units or particles into a body, mass, or amount: ie collective.

- "Chronic measure of violence determined" - It is about Chaos. It is determined (by the enemies of God) against those who belong to God.

- *"Solidify, quantify, objectify, notify".*

  Solidify - 1: to make solid, compact, or hard 2. to make secure, substantial, or firmly fixed <factors that SOLIDIFY public opinion> .

  Quantify - to determine, express, or measure the quantity of.

  Objectify - to treat as an object or cause to have objective reality. To give expression to (as an abstract notion, feeling, or ideal) in a form that can be experienced by others. It is the essence of the fairy tale to OBJECTIFY differing facets of the child's emotional experience.

  Notify - to point out.

Separation from others and knowledge of God and His ways, only to exclude His "Trump Card". (To note: The word "Trump". I had been hearing the Lord speak for 25 years at this point and never had He used this word before). It is the introduction and the first of many times that the Lord uses this word when He is speaking.

Which I learned later was Sovereignty. What He allows during the Trials of our Faith).

A Key to Winning

- The Lord spoke saying, *"You destroy the enemy's entire camp when you forgive **all** offenses."*

Offense is a snare that gives the enemy an opening. Judging others and judging yourself (in a self-condemning way). It is fertile soil for the Accuser. Offense gives way to blame. Blame, attracts and is from the accuser. The Accuser then, brings a Judgment.

"Then the master called the servant in. 'You wicked servant,' he said, 'I canceled all that debt (offense) *of yours because you begged me to. Shouldn't you have had mercy on your fellow servant just as I had on you?'*

In anger his master handed him over to the jailers to be tortured, until he should pay back all he owed. "This is how my heavenly Father will treat each of you unless you forgive your brother or sister from your heart."
Matthew 18:32-35

That's strong. The Lord did not speak these parables in vain. They are warnings.

The major key to overcome offenses is forgiveness. If we hold offenses against others, God will not use us to the degree that He has planned for us. And worse, He will not forgive us.

April 18, 2011

Man Made Laws and Gods Laws

We have been blind in part to God's laws because there are

so many manmade laws. Our own rules, our own ways of thinking, our own opinions. Making the laws of God of no effect by His own people (Romans 3:31). We removed ourselves from the agreements of God by **not doing** the will of God by Faith (saying one thing and yet doing another).

Yahushua said:

"And so you cancel the word of God in order to hand down your own (man made idea) *tradition. And this is only one example among many others."*
Mark 7:13, Matthew 15:6

He further said:

"Do not think that I have come to abolish the Law or the Prophets; I have not come to abolish them, but to fulfill them."
Matthew 5:17

I know this must be shocking to many of you. Yahushua, our Messiah, actually kept the law perfectly **as an example for us to follow** (*"As He is, so are we in this World"* 1 John 4:17). We are perfected through His Word in us and through us. Not by ignoring and transgressing His Word.

"In this, love has been perfected with us,
so that we may have confidence in the day of judgment that,
just as He is, also are we in this world."
1 John 4:17

In other words, if we walk in the light of His Word and His love, then the conviction of His Righteousness, His "Up Right-ness" is in us. The conviction of sin is present also, so we can make a choice. If we choose Him, we shun the evil and cleave to what is good. And we will not have to be judged by Him. That's the good news of the gospel in a nutshell.

- **Vision** – I saw Iron come in to rule. There was a huge gap. The ones that rise above are in "pride" (rich – not necessarily monetary) thinking they can do anything. The ones that fall below are in "self-pity" (poor – not necessarily monetary). The poor feel strength in it. It *feels like pride* to them both because they are the *"right fighters."* They are the ones with strong opinions. They moan and groan and complain about what is going on, so there is no receiving from God.

"But he (the one that comes to God)
must ask in faith without any doubting,
for the one who doubts is like the surf of the sea, driven
and tossed by the wind.
For that man ought not to expect that he will receive
anything *from the Lord,*
being a double-minded man, unstable in all his ways."
James 1:6-8

- The reason they will fall under the same power (rich or poor), is because it blinds the prideful and it wears out the ones in self pity and they both use pride to protect themselves.

- The Lord said, *"Do not fear what man will do or say to you. Be not afraid of sudden fear"* (Proverbs 3:25).

  Renounce listening to man over God. The only way you can judge (righteous judgment) rightfully or truthfully; is if you are actually hearing God and not yourself, others or Satan.

- Vision – I saw the clouds and then felt led to part them. Then I saw God high and lifted up with His divine Government around Him. They are ready to make verdicts. In their hands are scepters.

- For those that God is raising up with this power and authority, they are to judge the system, *NOT* the people.

- The enemy has been violating God's Law, so the Law is against him; he is judged by God's law (Deuteronomy 28:15-

68, 111 curses).

The Lord said, *"Changes are coming, changes are here. I want for you to know what is going on."*

Some main points the Lord is expressing during Intercession:

- The daughter of women - Israel and the church (Daniel 8:12).

- God is exposing the enemy's strategy.

- God has us pray in agreement with Him regarding movement, change, direction .

   The Lord Gave the following Words:

- *Regions*

- *Flexibility*

- *Spirit of Religion*

- *Structure*

- *Intercession*

- *Vision*

- We went over the word *Structure* and prayed regarding each meaning to get the mind of the Lord:

a.   Building (of the ministry)

b. Construction (made of God)

c. Framework

d. Makeup (the materials)

e. Arrangement

f. Composition (it belongs to the Spirit of God; to be in the ministry)

g. Anatomy (of those in the body of Christ) person or persons

h. Form (format Your desire)

i. Architecture (God is the Great Architect)

j. Humility and submission is the only way to win against the darkness.

May 28, 2011

- The Father said, *"My prophets' character will be shaken, tested, proven, tried in every way. My prophets have to be tried by fire. They must come forth as gold more than any other on earth. Prophets must be pure. Most people cannot abide the fire that long. I know it has been hard and you have been weak, but I have your strength."*

June 1, 2011

Exposing the agenda of the Anti-Christ System

The Lord began to give understanding regarding strategies of the enemy:

- Entities are manipulating the air waves to control the masses.

- They are projecting images.

- God developed and created all technology. He is the head of it, not them.

- God says, *"The battle is for souls."*

The Lord informed, *"Changes are coming, changes are here."*

Then He spoke regarding America's Politics: *"They have chosen their elected officials. They are fronting everything."*

The old Government (as we know it) is falling away like chaff and the new one will be in place before the other falls.

The Lord instructed, *"The religions of this world have become mans. Do not look to any man made religion for your source"* (Matthew 24:23-28) All religions on earth are manmade. The Anti-christ is coming through religion.

"It is not yet, but near." God said, *"it's at the door"* and I saw that His hand was holding it back.

> *"And you know what is now restraining him* (The Anti-Christ),
> *so that he may be revealed at the proper time.*
> *For the mystery of lawlessness*
> *is already at work, but the one who now restrains it* (The Holy Spirit) *will continue, until he is taken out of the way."*
> 1 Thessalonians 2:6-7

The Lord said, *"You* (His people) *are the light. What is the chaff to the wheat? If it needs to fall away,* **let it.** **Pay attention.** *This is your only role. I will fill you with the knowledge of My will."*

What those that work against His Kingdom are afraid of is the living, practicing, powerful, creative prophetic Word of God. It all starts with God's people hearing God!!

The Lord says, *"It's not as you suppose. The electronic age is not as it appears to be."* It is not regulated by who we think. It's being regulated on the earth by our Government and the enemy. God is the head of all information and technology, as He stated. God is standing strong over it all. He wants to give all knowledge, power, and His secrets back to us, His people.

The Word of the Lord is, *"It's a current. It is an image. They are used to no one seeing them. They will show you what is not real, but what appears to be. They will fall under his* (Satan's) *power. You* (God's people) *will stand as stars and teach many righteousness. I show you this so you don't beat the air. They want to project an image. I want you to know the Truth, so you can see what is really happening."*

All the signs, wonders, technology originated from God. The Fallen angels taught it to the people for their own advantage. It is in their power (in the World System) and they (regulate) give us as much as they want us to have. The technology revealed to us is nothing compared to what they have and are keeping it and the information for their agenda to use to manipulate and control mankind.

The Lord revealed, *"I am going to interrupt their flow by pouring out information and knowledge to My people and they will be bold and do the exploits"* (Daniel 12:9-10).

It is *not* to take down their system, but how to confront and interrupt their system. I need to interject here that the Church has thought it has power and authority in ways that God did not give them. The old teachings of warfare do not work here. .

The Church has as much power and authority, as they have Submission to God.

Let me say it this way, to what level of authority you want to have with God and man, will be the direct level of submission you will surrender to God. We just cannot wave a magic wand or shout some words or make up something because it sounds good and they work. We are under orders. *IF,* indeed, we can hear those orders.

God's instruction is then, *"Expose and disrupt* (the enemies kingdom and) *bring down* (God's Kingdom to the earth). *I am going to bring an everlasting Kingdom that will not pass away."*

The battle is for Souls. Yahushua will conquer the world system (Revelation 11:15). Every person that goes to battle must believe that they will win.

"A soldier refrains from entangling himself in civilian affairs, in order to please the one who enlisted him.

Likewise, a competitor does not receive the crown unless he competes according to the rules. The hardworking farmer should be the first to partake of the crops.

Consider what I am saying, for the Lord will give you insight into all things"
2 Timothy 2:4-7

God says, *"Your part is the proclamation showing His Kingdom over all kingdoms. It **trumps** theirs."* It doesn't undo it, but it sends a disruption and not all will default then to it.

July 11, 2011

God Bringing Great Re-Arrangement

The Lord began to speak about these things:

- 1990's Word about God elevating the laws (principles/precepts) in the last days. **Reveal the Laws of God.**

The Lord said, *"My Truth has been lost in this generation. I call you to rebuild "old waste places."*

"I bring great re-arrangement." It will start in the church then branch out to the world ~ 1 Peter 4:17-18.

I heard the word *"dispersion."* It's an impression, as if a huge lie will be exposed and it will mess people up (in their thinking and direction). It will be to test hearts of the people to see if they will seek God out. The whole world will be effected. I see a great shifting taking place into darkness, like it has become one with the Anti-Christ system.

- The old ways of God resurrected in the last days – Jeremiah 6:16, 18:15

- *"Some of you will rebuild the ancient ruins and will raise up the age-old foundations; you will be called Repairer of Broken Walls, Restorer of Streets with Dwellings"* Isaiah 58:12.

I received 3 words to look up:

- *Destruction*

- *Old Waste Places*

- *Former Things*

- There were principles that were lost to the people of God. The Lord said, *"You cannot build a structure without these principles."*

- The Church does not recognize the structure is torn down and needs to be built.

He says, *"No one knows how to get there."* This is because not enough people are seeking the Lord to hear what is on His mind.

We want to build the old waste places. This is part of our mandate. He says, *"It takes great faith to go here."*

- Our step of faith is that God is making us Master Builders. Crumbled and eroded down structures are where the people's faith level is. It takes faith to build this Kingdom.

The Lord spoke saying, *"David saw afar off, that's why he could build.* (This is where most fall short. They don't trust God to do it His way, but put their own hand in it) Luke 14:28.

And He says, *"That is why greater faith is not seen on earth today."*

*"...Nevertheless, when the Son of man comes, **shall he find faith on the earth?"***
Luke 18:8

I hear, *"Now hear a different aspect; behold all things have passed away, behold all things are new".* He glories that He is changing mindsets (a big shift in mindsets) He likes it! (2 Corinthians 5:17). I hear the word, *"realigning".*

July 19, 2011

Things to Come

- I heard the words, *'Crops and livestock'.*

- I see they are directly related to the Watchers, the fallen ones. Physical implications. Part of their program is to control.

- I heard *"Shaping the future and large deterrents'* (deterrent means to prevent someone from acting by intimidation, a hindrance or restraint).

- **Vision:** I saw people eating and there was fear and panic (because they are in agreement).

- I have a strong sensing it is American resources that will be affected and we will have to turn to other countries.

- **Vision:** I see we are so divided in our country (so angry) this could be a way to control us (Psalm 4:4 and Ephesians 4:26).

- I heard "*Watchers will reveal themselves physically*" (to people) in these days. We will not only need greater discernment, but we will also need to be more dependent on the Lord for our information (Again, that comes through Faith and Trust in His Word and the direction of His Holy Spirit). Not leaning to our own understanding, but acknowledging Him in *all* of our ways to make it in the days ahead (Proverbs 3:5).

- I heard the word, *"Influence"*. That we would be at the mercy of them. This could be the largest way to influence change through crops and livestock. But I do not say it will only limit it to that.

- I heard the word: "*Corruption*". It refers to the systems which will be fully corrupt and not redeemable (like last days Babylon).

- There will be prophets that arise and be part of the corrupt system. As was with Enoch, they (the fallen council) are afraid of the power and authority that will come through God's true prophets. As with Moses' confrontation with Jannes and Jambres. As with Elijha and the 400 False Prophets of Jezebel and Ahab. As with Ahab's Messenger and Micaiah the Prophet. And as with Jeremiah's confrontation with Hananiah.

  There are the few and rare that are hearing God with their integrity in God's Word and in serving the Living God.

Looking for nothing in return. God is their reward.

And then, there are the masses, all saying the same thing, to go with the Political Agenda of the day or oppose it.

July 28, 2011

More Things to Come

- Everything that can be shaken will be shaken and what you, God, desire to remain will be strengthened.

- I heard words, *"Shutdown and Calamity"*. Besides the obvious, calamity is ruin, disaster, casualty, hardship, trouble, misfortune, catastrophe.

I asked the Lord if we can change things during this Sovereign time?

- The impression I have is like a crash is going to take place with:
- 1. *Economic system*
- 2. *Crops*
- 3. *Livestock*
- 4. *Auto industry*

The Lord says, *"Rise up in your authority daughter. I will show you how to use it. I will show you how to overpower their system. Seeing what you know now is not enough, but I will pour out more knowledge."*

This Word from the Lord, should encourage all who desire to intimately Know, Hear and Follow the Lamb of God wherever He Goes and to be a part of His answer on the earth in the days ahead.

August 19, 2011

- The Lord said to me, *"Dawne, there are so many thoughts and opinions on the earth. I will use you to rightly divide".*

"And people will listen to you as they do and you will turn the minds of many and bring down opinions and strongholds of the wise and you will bring their counsel to nothing.

You will overthrow the darkness and stomp on it. You will be a victory for My Kingdom, for it to prevail in the minds of men and they will prevail.

You will be my mouthpiece to enforce strictness or strict rules of the Kingdom to enforce the victory. Strength and fortitude is yours. You're mind will be strong to finish the work.

Your faith has saved you and made you whole. Now take this faith and save many. Faith is the answer to everything. If you have faith, you can do anything.

I allow your faith to be tried for relationships to be real with Me.

I'm going to raise you up from the depths you plunged and nothing will be able to stop you, because I Am with you. There is no man that will be able to stand face-to-face with you and withstand what you are saying to him. Your words will be solid, seasoned with salt. They will be sharp and enter into the heart. You will provoke Kings of the earth to Good Works."

I heard, *"tribes or tributes. Tribes of the earth will be exalted to win end time battle."*

I heard these words: *"Locations, reason for change, transition, exactness, precision; and locations again."*

"My promises are yes and amen. I've taken down old

structures to build new ones and I've done it in you first. What you build will be great."

August 22, 2011

The Systems of this World

- **Vision**: I saw a city, like NYC, like Washington DC., very populated. It was regarding the World System. Also the Political System. The Lord had His hands on it. And then opened His hands and let it go. He is letting go of the system that is in the world. He was crowded out by all of our choices and it is time for the end of the system.

- I heard the words, *"Broken down system".* I heard, *"Channels"* (duct, conduit).

- *"Devices".* They will get information from the enemy (Watchers) and each other, now. *"There will be complete control over the people, no more ,* (God's) *Sovereign Rule"* (by their choice. Though He has not and will ***never*** leave His people. He is only leaving our System) 2 Thessalonians 2:7.

- *"They are switching the system over right now."*

"When the richest provinces feel secure,
he will invade them and will achieve what neither his fathers
nor his forefathers did.
He will distribute plunder, loot and wealth among his followers.
He will plot the overthrow of fortresses–
but only for a time."
Daniel 11:24

- God's judgment (on the World system and His people that have been partaking with it) **is His mercy**.
  "Don't team up with those who are unbelievers.

How can righteousness be a partner with wickedness?
How can light live with darkness?
What harmony can there be between Christ and the devil?
How can a believer be a partner with an unbeliever?
And what union can there be between God's temple and idols?

For we are the temple of the living God. As God said:
I will live in them and walk among them.
I will be their God and they will be my people.

Therefore, come out from among unbelievers
(those that do not do what God says, proving
they do not love Him) *and separate*
yourselves from them, says the LORD.

Don't touch their filthy things and I will welcome you.
And I will be your Father and you will be my sons
and daughters, says the LORD Almighty."
2 Corinthians 6:14-18

(Take note of the Father calling us Sons and Daughters here or Believers).

- But the Lord says, "*So now they are given over to their own devices. They* (those that are one with the System) *will get information from the enemy* (watchers and/or another Spirit) *and each other, now.*"

- Time of Defilement. The Time of Enoch (the Watchers), Judgment, Murmuring, Complaining. Keep our eyes on God, not man, in order to know what He is doing. God led to Jude verses 1: 5-25:

"Though you already know all this, I want to remind you that the
Lord, at one time delivered His people out of Egypt,
but later destroyed those who did not believe (unto faith).
And the angels, who did not keep their positions
of authority but abandoned their proper dwelling—

these he has kept in darkness, bound with everlasting chains
for judgment on the great Day"

(See: Revelation 9 – They are now released).

"In a similar way, Sodom and Gomorrah and the surrounding
towns gave themselves up to sexual immorality and perversion.
They serve as an example of those who suffer
the punishment of eternal fire.

In the very same way, on the strength of their (own fleshly)
dreams, these ungodly people pollute their own bodies,
reject (true) *authority and heap abuse* (blasphemy/slander)
*on celestial beings (*those having divine qualities).

But even the archangel Michael,
when he was having an argument with the devil
about the body of Moses, did **not himself dare to condemn**
him (Satan) for slander,
but said, "The Lord rebuke you!"

Yet **these people slander whatever they do not understand**
and the very things they do understand by instinct—
as irrational animals do—will destroy them.

Woe to them! They have taken the way of Cain;
they have rushed for profit into Balaam's error;
they have been destroyed in Korah's rebellion.

These people are blemishes at your love feasts,
eating with you without the slightest qualm-
shepherds who feed only themselves.

They are clouds without rain, blown along by the wind;
autumn trees, without fruit and uprooted—twice dead.
They are wild waves of the sea, foaming up their shame;
wandering stars, for whom blackest darkness has been reserved
forever.

Enoch, the seventh from Adam, prophesied about them:
"See, the Lord is coming with thousands upon thousands of his
holy ones to judge everyone and to convict all of them of all the
ungodly acts they have committed in their ungodliness,
*and of all the **defiant words ungodly sinners***
***have spoken against Him**.*

These people are grumblers and faultfinders; they follow their
own evil desires (live by their feelings);*
they boast about themselves and flatter others
for their own advantage.

But, dear friends, remember what the apostles of our Lord
Yahushua the Christ foretold.
*They said to you, "**In the last times** there will **be scoffers who***
***will follow their own ungodly desires**."*

*These are the people **who divide you,***
who follow mere natural instincts and do not have the Spirit."
Jude 1:5:25

Please don't let this describe you! And if it does, God has a remedy, before it's too late. Repent! Stop it right now and do not go back to it! Make an agreement with God to listen to and regard His instruction.

Find your Bible and Study to show yourself approved to God. A Workman that does not need to be ashamed, as you are able to prove respectfully, by your outward actions and works, that you are able to rightfully divide the Truth! 2 Timothy 2:15.

- **Vision:** I saw people on the earth talking with their opinions. The enemy is (using this) sending the flood out of their mouth. The Lord said to us, *"Don't believe the reports or opinions on the earth. All will be panicked. Listen to Me!"*

  "Then if any man shall say unto you, Lo, here is Christ, or there; do not believe it."

Matthew 24:23

In case you are confused by this: God wants the Words of our mouth to come out of our heart, the heart that He has inscribed His Word on. Not our own opinion, based on the Worlds point of view or agenda (Matthew 15:19, Mark 7:21). Yes, He has given to us a mind of our own. He does not control us. Its simply a choice we make to decide to be like Him and think like Him. Or not.

Monday, August 22, 2011

Divine Instruction

The Lord spoke these Words:

- Manifesto (public declaration of policy, a proclamation).

- Majestic (stately, grandiose, regal, kingly) He must increase as we decrease.

- Bound and Binding rebellion, indifference, familiar spirits against the people.

In prayer during the week God spoke to us about emotions. God led to a way of escape:

"No temptation has overtaken you
except what is common to mankind.
And God is faithful; He will not let you be tempted
beyond what you can bear.

But when you are tempted, he will also provide
a way out, so that you can endure it".
1 Corinthians 10:13

This is great news! We need more instruction on escaping!

God led to this for overcoming. Listen to this:

"His divine power has given us everything we need
*for a **godly life through our knowledge***
of Him who called us by his own glory and goodness.

***Through these** He has given us His very great and precious*
*promises, so that through them, you may **participate***
in the divine nature**, (by) having **escaped the corruption
***in the world caused by evil desires**.*

For this very reason, make every effort to add to your faith
goodness; and to goodness, knowledge; and to knowledge,
self-control; and to self-control, perseverance;
and to perseverance, godliness; and to godliness, mutual
affection; and to mutual affection, love.

For if you possess these qualities in increasing measure,
they will keep you from being ineffective and unproductive
in your knowledge of our Lord
Yahushua the Christ.

But whoever does not have them, is nearsighted and blind,
forgetting that they have been cleansed from their past sins.
Therefore, my brothers and sisters, make every effort
***to confirm** (guarantee) your calling and election.*
*For if you **do** these things, you will **never** stumble*
and you will receive a rich welcome into the eternal kingdom
of our Lord and Savior Yahushua the Christ".
2 Peter 1:3-11

This has to be one of the most exciting verses written by the one that knew what it was like to fail Yahushua, Peter! Verse 4 speaks of *"escaping the corruption that is in the world through your own evil desires"*. First, we have to acknowledge and then admit and confess being a partaker with it, for deliverance from being part of the world and against God, for our escape.

It's not magic. It's an offer of a miracle through a powerful God who consequently, wants a relationship with the Sons and Daughters He's created.

August 29, 2011

Coming out of Agreement and Renouncing

- We renounced the world system in order to help others to come out.

- Vision: I see a great shifting taking place into darkness, great darkness on the earth. Seeing those that have become one with the Anti-Christ system. I saw mass confusion on the earth; people bumping (mentally, spiritually, because of not paying attention) into each other. They don't know what is going on.

- The Lord speaking: *"They* (the Main Stream Religious Church) *will be in agreement with the Government. They are being used by the system. Deception* (darkness) *is on the rise and because of its increase, people cannot see in the dark."*

People will be "bumping into each other," in confusion (*"Come out from among them My People!"* 2 Corinthians 6:17). The Earth can't take it anymore. All the elements are in an upheaval. This is why the earthquakes, hurricanes, floods, ie natural disasters have come forth and will more so.

> *"The earth is utterly broken apart, the earth is split open,*
> *the earth is shaken violently.*
> *The earth staggers like a drunkard and sways like a shack.*
> *Earth's rebellion weighs it down and it falls,*
> *never to rise again."*
> Isaiah 24:19-20

> *"For we know that the whole creation groans and travails*

in labor with birth pangs together until now" Romans 8:22.

In hope since Christ was revealed, that the true sons and daughters of God will rise in their God-given authority.

- I hear: *"Deception on the rise."* Because darkness is increasing and the people cannot see in the dark. The land reels and mourns because it can't take it anymore.

  "All Creation groans and travails awaiting to see the manifestations of the sons and the daughters of God" ~ *Romans 8:19.* When will we rise up and listen to God?!

- *"If you agree with Me, My Words abide in you"* ~ John 15:7 This was said twice. The Word "abide" in the Greek is the word "Agree". *"Do two walk together unless they have agreed to do so?"* Amos 3:3.

- **Vision** – I saw several "ministers" rising up and "offering" the Bible. The Lord said, *"It's deception. I said, do as they say, don't do as they do."*
  "So practice and observe everything they tell you. But do not do what they do, for they do not practice what they preach"
  Matthew 23:3.

- They will be in agreement with the government. Many of (the believers) will be used by the system. I am reminded of what the Lord said in our meeting on July 11, *'I bring Great Rearrangement.'* It will start in the Church then branch out to the world. Dispersion. I sense it will be like a huge lie will be exposed and it will mess people up. Disorganize them. It will be to test hearts of the people to see if they will seek Him out. The whole world will be affected. I see a great shifting taking place into darkness, like it has become one with the anti-Christ system.

- I saw mass confusion on the earth bumping into each other. They don't know what is going on.

- I hear: *"Deception on the rise."* It's because darkness is increasing and the people cannot see in the dark.

- The land reels and mourns because it can't take it anymore. *"All Creation groans and travails awaiting to see the manifestations of the sons and the daughters of God"*. It is like the Martyrs under His throne, asking, *'Is the time yet, will you avenge our blood?'* (Revelation 6:10) The earth carries the testimony of God. The Earth is overwhelmed and He is saying finally, *"it is time".*

  He didn't send it, but He allows it to go ahead, because the intercession that it is carrying is so heavy, that it breaks out and breaks forth, whether it is under the earth with the quaking or in the atmosphere above.

- Vision – He showed the martyrs underneath His throne. How they were groaning and travailing and He has to have them wait because their vengeance does not come until the end (Revelation 6:10).

- The earth is breaking forth in a natural process because they can't take it anymore. It is part of God's procession. He has interaction with every living thing on the earth. He created it all for interaction. Everything living has interaction. As something grows in the soil, it is working together in unity with the components; it is a sign of how we are suppose to get along. On the Earth is there is so much division and offense, that the earth, soil and elements are in an upheaval with what we are doing (our sins). When we do all these things against other people and nature, we are sinning against them, because God created them for interaction with us. There is no more interaction, but division.

Making Agreements with God and with His Earth

- Then, the Lord said: *"Make an agreement with the Earth."*

'For the earnest expectation of the creature waits
for the manifestations of the sons of God.
For the creature was made subject to vanity,
not willingly, but by reason of Him
who has subjected the same in hope.

Because the creature itself also shall be delivered
from the bondage of corruption
into the glorious liberty of the children on God.

For we know that the whole creation groans
and travails in pain together until now.

And not only they, but ourselves also,
which have the firstfruits of the Spirit,
even we ourselves groan within ourselves,
waiting for the adoption,
to wit the redemption of our body."
Romans 8:19-23

- Earth is waiting for the manifestations of the (mature) sons and daughters of God!

- The Lord saying, *"You shall hear the Earth and the Earth shall hear you."*

- We made ourselves one with God's earth and His creation. It takes redemption, because it has been cursed. The Earth took on the curse with Cain and Abel (Gen 4:10-11). We repented of all the curses done against the Earth from Adam until now. That which has been lacking through a lack of understanding.

- How do we redeem the earth? We plant in the earth the fruit of the Spirit by what we, the redeemed of the Lord, do. Our true faith in action is by nature, redemption. It is the proof of your faith when you keep God's Word and do it (James 2:17-19).

- The Spirit of God said: *"I just gave you a major key to unlock the mysteries of God."*

- The Lord reminded me that people like us will stand out, because we think completely different. It will be entirely obvious. (Remember in Daniel's time there were only the 4 that stood out for God – Shadrach, Meshach, Abednego and Daniel.)

- The Earth is (according to the words in the concordance regarding Genesis 1:1) the country, earth, ground, land, wilderness, world, Nations). The air, water, fire, the soil, the sky. Earth in the thesaurus also says planet, globe and universe.

September 13, 2011

Exposing what's Ahead

- Revelation creatures - Revelation 9

- The Lord said, *"Words will be the enemy's greatest tool in the days ahead."*

- The Lord said, that is to say, *"words of judgment on others, opinions, assumptions, presumptions"*. Carnal Self-Righteousness. Using the Word of God to verify one's own lascivious ambitions.

I received the following words:
1. *"Magnetism* = Attraction, Force, Power; Signs & Wonders and Lying Signs and Wonders".

I was then reminded of 2 Thessalonians 2:9-10:

> *"Even him, whose coming is after the working*

of Satan with all power and signs and lying wonders,
and with all deceivableness of unrighteousness
in them that perish because they received not
the love of the truth, that they might be saved."

- The enemy's allure is real and it is strong. The only way to fight it, is to not have anything in common with it (John 14:30) and stay in the Word of God (Psalm 1:2).

- We then went to Genesis 1:4 and read the scriptures of what God created (dark, light, firmament, etc.). The Earth was cursed because of Adam's fall, so we are to take it back because of the dominion we have been given (Genesis 1:28). We carry forward what Yahushua started on the earth (John 10:10).

- Then we heard the words *"Signs and Wonders"* again. This time the word, *"Accuracy"* rose up, so I covered the words in prayer. *"Signs and Wonders"*. I felt this was a dividing of the dark from the light.

- A consideration on the word, *"Magnetism"*. Perhaps, that everyone that is out of the Earth will go with the Earth. Those that are made in His image and obey God are both Earth and Spirit. The Spirit and Earth will redeem the Earth. Those who are without the Spirit of God, there's a magnetism (a manipulation perhaps) with them. The Earth without the Spirit of God is not good. The Earth alone is cursed. The carnal mind, the earthly people without the Spirit of God, is in contrast with God and what He is talking about. Those who have God's Spirit can learn to take dominion to redeem.

"Heaven and earth will pass away, but my words will never pass away." Matthew 24:25

October 9, 2011

Dream – I dreamed that I lived in a home in a neighborhood. The **Government** came in to the neighborhood doing reconstructions inside of people's homes. Huge renovations. The people thought it was good. However, the government representatives were changing out electrical items, technical items, personal items, even such as shampoo and other things. They changed our homes and how we used things. They were serious about it and no one had choices. But most liked it or went along with it.

I was watching 'them' set things up. They acted in a business manner, like it was normal and they were normal and people accepted it, as if it were normal and ok.

I called a friend on the phone and realized that I could not talk on the phone because it would be recorded. My friend came over. I felt that everything in the room, the very atmosphere was charged with their 'knowing'. I was telling her what was happening, how it was unsafe and that we were being watched, listened to and controlled. I was in the loop and did not want to come under their power. There was danger in it.

October 15, 2011

- The watchers are on the 2nd heaven. The battle for souls and kingdoms are on the 2nd heaven.

- How do we be like You Father? Power comes from Heaven. I reached my arm upward and there was energy, fire and light (its shape was oblong and bigger than my hand). It was moving. I reached and pulled it down. God wants me to accept the challenges for the change. It's all for having His power. He has only given us so far, a piece of the puzzle.

- The Lord said, *"They are exchanging information right now about you! I am going to cause you to see a far off, so you will have the power to rope in their kingdom. Their kingdom is against My Kingdom. I am giving you power and authority to walk among them and see what they are doing and to stand."*

- I hear the word, *"Resolve"*. What do you mean? I have a resolve and I see power down in me and I become the resolve (a medicine).

- I heard the Lord speaking, saying: *"As I told you, the mouths are moving, don't believe them; don't believe any word, but Mine. That's why I have broken that down in you over the years. The people are going to believe the enemy, if they are not one with Me.*

  And I am making you a resolve for the people. Keep your eyes open. I'm going to show you many things, don't be taken by surprise. Changes. There is a great revelation coming which you need to be prepared for.

  The prophets from the foundation (all given a part) are carrying it and this is what they are all waiting for and they could see you were a part of this. They are rejoicing for it and you are ready to receive it. I declared My glory and you are a part of it. The Watchers see you among them because they are all on the 2nd heaven".

There was an experience I had, in which I wrestled or fought against a man in the spirit realm. He was wearing a suit. Though it seemed and felt real. The Lord said about it: *"he wanted to punch you, that's how he felt about you".*

They were exchanging information because they see what GOD is showing me. *"Their greatest fear is that one* (human) *would give up their will to do My will. It's a decision, not an anointing to do this. And that's what the prophets see. That power is in you to want only HIM and that is what they* (the Watchers) *fear. Changes are taking place."*

Lord, now what do I do with this power? Is it power and authority to bring resolve? *"There are many prophets that waited for this day, wishing they could be a part of it."*

I see two bolts that rivet into a structure. I saw rivet marks into my left shoulder. The rivet is like a bolt that cannot be moved for the kingdom of God. The Lord said, *"Your agreement with Me will keep you there unmovable, unshakeable, unstoppable. You live among them".*

November 9, 2011

- The book of Jude was read to bring our attention to the false teachers that were in the church. The Lord said, *"There are more of them in the church, than the ones doing it My way."* He is referring to this day that we are living in now.

November 23, 2011

- This overwhelming feeling I have is about what is going to face Americans. They will feel defeated and betrayed by our own Government. I need to stand against this force to tell them the truth. The Lord said, *"I've been wanting you to pay attention."* This has to do with teaching and training, what is coming on the earth.

December 22, 2011

- Says the Lord, *"The restoration of all things is at hand. I know things appear to look bad on the Earth. Don't believe every report and everything you see, because I will cause the Earth to help you."* Revelation 12:16 (Regarding understanding and overcoming, even the Political demands I see coming).

CHAPTER 9

THINGS ARE NOT AS THEY SEEM

YEAR OF 2012

January 9, 2012

Vision: I heard the word *"Economy"* and then I saw pipes connected with a joint and it came undone. *"System broken",* so there is no flow anymore. *"They will try to fix and repair the system, but it cannot be fixed. They will come up with a new idea."*

I heard the following words and I had a vision:

- *"Implementing new fixtures."*

- **Vision:** I heard the word, *"Currency"* (a system of money in general use in a particular Country). However, I am seeing money that looks different. It is paper and has a man's face on it to the right, not in the center. It's a different shape than the current money we have.

I heard the following words:

- *Note*

- *Federal Reserve •Stolen •Inconvenienced*

- *Changes •Seasons •Time*

- *Change •Nation*

January 21, 2012

- **Vision:** I see many well meaning people offering me pieces of their bread. It was like poor bread. The Lord said, *"Do not be a partaker of their bread, you have My Bread."*

January 23, 2012

I heard these words from the Lord:

- *"Shaking – things loose".* I see a strong structure and everything that can come loose will be shaken.

- *"Structures"* – something built or constructed.

- *"Economy"* – being set up for one world economy (the management of the income, expenditures of a household, government careful management of all, attention to resources, etc.).

- *"Massive fear and insecurity"* – all over our Nations. Strengthen us and prepare us. Pour out more kindness in repentance.

  The Lord said, *"The Governments are shifting and changing right now for a one world economy."* The governments don't care about people being insecure and fearful, they are going to do it anyway.

- *"Gender"* (Sexual Orientation).

- *"The love of money is root of all evil."* That is the root He is shaking on.

- *"Economic hardship"* – hard circumstances of life.

- *"Economic hard times".*

- The impression is like a massive test for our Nations and will reveal and expose what is really in people's hearts. The true character of people. He is the answer in the problem. We are the salt and the light. Brace us and give us greater wisdom.

- *"Massive jealousies between those that have and those that have not* (believers or non-believers both). The Lord says, *"You can't let others destroy you. What do you think I'm doing next for America?"*

- **Vision:** I see the arrangement of America on a level and then I see the ground opens up (from the shaking). I see people and things falling through; they are prominent people, in political places. It's a part of the shifting.

February 12, 2012

- **Dream:** It started out where I was talking to someone who had been to Heaven or was still in Heaven. It didn't seem that I had direct contact with them, it was either off and on or in and out, either in person or in the spirit realm. I don't know. It seemed to be like my grandmother (Today is her Birthday on President Lincolns BD).

   So, she was telling me all kinds of things about Heaven. I was not getting it all and I kept asking her a plethora of questions. She told me that the reason I don't understand it all, is because I was too focused on the pain that the Lord has allowed me to go through on the earth. My attention and focus was still too much on me. But the things that she told me were amazing. What I understood the most was, how much Heaven was like here, in that every one lives, has a roll, a purpose and a calling, even in Heaven. How very much a real life they live there. One that is fulfilling and has deep meaning.

   Next, I was talking to my ex-husband. He was in Heaven. I

was asking him all about it. He told me that he had a 1500 sq ft. home there. I asked if he lived alone and he said he did not. There were others that lived with him. It was a 3 or 4 bedroom house. He seemed reserved, but fine. I marveled that a developer/builder living in a large house on the earth, had such small house in heaven.

It seems I talked to my spiritual mother too, who also had gone to Heaven and was sharing things with me. I am not sure. But these were people I knew.

Then, I walked into a school. There was a teacher in a class room. I could not tell how old she was. She was a mature woman, not old though. She was telling me all about a Strategy that Heaven had and how it was being carried out. What she shared with me was lengthy and amazing.

She was from Heaven, but living on the earth, as a School Teacher. That was her regular job, but her calling was much greater. There was so much she was sharing, it was life and death. I was asking her in detail, as I did my grandmother, how things worked. I was asking the same questions to see if I could understand any better, because I had not the first time. As she was going into detail more, I understood more. But it was all so surreal to me.

She was telling me of Kingdom things that had to do with the earth. In fact, everything there in Heaven had to do with the earth. They were in one accord. So, she is telling me these things and I recall this one part: It was about Attorneys on the earth and evil and acquisitions in the Heavenlies and something about a big mission to expose evil. It was bad. Life and death.

It was a secret, but I was being told. I wanted to know so much more. It was as if I were starving or insatiably thirsty for this knowledge. I kept asking more and more, but class was about to begin and people started arriving. I asked her if she worked there, in Heaven? Did she mean that all this work was being done in Heaven? She said, *No, that they are working all this on the earth.* It was as if I needed clarification as the last conversations had to do with things in heaven only. She had to go. I held out my hand to shake hers and she did not extend her hand back. She said she needed to go wash her hands before class and was courteous and kind. She then handed me her business card. That was the end.

March 25, 2012

- The Lord speaking to me said, *"See how the land quakes, see how the earth mourns? It is looking for a redeemer. It is looking for their salvation. I caused you to be as the land that is reeling to and fro, not understanding the darkness that is over it."*

- God let me experience being one with the land because it takes on intercession. There is only two ways of cleansing the land, fire and water.

- The Lord said, *"You are the water and fire prophet. The spirit realm recognizes you and knows who you are. They* (those that oppose the Lord) *will try to stop you, but you have power and authority over them."*

- There are ranks against me, so it looks like I am not victorious, but I am. He says, because there are more than one or two hitting me up at the same time (but two put ten thousand to flight). The heights that He has brought me to, I will go to the same depths. And all of my depths determine my heights.

- He says, *"I'm giving you power over life and death."*

- I hear the Word - *"Division".*

April 28, 2012

- **Vision:** I see that America is going to be a mere version of its self. It is going to be a shadow, not substance, of what it is supposed to be; Only 10 percent; a division. When I saw the percentage slip away, the people were in the percent and crying and suffering because there is no more help for them in America and no more purpose for them. I'm seeing the rich and poor division again (monetary, but in thinking as well).

- The Lord instructed: *"Redeem the people out of it."*

- **Vision:** I see people on my right and I am wrestling with the enemy and I have such a calmness and peace and no judgment on the people. Says the Lord, *"I've caused you to understand so you won't judge the people and you'll have nothing in common with them* (their flesh, evil thoughts or deeds)."

May 12, 2012

- One night, the entities during the Dark Night of the Soul were present. They do not react as demons do. I asked who they were and why were they here. They spoke and I heard: "We want what is inside of you". That was creepy.

- I carry and collect information from the Kingdom of Heaven. I had an impression of the radio towers (the ones that go up to a point and are metal). If you take out the master tower, you weaken the smaller ones and it becomes less powerful.

- Each and every one of us is important in this last days battle. Heads up to God and be in His Word. Ask the Lord to lead you, to those that know God and can hear Him for these days ahead.

June 4, 2012

- I hear the Lord saying, *"Daughter, These are the last days of the Nation* (as we know it). *People's good intentions are not going to count. Your life is not your own. You can't take it personal. That is what people do* (default to their fallen nature, when they do not pursue God). *It is not about you."*

June 25, 2012

- I have an impression of something bad coming. It feels like the enemy is trying to pivot me to turn and look at ruins of what is coming in the world system. By me focusing in on that, it would shut me down from what God wants me to know, by keeping me in the negative. I took the enemy's power away from him against me, by relinquishing my rights to God to surrender to Him, to see and to understand the negative. I am reminded that Yahuwah told Jeremiah, *"Don't look at their faces"*. None of that is my business. What I hear the Father say and what I see Him do, is my business.

July 20, 2012

- I had a strange foreboding of my rights being taken away.

- **Vision:** I see an eye in the Spirit looking at me. The Spirit of God told me, *"They are watching you. You are being watched."*

- *He further emphasized, "A major shift is going to take place in this election. America going into a kind of captivity. It's here now."*

  I then Heard the following Words:

- *Fight your battles.*

- *Shape shifting.*

- *You're going to see a lot.*

- I prayed, what do I do Lord? He said, *"You can glory in your infirmities that the power of God can rest upon you"* (2 Corinthians 12). I felt a bit defeated with that answer, though I choose it anyway.

- So, I prayed in spirit and I heard that, "the Nephilim and Watchers are so strong on Earth now and they know that I am opposed to them. They want to take me out (down). The Lord tells on them: *"They are gathering information to use against you"*.

July 27, 2012

- **Vision:** I see a vision before me, of when God made a (particular personal) Covenant with me in the Fall of 2008: Then He said to me, *"Your life is to choose My will, anything else is death."* I am completely finished – undone. He continues, *"This is what it has cost you, that you would not see things naturally anymore, but My purpose for them."*

- **Vision:** Then I saw a vision of a chess board (similar to a print I had framed above my mantle in a former home, of a chess game being played from Heaven and earth). It's a strategic battle right now. I recognize God is in control. God says, *"That is what the enemy fears; he fears those that **know** I AM in control."*

I am reminded of the 1940's history I read about. I learned that the Nephilim (part of the fallen council) had the plan and pattern for our country and the leaders were in agreement at that time. However, the Lord intervened. All leadership in America is on board and in agreement with it now. It's all about power, they are one. The Lord says, *"And so that is the way it is going to go. I want for you to understand, **None of it,** is My system."*

- Democrat and Republican won't exist. It's here, done deal and changes are next. The prince of the power of the air is working very strong through our telecommunications. It's all in the air. After the election, everything will be changed.

July 28, 2012

- I am hearing that: *"The time is short."* I saw it condense itself from tall to short. He (the Anti-Christ) *"thinks to change the times and laws"* (Daniel 7:25). And Revelation 12:12: *"The devil knows he has but a short time."*

- **Vision:** I see blinders over people's eyes (black eyes that can't see) and can see nothing. The god of this world has blinded the minds of those that would believe (God's Truth) – 2 Corinthians 4:4.

- The Spirit of God spoke saying, *"People do not know that who they are agreeing with, **IS** who they are connected to. They don't understand."*
They agree and are connected to the Prince of the Power of the Air (Ephesians 2:2). I prayed earnestly, Lord, what do we do?

August 5, 2012

- The Lord spoke to me, *"The metaphors of the wise will bring trouble/dissension. But deep calls to deep at the noise of your water spouts to others to bring change"* Psalm 42:7.

- **Vision**: Intrinsic; I saw depth and water. *"Water is the element that is unstable; which is also symbolic of the emotions.*

August 15, 2012

- Yahushua speaking, *"When I return, the people will be shocked that they were not in faith."*

  ".......Nevertheless, when the Son of Man comes, will He really find faith on the earth?" Luke 18:8

Listen very carefully:

"Lord," someone asked Him, "will only a few people be saved?"
Yahushua Answered,

*"**Make every effort** to enter through the **narrow door**.
For **many**, I tell you, will **try** to enter
and **will not be able**.*

*After the master of the house gets up and shuts the door,
you will stand outside knocking and saying,
'Lord, open the door for us.'*

*But he will reply, '**I do not know where you are from**.'
Then you will say, 'We ate and drank with you,
and you taught in our streets.'
And he will answer, 'I tell you, **I do not know where you
are from. Depart from me, all you evildoers**.'*

*There will be weeping and gnashing of teeth
when you see Abraham, Isaac, Jacob, and all the prophets
in the kingdom of God, but you yourselves
are thrown out.*

*People will come from east and west
and north and south, and will recline at the table
in the kingdom of God. And indeed, some who are last
will be first, and some who are first will be last."*
Luke 13:23-30

If we read carefully God's Word and receive it for ourselves personally, for today. To read entire passages and investigate the Bible, we will come to know the heart, mind, will and intent of the One who chose and accessed every day people, like us, set apart to Himself to write His Word.

September 5, 2012

- The Lord spoke to me saying, *"Daughter, Only those that listen to the sound of My voice will make it. I've said in the gospels, My sheep know My voice"* (John 10:27).

- *"Pay attention"*. I see like a squeezing and intensity and feel like what is going to happen is a quickening (speeding up) so it can infiltrate and take over faster.

- *"He* (the Anti-Christ) *thinks to change the times and Laws."* That system in America, belongs to Satan. *"Don't try to save that system, I'm after souls."*

- *"Daughter, they (*Christians and the Republicans) *are going to think they are going to rule in the world". They're thinking they will have all power and authority to do what **they want**"*, because they have grown so large (prideful).

- *"I have shown you much evil. The overtaking of evil has saturated America. There is no separation* (that) *it is not in."* Many shiftings and adjustments have to happen.

- *"It's going to make your job harder, so you must look to Me and obey every Word I say."*

- *"Changes are rapidly occurring, accelerating; accelerating on the times. I'm showing you this, so that you understand the time, what time it is. Changes occurring quickly, rapidly".*

*"Among the mature, however, we speak a message of wisdom—
but not the wisdom of this age or of the rulers of this age,*
who are coming to nothing.

*No, we speak of the mysterious and hidden wisdom of God,
which He destined for our glory before time began.*

**None of the rulers of this age understood it.
For if they had, they would not have crucified
the Lord of glory.**

*Rather, as it is written:
"No eye has seen,
no ear has heard,
no heart has imagined,
what God has prepared for those who love Him."*

**But God has revealed it to us by the Spirit.
The Spirit searches all things, even the deep things of God.**

*For who among men knows the thoughts of man except his own spirit
within him?*
So too, **no one knows the thoughts of God
except the Spirit of God.**

*We have not received the spirit of the world,
but the Spirit who is from God,*
that we may understand *what God has freely given us.*

*And this is what we speak, not in words taught
us by human wisdom,*
**but in Words taught by the Spirit, expressing
spiritual Truths in spiritual Words.**

The **natural man does not accept the things that come from the
Spirit of God.**
*For they are foolishness to him
and he* **cannot** *understand them,*

because they are spiritually discerned.

The spiritual man judges all things, but he himself is not subject to anyone's judgment.

*"For who has known the mind of the Lord,
so as to instruct Him?"
But we have the mind of Christ."*
Corinthians 2:6-16

September 8, 2012

Vision: I see me walking into an arena where bumper cars were and I was disconnecting their cable that is connected to the ceiling. It was connected to the prince of the power of the air.

- I will have to open my mouth and speak what God is saying to them as the Lord says, *"Its life and death."* The scripture in Ezekiel, if you know that they (practice) sin and do not warn them, their blood is on your hands (Ezekiel 3 and 33).

- So the Lord says to me: *"I've given you much practice. And you have not told anyone's business. Purity is the only one that can pronounce judgment and bring accurate* (God's viewpoint) *exposure."*

September 9, 2012

- I hear the Lord saying, *"Daughter, Do you know the laws of darkness? Do you know the laws of Darkness seek to seize you? There is nothing you are going to say that will convince them of their evil; evil begat evil. All your good works and good conscience **will never** convince them of the Truth. That's why you have to keep walking in the midst of them as Christ did."*

- I heard the word *"broken"* in prayer for weeks. God tells me: *"The system is broken and you cannot fix it. I did not come to fix it. I've come that they might have life and have it more abundantly. Christ is a reflection of the Father. Love and kindness for others is the example. It's not about the ones that don't receive it. He never went after those that did not want Him."*

- *"They have their laws they work by and their laws work. Those that don't acknowledge the laws of darkness are taken captive by them. You have to have a respect for the laws. You're only here to expose it. Even I didn't take down the kingdom that existed when I was here."*

- *"Life and light are with you and in you. Remember, you won on the Second Heaven and I call you a brilliant warrioress."*

September 15, 2012

- **Vision:** I see "bracelets" on wrists and ankles. It's like a control thing; who you belong to; a system; being owned, like slavery. The Lord asked, *"Do you know why? Because the system wants to tell you who you are."*

- *"Jealousy"* I heard it loud, four times. Satan is jealous. *"Everything Satan had, I gave to mankind. That was the test, I gave you everything instead of him and he is jealous."*

- *"Loosing the bands"* has a feel of intercession.

- **Vision:** I see trouble like **never** before, fear on every side. It will be a grief just to hear the daily report.

- I heard the Words – *"Cancel out the cross"*. If there is no cross, there is no death, burial and resurrection and then we are yet in our sins. Christ would have died in vain. It's their plot. We cancel out the cross by hearing the Words of God and not keeping it (in our hearts with action). Listen to this:

> *"If we **deliberately go on sinning** <u>after</u> we have received the knowledge of the truth, **no further sacrifice for sins remains**, but only a fearful expectation of judgment and of raging fire that will consume all adversaries.*
>
> *Anyone who rejected the law of Moses died without mercy on the testimony of two or three witnesses.*
>
> *How much more severely do you think one deserves to be punished who has trampled on the Son of God, profaned the blood of the covenant that sanctified him and insulted the Spirit of grace?"*
> Hebrews 10:26-29

That's a rhetorical question.

September 20, 2012

- I heard *"closed doors"*. The connotation attached was, the enemy is coming down and locking them. I hear the Lord say, *"But you have the key."*

- The Lord spoke saying, *"The blood* (of His Son on the Cross) *sounds ridiculous to those that don't believe."*

It reminds me of:

> *"For the message of the cross is foolishness **to those who are perishing**, but to us who are being saved it is the **power of God.***
>
> *For it is written, "I will destroy the wisdom of the wise;*

the intelligence of the intelligent I will frustrate."
Where is the wise man? Where is the scribe? Where is the
philosopher of this age?
Has not God made foolish the wisdom of the world?

*For since in the wisdom of God **the world through its wisdom did
not know Him, God was pleased through the foolishness
of what was preached to save those who believe"***
1 Corinthians 1:18-21

- **Vision:** I see the whole (front) upper part of the church. The pulpits on stage. The Lord says, *"I'm getting ready to do a sweeping."* As if a flood is coming through in the leadership. *"With what is left, I am going to need somebody to stand up and instruct the people."*

September 23, 2012

- I hear: *"Acquisitions"* - the act of contracting possessions

November 10, 2012

- Human and Nephilim —when they show up what do I need to do? God's answer: *"Seek Me with your whole heart, that I may be found. Only mankind has* (legal) *authority* (on the earth). *Those that agree with Me, bring the Kingdom of Heaven to earth. In the jungle kingdom, lions know their position and all other animals respect it."*

"They (the Nephilim) *think they are like you, but they are not. That's what makes them so convincing, because they are deceived."* The Nephilim nature is to be like us. *"What does that make their* (Human and Fallen Ones) *nature, if they had gone on to next realm without Christ; unredeemed and carnal."*

"What did I tell you regarding people who are not thinking

like Me?"

I asked, are we able to command lost souls in the spirit? The Lord answered and said: *"You have power and authority to make decisions, they do not. They lost their rights to make decisions on the earth* (when they physically departed the earth). *They don't have to obey, that is their nature. The nature of the person remains with them when they depart and is the same when you are dead. They have no authority that you don't give them. Don't agree with them."*

November 12, 2012

- I heard the words: *"Balance of Power".*

- **Vision:** I saw and heard: *"Obtaining the earth's resources for a balance."* I see scales tipping and trying to balance back and forth. I am reminded of the dream about teaching acquisitions (attorneys and intercessors are synonymous as they both stand in the gap for others).

- I hear, *"Interception"* – As if He is intercepting (taking) people from the earth (example – through death). No one considers that God takes the righteous from the earth, from the time to come. Not necessarily because they can't handle it. But God needs them in Heaven.

"The righteous perish,
and no one takes it to heart;
devout men are swept away,
while no one considers
that the righteous are guided
from the presence of evil.
Those who walk uprightly enter into peace;
they find rest, lying down in death."
Isaiah 57:1-2

- A Balance of Power. He is getting ready for a revealing. Like a drape or cover being taken off to see clearly. That is getting ready to take place; an unveiling. But He says, *"This is something that will separate."*

- **Vision:** I see a type of gases being emitted on the Earth; toxic. I do not know where they come from; a poisoning.

November 19, 2012

- I heard *"Troubled times."*

- **Vision:** I heard and saw: *"Things are not going to be as they seem."* I saw a gap between what He said and then something fell away. *"There will be a great falling away"* 2 Thessalonians 2:1-12 and Hebrews 6:1-6.

- *"Things changing shape"*

2012

- **Vision:** I see that some old has to go, shaking things will fall for new things to come (Governments). The Lord says, *"The old is being done away with and the new is coming in."* They introduced a new structure. He says, *"The land is mourning and reeling to and fro because of that."*

- The new shift will affect the economy. I then heard this *"Do not take that chip"*. Run away to the hills. It's starting this year (the beginning of the end).

- **Vision:** I see "radar" - the earth is set up in every populated area. Radar, ie all systems are in place now to track people. (Tracking GPS in cars, phones, Credit Cards, Drivers license, Personal Computers, Street Corners, etc.) Radar is now on the earth, everywhere we are. And I see that it is connected with a one world currency.

I hear these Words:

- *"Globalization"*

- *"Global economy"*

- *" Global oneness"*

This is how they make us one with the economy.

- I heard, *"Lies.....be told."* Lord, do you want exposure on the lies?

- **Vision:** I see that they know what they are doing and they will lie to us. It's about power, not about the people.

- The Lord says, *"I'm going to give you greater technology information than what you have right now. The majority of "believers" will fall away* (from truly knowing the Living God) *and not give up the technology, thinking it is God. Do not let your hearts be troubled, do not be afraid, I would not tell you this before if I did not love you."*

- *"Associations"* (a connection between ideas, sensations etc. companionship, fellowship, partnership, having common interests, purposes, etc.) Anything connected to us whether human, animal, technology, anything tied to us. We need accurate discernment.

- I hear: *"Challenges for change"* and *"choices for change"*.

- The Lord says, *"In the days ahead, your choices will be placing a challenge on you, so you can make appropriate decisions and change."* Grant me wisdom when to say it, through the scriptures. It's here. There is no intercession, but preparation to receive from God for what we need to do.

- **Vision:** I see something with gasoline (resource).
  I also hear the following Words:

- *"Bank accounts"*

- *"Corn"* (see it as an elevation of it).

- *"Synergy"*

- *"Resources"* (something that lies ready for use or can be drawn upon for aid)

- *"Tracking"*

- *"Immobilizing"* – to prevent the movement of.

- *"France"* - their power was taken away. They were separated from the world in a lot of things they do, more independent and not dependant on others.

- *"Guideline"*

- *"Restitutions"* - giving back to rightful owner. Something that has been lost or taken away.

- *"Deliberate"* (Dee- Liber- Ate or De-lib-er-at – two ways to say it) - carefully thought out or done on purpose.

- *"Stupefy"*- to make stupid, dull or lethargic.

- *"Regime"* – a political or ruling system. Political system.

December 1, 2012

- **Vision:** I see a parting on the left and on the right and it sounds like *"Whose Left?"* Those that are left are the goats. They that will not believe you, those that are carnal minded. On the right are sheep and they are ready to be herded and need a leader. (*This is not a political reference of right or left)

December 4, 2012

- The Lord says, *"More grace for those **who will receive** it."*

CHAPTER 10

IT'S TIME

YEAR OF 2013

January 2, 2013

- **Vision:** I see a Scientific Field.

- Words Received: "*Laboratory*" and "*Escalated*".

- **Vision:** I see people in white lab coats and they have test tubes. They are working on things.

- I heard the Words: "*Disabled*", "*Disengaged*", "*Separate*".

- **Vision:** I see 2013. Something coming bad by Fall of 2013. For the first time, the people will see the evil in our Government and Agencies through injustices done to them by the people. It's worse than offense, it will come by an action. God, Prepare the people. When people are offended, the love goes away. Hard heartedness, hearts growing cold. America is under the Anti-Christ system. God is no longer in the American system.

- I heard: "*Disagreements, Disabled, Disengaged*". This impression I'm sensing is so huge and so large, that I can't stay here. Show us our part, what we can do. The Lord says, "*It's not by strength or by might*" (Zechariah 4:6).

January 17, 2013

- **Vision:** I see to write down the sins of the people in our society right now. An intercession, not an accusation. What is in the way for God to come down mightily on their behalf.
- He wants to change up the game plan. The people are calling good evil and evil good and they don't know the difference anymore (Isaiah 5:20).

- God says, *"It's time"* (the beginning of the kind of work from what he showed 26 years ago).

- **Vision:** I see a shaft of wheat. In the center is a lightning rod from Heaven and it splits down into the very grain of that wheat. It reminds me of rightly dividing, what looks acceptable verses *what is* acceptable with God. The Lord states, *"What the church has seen as a grain of wheat, is not accurate. I don't accept manufactured grain* (man made, through the system of the church), *it's not pure."*

January 20, 2013

- **Vision:** The planet has been over taken by gases, they are coming up and polluting the earth and it is being saturated with it. It's the sins of the people on the planet. I see a toxicity coming out of the people's mouth and going up. Lord, purify your people after the shaking, separate them for your use, continue to let us see the time and the hour for what is coming.

- **Vision:** I see something like a bomb cloud. Destruction, annihilation, devastation, unrecoverable because the people are hooked up with the enemy.

- I hear: *"Justification". "And they* (the children of God), *are going to have to believe this to make it. Eye has not seen, nor ear heard, what God has in store for those that love*

Him" (1 Corinthians 2:9). The sensing is that it will be - stand strong, don't worry for what is to come, because something greater is coming!

- **Vision:** For elevation with Him, we have to go deeper with Him.

- I hear two Words. It might be a sign of the collapse of the economy: *"Toyota", "Collapse".*

I heard the following Words:

- *Equilibrium* – interlocking puzzle.

- *Equinox* – (happening March 20 and Sept 22nd regarding tilting of the earth on its axis (there was more that I did not quiet hear).

- *Parallel*

- *Adjacent* – near, close, neighboring.

- *Connected to and united with.*

- **Vision:** I saw something break away and off to the right of these words on the left. The right side moved away. God says, *"It will look to be a certain way, but it's not that way, it's a lie."*

- He reminds: "That man of sin should not be revealed until there is a falling away" (2 Thessalonians 2:3).

- The Revelation of all these words will be revealed when a falling away comes.

- **Vision**: I see that the Lord is showing, choosing forgiveness more for the days ahead, because the offenses will abound. He says, *"They choose their own, that has nothing to do with you."* It's not God's fault.

- **Vision:** Those that are unfaithful in this last dispensation with what *they* wanted to do instead of what He asked them to do, He will take the authority of what they are doing, from them.

I see that they are coming to a low place and giving over to the next generation (those prepared in spirit). It's part of the proving process, testing and trying. The valley of decision. They refuse correction. In pride, they refuse it, so they will have to stumble over the Rock of offense.

Satan already has them captive. I see them in cages. They keep their offenses because of unforgiveness. There is no faith in pride, nor is there forgiveness.

- This is what the Almighty says, *"This is the great falling away. And it is in their* (regarding their) *faith.* Those with mixture will get beat up. *That is why it is important that those that make it,* **have to hear Me** *and* **think like Me,** *because it will be too confusing on earth, as the enemy has increased; And the people are in denial and they are denying My Word* (through word and deed). *"*

  "Challenge the people for this change and stand in their way. The people will think they are <u>so right</u>, that they will fight you. The prince of this world has keys to all those people (captive) *because they are in his prisons."*

February 15, 2013

- **Vision:** I saw the Word of God or Writings being deposited like coins in a bank account. But it was the Word of God or Writings.

February 16, 2013

The Lord was speaking about "*Nations, People starving. Writings. Investing on the Word. Send or sent*".

March 8, 2013

- I heard the Words:

- *"Ego-Engineering"*

- **Vision:** I saw mechanical movement in this Word above.

- I heard: *"Manufacturing"*. The sensing is, that it is like a whole group in the spirit realm are working together to program this mindset; as if in cloning a certain mind set.

- The Lord says, *"Only those that are in covenant with Me are going to get this. Agreements are a form of covenant. If you covenant with Me, that is your choice/decision. It's a system we don't belong to and I want for you to be aware of it"* (The Ego-Engineering).

- *"These last four years are about teaching you how to not be moved"* (Stability in the midst of all chaos).

- *"It's not meant for everyone to understand."*

    "Rather, we have renounced secret and shameful ways; we do not use deception, nor do we distort the Word of God.

*On the contrary, by setting forth the truth plainly
we commend ourselves to everyone's conscience
in the sight of God.*

*And even if our gospel is veiled,
it is veiled to those who are perishing.*

The god of this age has blinded the minds of the unbelieving
(not faithful because unpersuaded,
i.e. not convinced; describes someone who rejects
or refuses God's inbirthings of faith)
*so that they cannot see the light of the gospel that displays
the glory of Christ, who is the image of God."*
2 Corinthians 4:2-4

- I heard: *"Conditions".* It is said that God's love is unconditional. But the terms and conditions of His covenant are conditional for **both to be in agreement**. We won't get the reward (promises) of the covenant, *unless* we are in agreement with Him through it.

April 18, 2013

Developments in dealing with spirits over my head at night: I identified that they were flying snake types the last months. They have been around for a couple of years or so.

At any rate, they fly. I used to call them "dream weavers" because they darted above my head.

A Theological Professor friend identified them in the breaking down of the Hebrew scriptures and additional Hebrew writings as "Seraphs". Snakes with wings. They fly *and* are snakes.

On Monday, they showed up and I called them out as Seraphim. They not only reacted, as they do when I catch them in the act, but, they did not come back! On Tuesday, the smoke odor showed back up. My Theologian friend told me that, one type of Seraph is the snake and the other is the fire breathing dragon. So, I rebuked it as such. The smoke did not stop. However, it was the first night in a very long time that I actually got a full 8 hours of sleep.

On the weekend, there were spirits that were large, very large and they wanted to kill me. Also identified by my Hebrew Theologian Professor as (fallen) Cherubim. These are all the fallen ones, of course. Not the ones that stayed with God.

And there is so much more to talk about on this subject. Perhaps if I write another book, if the Lord wills, I will expose these so the people of God know how to do relevant warfare.

May 13, 2013

- **Vision:** I see the earth quaking, grounds shifting underneath. For those that are the Lord's, I feel it is a help. Through the instability, it will shift us to who we are and where we need to be. I heard the Lord say: *"The earth is full of My glory."*

May 31, 2013

I heard the Words:

- *"Overthrow the system".*

- *"The heavens are declaring and decreeing a testimony of the King of Kings and Lord of Lords. A great host for the battle. There will appear signs in the heavens and on the earth beneath. Signs of a great battle and struggle between darkness and light."*

- *"Evil will not prevail."*

- *"All destruction is not evil"* (it's a cleansing of the land and destroying evil).

- *"Timber"* (Yelling out the warning: because something big is getting ready to fall).

- The saying, "you can't see the forest for the trees". The people can't really see without a cleansing of the purification of the land. Then they realize what is important and live more simply, their entire lives are changed.

- *"Challenge"* (Sound the alarm).

- *"Sweeping"* (USA cleaning house).

- *"Changes"* (so we have lasting change).

- **Vision:** I see a watch and the Almighty God is tapping on it and indicating that *"it's time".* I see a large watch with a second hand moving on it on a man's arm and he is taking his finger and thumb and bringing them together, as if to indicate *"The Time is Short."*

- What are we to do Father? I heard, *"It's time to shake the heavens and Earth. I will cause to be revealed what is in them* (Heaven and Earth) Hebrews 12:26, Isaiah 13:13, Haggai 2:6, 21, Joel 3:16). *Things are going to be revealed that you will not believe."*

- *God says: "Be persistent".* Press into Him for the Truth.

June 8, 2013

I heard the Words:

- *"Right of way"*

- *"Passage"*

- *"I've brought you here for such a time as this, to prepare you for a future. It's not to your left or right but right in front of you.*

   "It's important for you to know for the days ahead (big battle ahead) who you are. Remember, I said it's not on your left or right, but right in front of you."

   "There is so much for you to see. I brought you here to see it and you will never believe it, if it were told to you. You have to see it."

- *"Time will tell. You have much to know and much to find out."*

- *"Courtship"* (see a court at a house).

- *"European empire"*

- *"Hierarchy"*

- *"Chain of command"*

- *"European nation"*

- *"Royalty"*

- **Vision:** I see where Kings and Queens sit up high, on a throne and I see a see a Lion with a crown on his head and seated on a big throne.

- *"Agreeable"*

- *"Agreeable for (four?) records".*

- *"Tri Top"* (coming up to a point).

- *"Records"*

- *"It's in the records".*

- *"Obvious place".*

- *"Well-preserved & protected".* What is? The records or land? The secret that I don't know, has been kept well-preserved and protected to reveal what I'm suppose to find out.

- *"Classical literature"*

- *"Performing arts"*

- *"Julianne"* English language derived from Latin.

- *"So much for you to see"*

- *"All going to tell a story"*

- *"Trouble"*

- *"Shape shifters intervening"*

- **Vision:** I saw a scepter given to a hand.

- *"Changes will occur quickly"*

- *I'm shifting and shaping the times. They will come (shape shifters) out of the Earth to interrupt it.*

August 12, 2013

- The Lord spoke saying, *"Purpose in today's world is an idol".* God has been working with me the last five years to drain me of my own life. No idols (which for me, was purpose). It took 40 years for God to get the purpose out of Moses, so He could put in His own.

- He says, *"If you brag about your abilities, it's no longer I, but you. If I do it, you take no glory."* If He does it, then they have a reason to fear.

- **Vision:** I can see all over the earth in different groups (political, religious, families, etc.) and I see divisions, cracks, dissentions. The Lord says, *"You cannot be divided in your way of thinking at all. The only way to get through to them is to think like Me".* Without Him no one can.

- The Lord is saying, *"This is why I* (have) *allowed you to suffer, so you know what it feels like and you're not affected when you go back into it* (to help others). *I don't want you to lose heart or faint. I have never left you. What you thought was for ruin or demise is actually for strength and virtue, a power in the earth."*

- *"The earth is never going to be the same."*

August 29, 2013

I hear the Words and see the following **Visions:**

- *"Fire"*

- **Vision:** I see a jail or prison.

- *"Flies"*
- *"Trouble the waters"*

- All those flies (Beelzebub) are the counterfeit and the people will think it is God's presence and it is not. All the things they are going through and it is not going to be Him, but the counterfeit.

- **Vision:** I see abiding the furnace of affliction; the people have to be purified.

- *"It's coming"*

- Flies - demons. I am reminded, there are as many of them as are of you. Bondage, prison.

- Fire – purification

- Highly emotional time. The people being led by how they feel.

- I see that we will have to be watchful of who is who.

September 13, 2013

- The Syria/Russia/USA thing could be the September/Fall thing that God was talking about, that would change the structure of the system eventually.

I asked the Lord for direction in His Word and that He would speak to me about what He wanted to talk about. The Bible opened to 2 Kings 20. The Title – The Syrian Army Surrounds Samaria.

September 30, 2013

- I feel before I come out of my own personal Dark Night, that there will be an all out assault of the enemy against me (*Author note: which occurred January 2015 and again in May 2018).

- *"Troubling the waters"*

October 15, 2013

- The Lord said, *"It's going to be harder to save them* (those that have not accepted Him) *because they don't want anything to do with Christianity on the earth today. But the people will need to believe."* He said before, there are as many of them (the enemy that opposes) as there are of us (the workers of righteousness).

  - *"A forfeiture"*. It's the sense of becoming "nothing" or suffering loss, so that Satan no longer has access.

  - God says, *"I do My works in secret* (in darkness Genesis 1) *so corruption can't get to it."* For example, creating life in the womb.

I asked, "Darkness is good then"? Yahushua went down to the dark in the lower regions. He was the light in that place of darkness. He had power over them; He had the keys too. It is in that darkness we take back our power and authority. It's before the resurrection power, before He rose again.

> *"That I may know him and the power of his resurrection,*
> *and may share his sufferings, becoming like him*
> *in his death, that by any means possible*
> *I may attain the resurrection from the dead.*
> Philippians 3:10-11

- **Vision:** I saw people that had been burdened down with depression. I saw them leave their body and go to Heaven. There is no burden in Heaven. I see their body on earth, it's cellular. They carry generations of depression and sins; it was cellular and in each generation it was carried down and it became heavier and weightier.

> *"Cast your cares on the LORD and he will sustain you;*
> *he will never let the righteous be shaken."*
> Psalm 55:2

Then Yahushua said, "Come to me, all of you who are weary and carry heavy burdens, and I will give you rest. Take my yoke upon you. Let me teach you, because I am humble and gentle at heart, and you will find rest for your souls. For my yoke is easy to bear, and the burden I give you is light."
Matthew 11:28-30

"Beloved, I pray that in every way you may prosper and enjoy good health, as your soul also prospers."
3 John 1:2

God created us to live a full life here. A life in relationship with Him. With peace and with joy. There is no reason to go home early! Unless we are just not equipped and prepared to keep His Word in our hearts, that our soul would prosper and therefore our health would prosper. Let go, trust God.

A GREATER WEIGHT OF GLORY

October 19, 2013

God gave to me today: 2 Samuel 24 and 1 Kings 1. Upon reading, I realized a huge problem I have. I mean, really freaking big. I am offended by God's Sovereignty. I was so offended reading those chapters. I didn't realize that, 1. I was offended by this before. And 2. I didn't realize to what extent that this has been the problem. Sovereignty. Although, that is what He has been talking to me about now for the last months. I knew that I didn't understand it well. And I asked for Him to show me more.

The Lord also gave to me Job 36 - 38. I discovered that this is what Job was offended by as well. God's sovereignty. It is highly offensive. But, I prayed and I asked God to forgive me and I repented of this. It hurts. But I am learning to embrace pain and great sorrow. I feel I have so far to go with this. But, I don't think it comes so natural. I believe it's a supernatural work. God *"working in me both to will and to do of His good pleasure in order to fulfill His purpose"* Philippians 2:13.

Job also was always very blessed, like myself. Maybe some pride was lurking. Although God did call him righteous. I just don't think that anyone really understands or knows God. Not really. And that is exactly what He is looking for. That is my issue. No one really knows or understands me. Imagine how God feels!

I find, and what is further angering is, that He has not chosen others to know sovereignty intimately, like He has chosen me to. I am mad at that. I mean, this separates me more than before! How are they ever going to know or understand when God does something sovereign in your life and He doesn't do it to or for them? It's like being supernatural or an alien or something. No one knows how you got that way, because they are not like this!

So, in reflecting on Sovereignty, pride will fight against it. I think about my dream last night. I fought against the ways of the boss, because I thought I was right! Until I had time to reflect afterward and the issue wasn't even what I thought it was!

There is a way that is right and the boss knows the way, even if we do not get it at the time.

So a lack of understanding will fight. That is pride.

To accept in total compliance and acquiescence is hard. The only thing I know, as God has now taught me, is to embrace even what I have hated. The pain, the suffering, the sorrow. And who knew really, that even that, would be of God?

I worked so hard at knowing Him. Finding out His ways. Finding the laws of the Kingdom and the supernatural. The keys, if you will. Not realizing all along that He still holds the "Sovereign key". Five straight chapters (Job 38-42), God reproved Job after all he'd been through! I don't know how that man was standing at the end.

Considering and hoping, that as the Lord has given me these chapters today in all, if it means that I am close to the end of the dark nights of my soul. (*Author note: It wasn't, I still had 4 1/2 years to go).

The Last Chapter God gave me today was: Jeremiah 12. Entitled – "Jeremiahs Complaint and God's Answer". I am utterly saddened that I cannot even be the good friend of God that I thought I was. How can He trust counsel that does not think like Him? Jeremiah's complaint seems so valid. And God's answer to Jeremiah, was to repent for not thinking like Him (Jeremiah 15).

One cannot even live without breath from our Creator. And nobody (naturally) knows this because, He has set it to happen so 'naturally'. So that all natural events, they do not even think are Him. Even the wisest man of his time, King Solomon realized:

*"I saw all the work of God, that man cannot find out
the work that is done under the sun. However much man may toil in
seeking, he will not find it out.
Even though a wise man claims to know,
he cannot find it out."*
Ecclesiastes 8:17

*"What exists is out of reach and very deep.
Who can fathom it?"*
Ecclesiastes 7:24

Unless the people see and experience miracles, they do not believe. I am angry at this also. I cannot make anything happen, nor can I make God do anything whereby they believe.

I really hope the next step is that I am healed, set free and delivered from this anger and opposition that I have carried within. I am so mad that they do not love God and serve God and acknowledge Him.

I am mad that they walk away and forget Him and what they have been taught. I am mad that their minds do not work at full capacity (as if mine does). But I don't know why I am so obsessed with Him. That I *have to know Him*. That I *have to* find a way to submit to Him, even though it will kill me. And it has. I don't understand it.

And I am madder that I don't like everything about Him! What a revelation. Like being married and coming out of your honeymoon and you find out things about your spouse that you are appalled at! You'd think this would have happened a lot sooner than in 27 years! Maybe I was in denial. Lol, I make me laugh.

And when I was reading in Jeremiah, I was thinking, why doesn't He just leave us all alone to do what we will and see how it turns out? Much like He does seed time and harvest? I am just so educated on *His Ways,* that I forgot His Sovereignty! How sad for me. Mostly because, it's still a mystery. Especially now that I don't get it at all! I wonder, why would He even choose me? And for what? And maybe He didn't. How prideful of me.

Honestly there are times I cannot even stand that I have wisdom. What has it profited? Separation from others and knowledge of God and His ways, only to exclude His Trump Card.

"But as I looked at everything I had worked so hard to accomplish,
it was all so meaningless—like chasing the wind.
There was nothing really worthwhile anywhere."
Ecclesiastes 2:11

October 24, 2013

- The Lord spoke to me saying, *"Kindness is a commodity."* A brand of heaven that will stand out. Kindness alone will be a stark contrast of the reality of the darkness on the earth. It will be what connects people to the Kingdom.

It's like oil and a bridge. Kindness runs out of the people's mouths and goes under others feet and it becomes a bridge for them to get to the other side. Kindness will stand out. It is the Kingdom's policy. If people can be kind, it comes from a place of substance.

Kindness is a respect, it requires patience and for you to pay attention. Kindness is not selfish. Kindness is proof of God's love.

One day in 1998, the Lord spoke to me about a situation that I was agitated over saying, *"Daughter, be kind"*. I retorted, "Kind?! Why should I be kind?" He gently responded, *"Because I Am kind"*. I argued for a while, but we know how that turned out.

October 29, 2013

I was harassed last night by (Fallen Council) Ophanim or Seraphim and they kept me up and imposed visions that were like news reels that would not quit in my mind. They force a type of mind control, I will not accept.

And the only way they can try to get to me, is when I am asleep. But, I cannot sleep when they are around. My spirit man is too privy. But they wait and wake me in the middle of my sleep. Non-stop.

I had more patience than I normally have. I did my battle with them as the Lord has taught me, but finally, I was able to not feel irritated or upset about it. Just understanding, that this is what they do, this is their function and so I stayed consistent and diligent in the fight as the Lord has shown me to.

Revelations today from the Lord:

- I asked Him why I don't feel like going anywhere with anyone or do anything? It's like, I don't enjoy people anymore and I hate that, as I am such a people person. It doesn't make sense to me. I do realize that I used all my energy to be around things and people that did not profit and I ran out of energy for those things (So I thought). But, the Lord said to me today, *"It's not that you don't want to be around people, it's that you see what is in them and you don't prefer that"*.

- **Vision:** And then He showed me a sea of people and they were all the same. And He was right. I love people. I have no more energy to give out. I am drained myself. And when they have nothing to offer and only take because of what is in them, I have no desire to be around it at all. I am glad for Him telling me. It's been so dark and I've been in adaption through this dark night of the soul. I don't really understand everything. I just know that it is so.

- Today, when I was in prayer, I heard the Word, *"Change"*. So I began to pray it (as I have for sooooooooooooo many years now. It's the same Word for years isn't it? Agggh, when will I get it?) and then I waited and I heard the word, *"Revolutionize"* and became aware that I didn't know what it meant. So, I looked it up and the first word was, *"Change"!* Then He said, *"Transform, Shake up, Turn the world upside down, Metamorphosis"*.

- I also heard, *"Sanction"*. So we (Intercessory team) prayed according to the Words given.

November 6, 2013

Today I heard the Lord saying these Words:

- *"Those in the system who hear another voice will not believe God."*

- *"Cleverly disguised"*. Something in our Government is cleverly disguised.

- *"Package or package deal"* Associated with the Affordable Health Care Act? Not sure.

- The Lord says regarding the Government: *"Eye has not seen, ear has not heard. They have something similar, a deceiving, a duping. They know what they are doing and are doing it on purpose. It is evil what they have in mind."*

- *"Challenge for change"*

- *"Choices"*. The word was illuminated. He will elevate many things; a lifting of darkness for people to have a chance for choice for change.

Lord, I pray Sovereignty for deliverance from anything we put before You. Sovereign deliverances.

November 14, 2013

The Picture becomes a bit clearer

- Vision: I see President Obama in a vision. I had a concern when I saw him in pictures for the last two to three days.

  I see the oval office and then a man, that is the President; but I saw a fallen position, he had fallen. He is not upholding his office, (he is beside the office); and he is not the man who was elected, but has his own agenda. He is not as solid. He has fallen short. It feels he won't do anything but ride it out.

- God said, it is *"Set up for the next one"* He has stepped down and aside so one stronger can come in.

- It's a set up for him to mess up the system, so that in 2016 someone comes in with a "better idea". This is not good. What do we do? I hear: *"That the man of sin should be revealed."* The Man of perdition - 2 Thessalonians 2:3. We pray the man of perdition be revealed, a revealing.

- *"Trying times"* ahead.

  What is our position at this time and how do we pray?

- Stay attentive, be alert. Ephesians 6:18, I Peter 4:7 and Chapter 5, Mark 13:33, Colossians 4:2, Acts 20:31, I Corinthians 16:13, Luke 21:36, Mark 13:37.

- *"Be Kind, because it is a sign and wonder when everyone is angry; it stands out."* Pride and self-pity are a part of the fallen (nature) identity.

- *"Trouble the waters and align the meridian".*

- Seek first the Kingdom of God and His Righteousness.

November 22, 2013

- **Vision:** I sense something coming stronger and stronger in the earth. I see a fog coming in and you can't see clearly and it drowns out all the presence of God. It crowds out God, people are so busy with other things, that they are not paying attention.

- **Vision:** I see corporate America. The system is like a crime group, like mafia, they know what they are doing. The agenda is crime to man and to the system, it is criminal – robbing people and "corrupting" God.

- I hear the following Words: *"That's what you are sensing on the earth."* I see a dome covering the USA.

- Hearing: *"Subliminal"* through any of our five senses it can come - see, hear, feel.

- *"Elements"*, i.e, Component, constituent, atmospheric agencies; example the weather.

- *"Discharged"* – A release, a burden or contents, unload.

- *"Changing dimensions"* – Dimensions in wiki says: math and physics 666

Dimensions project something not there. I see in the spirit, which is another dimension.

- *"Accessing dimensions"*. Are you saying our Government is doing this?

- *"Making something appear what it isn't"*. I see some people walk in extreme bright white light with full knowledge of it.

- *"Illusional therapy"*. Sounds on I cloud, makers of Apeople, illusional, false or leading impression of reality therapy, curing or healing, treatment (*Author note: the words above that seem to be mis-spelled, I am not sure. I had a note taker. I consider if God was saying icloud or a cloud. And Apple or a people).

- *"Classification"* Mathematics, media, science. It's happening right now.

- Hearing: *"radio frequencies"* Airwaves.

Oh, Lord, how do we live this life successfully in the days ahead?

CHAPTER 11

DEEPER INTO THE SPIRIT

YEAR OF 2014

March 1, 2014

- I hear the Lord saying, *"There are as many of them as there are of you."* They are here because of the strongholds and wills of men. Their (the enemies of God) strength and power come from human agency, the wills (decisions, choices) of mankind. God's will is done on the earth, **when** His people agree with Him.

- *"Interchangeable"*. We can't tell difference between them.

- Without the dark night of the soul (sovereignty) I would not have been able to identify them.

- *"Treatment"* (The deadly wound of anti-Christ?).

- *"This time"* pointing at a big face of a watch - Mark 13:19 and Matthew 24:21.

"For those will be days of tribulation unmatched from the beginning of God's creation until now, and never to be seen again. If the Lord had not cut short those days, nobody would be saved. But for the sake of the elect, whom He has chosen, He has cut them short."
Mark 13:19-20

- *"It's so important* (for the days ahead that) *you have the right Name."* **YAHUWAH**. We will have to have the right Name to pierce the darkness. It carries God's pure power.

March 9, 2014

- I gave up I offenses of certain people. I am mad at stupidity and jealousy. The Lord says, *"It's not going to do you any good."* I feel devalued; but so was our Lord on the cross.

At the point of greatest weakness, when you feel you are losing, you are winning. Like Christ on the cross, for God's sake, when He was high and lifted up, in His deepest pain and darkest most alone hour, that was when He was winning the battle.

When He ascended to the Kingdom of Heaven, He took His blood and spread it on God's mercy seat, so that God remembers mercy over the people. He now looks to us, those whom He can call on and trust on the earth to fulfill the sufferings of Christ, as Paul said:

"Who now rejoice in my sufferings for you,
*and **fill up that which is behind of the afflictions of Christ in my flesh** for his body's sake, which is the church."*
Colossians 1:24

*"And if children, then heirs—heirs of God and fellow heirs with Christ, **provided we suffer with him***
in order that we may also be glorified with him."
Romans 8:17

"That I may know him and the power of his resurrection,
*and **may share his sufferings, becoming like him in his death,***
that by any means possible I may attain the resurrection from the dead."
Philippians 3:10-11

The Lord says,

"The answer is not in suffering,
but what comes from the suffering."

If He is the one that leads us to suffering, we can be assured He has a plan for an outcome, a huge outcome, a Kingdom outcome. Don't get stuck in the suffering. Don't break down, watch out for pit falls. There's no other way to bring the Kingdom here to the earth, except to go through this suffering, this dying to the carnal nature. You can't get it *when* suffering; you have to go *through it,* as Yahushua did. There's a plan. There's a follow through to the plan. Keep going.

- He says to me, *"Such is the Kingdom, in the face of all adversity; you stand. There will be persecution, but I don't want you to pay attention to that".* Stay focused on Him. *"This has been your training...."*

THE ACCUSER IS HERE, ON THE EARTH

April 17, 2014

- I hear the Lord say, *"There is a divine shaking of the Kingdoms."*

When we see the kingdom of man (the world system) falling, this means the Kingdom of heaven in coming! Yes, this is a good thing! Something is coming....it feels from the Right – East – Judgment, wickedness (spiritual).

*"And I heard a loud voice in heaven saying:"***Now have come***
*the salvation and the power and the kingdom of our God,
and the authority of His Christ.*

For *the accuser of our brothers has been thrown down—
he who accuses them day and night before our God.*

They (God's people) *have conquered him by the blood
of the Lamb and by the word of their testimony.
And they did not love their lives*

so as to shy away from death.
Therefore rejoice, O heavens, and you who dwell in them!
But woe to the earth and the sea; with great fury the devil
has come down to you, knowing he has only a short time. "
Revelation 12:10-12

Per God's Word, His Kingdom comes here *in the midst of* the enemy being here. God's people, through the blood of the Lamb (Christ's Work on the Cross), the word of our testimony (our own personal overcoming) and not loving our lives to the death (done by faith), is how we win.

- It's a darkness that comes of lies and deceptions. They will be covering us like a fog and it will strengthen the people to believe lies and nothing is going to be as it seems. It's huge and thick, like a dust storm! It will cover the people and set up for the Anti-Christ.

Lord, how do we secure ourselves at this time? How are we going to make it?

The Lord answered:

"Constant Repentance. Greater Love. Put on the full Armor of God." Stressing the Breastplate of Righteousness, which covers the heart. Guard your heart. The enemy will target that area! *"Guard your heart above all else, for it determines the course of your life"* Proverbs 4:23.

- *"And this is the reason, lies and deception will strengthen them for the end time battle, to fight against the Lord."* The enemy will use the lies and deception to rally against the Lord and His people.

The Lord instructed: *"Stay in intercession and greater love".* When lies and deception is enforced over the people, they will "right fight" against everyone that truly knows and walks with God. It will separate the sheep from the goats.

I then heard the following Words:

- *"Roman times"*

- *"Brutal rule and force"*

- *"All being taxed in*

- *"Bondage"*

- *"Bringing a Nation to its knees"*

- **Vision:** I see America in servitude to a dictator not Yahuwah (though they attribute it to God).

- "Setting you up for a fall." Through lies and deceptions Many people we love will fall away. They do not agree. There will be rebellion against the Government. *We need to know who is who.* Sheep verses goats. Don't stay with them to keep the peace. This will be after the Lies and deceptions (it's not this year).

- *"Separation".* He is forcing a separation to see who belongs to God and who doesn't. Who thinks like Him and who does not.

- **Vision:** I see a separation and division. Something coming down from above. Separating chaff from wheat. *"This division, this separation for a time."*

- *"Changes"* - **Vision:** I saw a clock and clock parts and said over and over… *"changes".*

- *"Summary of parts".*

- *"Collections".*

- *"Making up the whole".*

- *"Holy"*

- *"Holidays"*. I looked up Holy holidays. Could be (a part) regarding lies and deceptions.

- He is saying, *"At an appointed time"*.

Are we supposed to be interceding to change this? The Lord spoke: *"I Am simply preparing you with the information. I have given people, for years, a chance to come out and I have reasoned with them."*

April 17, 2014

- The I AM says, *"And My Kindness leads to repentance. Forgive them their trespasses and I will forgive yours. Huge offenses such as the world has never seen!!!"*

- He says, *"No blame"*, because the accuser of the brethren dwells in blame; that is his domain; that's his thing. That is why offenses cannot be tolerated, because there is blame in offense and Satan dwells there; we cannot have it.

Consider this passage. Paul speaking here about communion with the Lord:

"So then, whoever eats the bread or drinks the cup
of the Lord in an unworthy
(unworthy of God, not accepting His righteousness
for your own) *manner, will be guilty*
(held liable) *of sinning against the body*
and blood of the Lord.

Everyone ought to examine (put to the test to reveal
what is good and genuine) *themselves before they eat*
of the bread and drink from the cup.

*For those who eat and drink **without** discerning*
(investigating, judge thoroughly – literally, judging "back-and-forth",
to doubt) *the body of Christ, they eat and drink judgment*
(Emphasizing its result. This is everlasting damnation or torment
for the unredeemed. It dramatically links cause-to-effect.
Every decision (action) we make carries inevitable eternal results
on themselves).

*That is why many among you are weak and sick
and a number of you have fallen asleep* (spiritually
or have actually died). *But if we were more discerning
with regard to ourselves, we would not come under such judgment.*

*Nevertheless, when we are judged in this way by the Lord,
we are being disciplined so that we will not be finally condemned
with the world."*
1 Corinthians 11:27-32

May 28, 2014

- God says, *"Knowledge will be poured out. There will be
  'other knowledge' and it will corrupt everything* (be
  twisted) *and fight God's* (true) *knowledge. In the dark,
  you will need to know what to do, because it* (God's
  knowledge) *will equip you with what to do."*

- **Vision:** God is showing the dark side. The enemy will try
  everything he can to corrupt, because he is here, the race is
  on. He knows what time it is and knows he has but a short
  time - Revelation 12:12. A reminder of corruption. It may not
  always be what it seems. The Anti-Christ uses flatteries
  (Daniel 11).

- *"Great, great, great changes are happening in this time* (of
  darkness). *This is all good."* God calls this good. Who am I
  to disagree? I will glory in His purpose.

- **Vision:** The Lord is showing: how people will be key players, like marionettes on strings. The strings are a stronghold over them (by their will having something in common with the enemy and not in God's nature) and are controlling moves and actions. So this power will empower what is in them. Their undiscovered carnal corrupt nature. If we are empowered with God, we will be stronger! Decisions will be solidified in that time.

- *"Specifics"*

- *"Dimensions"* (Revelation 11).

- **Vision:** Declare and Decree the way of the Lord. I see You are showing me Treasure on Earth. The revelation of treasure. Making room, making way. In the Old Testament, it was a treasure of the Lord. There is a secret chamber and it is closed off. I think of: *"Now we have this treasure in earthen vessels, to show that this surpassingly great power is from God and not from us."* 2 Corinthians 4:7

- I am reminded of the Dream I had of attorneys on the earth, acquiring divine acquisitions.

- The Lord spoke: *"I don't want you to feel that you won't have everything you need. You will have everything you need."*

- *"Take heed"*. I heard this three 3 times. A warning to pay attention.

- **Vision:** I see dimness over the treasure. It has someone escorting it, like watching over it and he looks like a high priest. He looks royal and rich with crown of jewels on his head, but he is not a king.

- God revealed, that we (His Covenant people) are making a way for You to abide here 1000 years. You are setting up

Your Kingdom right under the devil's nose! Just like Satan missed the point - God's secret, right under His nose - regarding the Messiah. Otherwise Satan would not have brought Him to execution. Right after that, the King of Glory made His way to the underworld , to take the keys away and set up an everlasting Kingdom coming on Earth . It truly was the beginning of all things new.

"When He ascended on high, He led captives away
(from the god of the underworld – Satan)
and gave gifts to men."

What does "He ascended" mean, except that He also first descended to the lower parts of the earth?

He who descended is the very One who ascended above all the heavens, in order to fulfill (complete) *all things* (written of Him).

And it was He who gave some to be apostles,
some to be prophets, some to be evangelists,
and some to be pastors and teachers;
to equip *the saints for works of ministry*
and to build up the body of Christ,
until we all reach unity in the faith
and in the knowledge of the Son of God,
as we mature to the full measure of the stature of Christ."
Ephesians 4:8-13.

And we are now reaching that pinnacle – the culmination of all things. What God has been waiting for. The manifestation of the Sons and Daughters of God to rise. Get mature. Grow up now. It's time.

- So, the Lord says, *"And now, it's all about the equipping"* (Ephesians 4). His glory will be revealed during that time.

- I said, Father, You do miracles for unbelievers to prove You are God. He is happy about it. He is proud to be able to bring it to this time. He is undermining Satan.

- He says, *"My people will be willing in the day of My power* (Psalm 110:3). *There will be a phenomenon during that time. Do you know what that means?* (I answered: Revelation 12, the woman clothed with the sun, the moon and the stars?) *I am giving her all power and authority".* She is the church, people who walk with God. Could this get any better?

- Keepers of the Treasury. We declare and decree (Job 22:28) that we have your provision into the earth; that what we have need of comes from You. Open our hearing and heart to receive from You more.

June 4, 2014

- I sense God's presence and His attention is on Russia. There is a distraction. He wants us to be watchful.

- The Lord says, *"I have said, let not your heart be troubled, neither let it be afraid. I already told you perilous times, wars and rumors of war, famine, desolations, many troublous things on earth. It's My Kingdom that leads to repentance."*

  Reference - Matthew 24. I am finding interesting here that He did not say, His Kindness leads to repentance, as the scripture says (Romans 2:4) and He often brings up the subject of Kindness. But here, Kingdom. My consideration on this is, that those of another "kingdom", one that says they are of Him, but are not, **will not** repent." Food for thought.

- That's why choices (God's gift of making our own decisions from the beginning) are being poured out. It enables them to make a choice, to enable them to change their minds (a grace).

- The Lord shared something that I was coming to learn through the specific method of warfare that He taught me with the Fallen Council. Regarding the fallen council and their plan, *"They can't be defeated because it is purposed."*

Again, this is sovereignty. As in the book of Job. He could not change a thing, though he tried. In Jeremiah, for Jonah. This list could go on. There is some intercession and prayers God will not listen to or hear because of the accumulated sin, the separation of people with Him on the earth.

"As for you, do not pray for these people, do not offer a plea or petition on their behalf, and do not beg Me, for I will not listen to you."
Jeremiah7:16

Then the Lord said to me: *"Even if Moses and Samuel should stand before Me, My heart would not go out to this people. Send them from My presence, and let them go."*
Jeremiah15:1

The Psalmist lamented:
"If I regard iniquity in my heart, the Lord will not hear me"
Psalm 66:18

- Vision: He is showing there is a system coming from the 2nd Heaven, where enemy has ruled, to the Earth. It is not implemented yet, but it is in place.

"Don't underestimate the power of your obedience to Me".

June 16, 2014

I heard the following Words:

- *"Prerequisite"* something necessary to an end or to the carrying out of a function.

- "Requisition" an act of formally requiring or calling upon someone to perform an action.

- **Vision:** I saw arms out, hanging on too tight, frustrating, letting go.

- "Shaking loose" (let go).

- "No man"

- "Condition of the soul".

- Scripture: *"Eye has not seen, ear has not heard, what God has for them that love Him."* 1 Corinthians 2:9

- **Vision:** I see a plot of land and it is not in good condition. The earth is affected by our sin, it is contaminated.

> *'The earth mourns and withers; the world languishes*
> *and fades; the exalted of the earth waste away.*
> *The earth is defiled by its people;*
> *they have transgressed the laws;*
> *they have overstepped the decrees and broken*
> *the everlasting covenant.*
>
> *Therefore a curse has consumed the earth*
> *and its inhabitants must bear the guilt...."*
> Isaiah 24:4-.6

- **Vision:** A development of something political. It's going to happen in the fall (September or after) like a swelling, through the media. The political side is in agreement with the darkness.

June 17, 2014

I hear a declaring of these Words:

- *"Sovereignty"*

- *"Indulgence"*

- *"Glutton"* giving into their desires.

- *"Desire"* a sense of seduction.

- *"Appetites"* a neediness, ravenous appetites have increased.

- **Vision:** I see something regarding the prophets that I have esteemed in the Church. I see them. I am hidden. The Lord says to me, *"You are not like them, I have kept you separate and you will speak hard core words and they* (the other prophets) *will not agree with Me."*

July 15, 2014

- **Vision:** I see that those *who live by* their Faith will be in a different cycle from Heaven.

- *"Political campaigning"*

- *"Arrival"* this might be connected with Word which was received few months back about the political scene.

- *"Plots and take-overs"*

- *"Agenda".*

- It feels like You Lord, are telling on the "King's business".

July 24, 2014

I hear these Words:

- *"Mark of the beast"*

- *"Don't forget the power will be here for the enemy too."*
- If we are not in agreement with the system (of the world) we will be shunned and fought against. The Lord says, *"Most people will go along with this."* Because mainstream Christianity and the Government will agree together.

- *"System implementation"* execution of a plan.

- *"Treasury"*

- *"Trickles"* slowly things coming on us.

- *"Weights"* burdens on us.

- *"Program detection"*

We tore down all things that think to gain power over us and came under the things that belong to the Lord.

July 28, 2014

I hear the Lord saying:

- *"Trouble the waters"* Stirring up things that need to be, to bring about healing. Reference John 5:4

- San Diego, California is coming before me very strong. What is it? Have your way, do your will in San Diego. Your presence Father, over San Diego.

- I sense what is getting ready to happen is so big. Transitional over the next few months. It's like a big bubble over us. It's here, but not released yet. It's good. It's an energy and it contains power.

- Our will, plus Your will is Power on the earth. The Lord says, *"The time of transition is here"*. As in the days of Noah (Matthew 24:37). Supernatural power on Earth.

- *"Restoration"* The Garden is a restoration. They were perfect in the Garden before they broke their agreement with God. The power coming in, will bring the Restoration. The recovery of all.

- **Vision:** The power source looks like water. Trouble the waters. But it is more of a substance and it is above our heads flowing and the word *"Restoration"* was in it.

- In the beginning, the Spirit of the Lord hovered over the face of the deep - Genesis 1:2. But now, the water is above us. He is announcing the end before it begins. He is announcing the restoration of God in the earth right now.

- The key is as simple as *paying attention and being willing* to do it *His* Way.

August 13, 2014

I saw and heard the following:

- **Vision:** I see a crematory dark and gray with smoke rising and ashes of people everywhere. It had to do with Government taking and burying, throwing in a pile. I see buildings and structures. I sense it is an Anti-Christ spirit, moving everything around.

- *"Chosen Vessel"* is a carrier for a cause.

- I recall Chuck Pierce saying, "Warfare is only won through Covenant War", It is only through keeping covenant with God, that we will win the war.

- Regarding the Words about September and Fall, we need more than anything, faith and patience.

- **Partial Vision:** A Goat or a ram with long horns (black?) and fur that is an orange-brown in color.
- *"Separation. "This separation is going to create a whole new level or type of warfare."*

- Father, you have said to me that, "You are raising up those in this hour who will not take "no" for an answer". You have been preparing and training your people for this. A new level of warfare will create division. In the last days, the book of knowledge will be opened and poured out (Daniel 12:9).

- *"Teachable"*

- *"Training"* The anointing to train others and we are teachable by You and can do this for others. We need this anointing to break the yokes and unplug them from the System.

August 22, 2014

I heard the following Words from the Lord:

- *"Coercion or Conversion"* Coercion is persuading people to do something by using force or threat (such as martial law).

192

Conversion is change from one religion, belief, political party, etc. to another.

- *"I'm tearing down old structures".*

- *"Transitional phases"* from one state or condition to another. In between the process there are changes going on.

- *"Moon"*

- *"Times and seasons".* Lord, raise us up to know.

- *"Cleansing"*

- *"Purifying the altar".*

- *"Synchronizing"* to operate at the same time or rate.

- *"Time lapse"*

- *"Tablets"* Moses

August 27, 2014

The Lord said, *"Destruction of the system"* and *"to prophesy to the 4 corners* (of the Earth).*"*

September 3, 2014

- **Vision:** I see openings in the USA (compromised in our protection); a boundary line with cannon balls firing against America at the ports. War or warfare. Six or Seven cannon balls. Three are coming to my attention and they are strong. They are at every opening.

September 15, 2014

- I heard the word, "Chaos" in my prayer language twice. Out of chaos comes order! Chaos is complete disorder and confusion. Chaos comes before creation. Genesis 1:2 is creation.

September 22, 2014

- I heard the Word, *"Cache"*. It means: In computing, a **cache** (/ˈkæʃ/ *KASH*) is a component that transparently stores data so that future requests for that data can be served faster.

  The data that is stored within a cache might be values that have been computed earlier or duplicates of original values that are stored elsewhere. If requested data is contained in the cache (cache hit), this request can be served by simply reading the cache', which is comparatively faster. Otherwise (cache miss), the data has to be recomputed or fetched from its original storage location, which is comparatively slower. Hence, the greater the number of requests that can be served from the cache, the faster the overall system performance becomes.

October 6, 2014

- **Vision:** I saw a blonde woman put some kind of covering over me. As I was doing warfare against what she was doing, I heard her say "Columbia and Lima" in her language, with her accent.

  And then I heard the enemy say, "We know more than you." (But I already know that and I don't care. He sounded threatened though).

- Regarding President Obama: I sense he is tired (not physical) and weakened in his position and resolve on some things. We prayed for his strength and God's wisdom for the well being for America.

- I have heard the Word, *"Gemini"* now at least twice. I think of two faces; beast and false prophet. Someone who represents him.

- My thoughts for those that accuse President Obama of being the Anti-Christ is this: There would have to be rule by one person long enough to have a switch over to the One world system and he would have to do that and rule it. Furthermore, establish something in Jerusalem for the Temple to be built.

- I see that he is considering, contemplating a new idea that is not good. I see him looking at, that our system is so weak, that he does not know what to do and how to overcome it. Heavy pressure – not decided yet.

- I see that alot of people judge him unfairly that he does not care. I hear the Lord God say, *"He does care"*.

- The Lord showed the corruption of America is through our speaking against America throughout the years. We eroded it because of our (hate) speech. We, the people, have been the ones who have endorsed evil. Our elected officials are representative of **our own ways of thinking.** They come from among us.

Hear the Word of the Lord

October 10, 2014

- **Vision**: I see needles in packages not opened yet. *"Mandatory injections."*

- I see that they are injecting something, i.e. microchip, tracking device. Emergency. They call an injection "an emergency". What are they working on right now? While this Russia investigation is going on? Health care. Mandatory injections, microchips, emergency.

October 14, 2014

- I heard, *"ISIS annihilated!"* (?) If there is a conspiracy bring more exposure Lord.

- **Vision:** I saw Russia here on this level (bottom). Something above Russia comes over and expands and excels Russia. (Be watchful) Above Russia and beyond Russia, is the USA on the 3rd tier or level. It is competing for the finish line or to catch up. They (Something above Russia) sped past Russia, but not quiet coming where the USA is. It's not much farther for them to go though.

> Level 3 – Top - USA
> Level 2 - Speeding fast forward toward USA ? This is the one to "be watchful"
> Level 1 – Bottom - Russia

- I heard *"Prescription".*

- *"Who shall lay anything to the charge of God's elect?"* Romans 8:33.

When God's people are in accusation (which is a form of agreement with the enemy), Satan uses this for a stronghold. A stronghold is formed by using the natural and spiritual connection. An agreement between the two.

The accusations against Job were locked into place, until Job came out of his thinking during his dark night of the soul, with God confronting him for five entire chapters. Then Job prayed for his friends, as God did not want to judge them, but to give them the opportunity to see something different than they thought they knew.

November 2, 2014

No one person can die (in their flesh) to the extreme without God's help. Humiliation produces humility. Love brings you to death of old self that fights God.

It's surreal that, it is "that time" that God has talked to me about for all these years. The time the Bible speaks of as the last days (of America as we know it). I am having a hard time believing, it is the End Times. How do I accept it? It is about changing who I am completely, I think. Oh God, help me!

- *The Lord says, "One works and one doesn't. You want a solution. You have to do the one that works. I have not called you to be like everyone else."*

November 19, 2014

Vision: I saw the Lord carrying the cross, bleeding. *"Not everyone can receive this."* He felt defeated. He was publically humiliated.

The Lord said, *"Accepting My Way is power."* God's Way for Christ to do the will of God, was the cross. We all have to be more flexible with God, to do His Will, His Way.

The rebel and harlot church. They rebel against God every day because they do it *their way*.

Entering into His rest, is to do it His Way. That carries proof of faith that the angles stand in awe over and the demons tremble at.

197

December 10, 2014

Forgiveness is the greatest weapon. Everyone we forgive, we set free. I sense so strong, that You, Father, are announcing Your Kingdom. Make the paths straight through repentance and forgiveness, for the King of Kings to come through. It brings the power of God to us. Nothing can hold us captive. We continue to look to You, not stopping, every day we agree with You.

The times that things are hard, we need to consider, is because we hang onto things and we fight God. Father, break our agreements, so that we don't withhold from you. Don't let us be like Balaam. Nor like Esau, both selling out their birthrights. Through our weaknesses, submitted to You, humility will be perfected. This is power and it wins with God. Perfect your humility in us God. Humility accepts (surrenders) and doesn't fight against God.

I am remembering divine acquisitions (the mediators). Mediators to rise and to bring God's Kingdom to earth.

I then heard these Words:

- "Celebrate - *The world will be celebrating the wrong thing*". They did this as well, before Yahushua's first coming in Malachi. "I'm giving you the answer" (in reading Malachi).

- The answer is in forgiveness and humility. Humility repents and forgives.

- *"Elements"*

- *"Weaknesses"*

- *"False advocacy"* (advocacy: public support for a cause, ie false public support).

- *"Darkness permeating"*.

- **Vision:** I see a campfire in midst of us. His people are waiting on Him. We are not part of what they (the world and the church that is worldly) are doing. The Lord says, *"My people will be willing in the day of My power."* Like the upper room. The chosen are the Kingdom builders making straight the path for His 2nd coming.

So we have to be willing. Submission to Him is our greatest gift.

"Your people shall be willing in the day of your power"….
Psalm 110:3a

Not all people recognize this gift. It won't be popular. One major key is patience. Patience has everything to do with success. Waiting around the fire. We are willing, because we have been patient.

The darker it gets, the greater the signs and wonders will be. Like fireworks late at night. Great faith works through His authority. The law of faith and submission are synonymous under your authority.

- **Vision:** I see a clearer distinction and the way is being made in the spirit first, building this Kingdom. The rest of the world being captive by Anti- Christ spirit, while true believers are being set free. The chosen few are the Kingdom builders, making the path straight for His second coming.
- Divine acquisitions are end game of the two witnesses (Revelation 11). Lord, bring us there where we have nothing in common with anything but You and Your Kingdom.

I heard:

- *"Gravitational pull"*

- *"Vortex"*

- *"I want for you to know about it. It's about law." Don't forget to read Malachi."*

The same thing is going on now. He is at work to bring all these things about. Make His path straight.

God is setting it up. The Anti-Christ (spirit) is a tool. God is allowing the enemy to get stronger on the earth. We need to be so careful, not to be part of it. Repent, as it is an opportunity for change when we are thinking wrong. If you feel stuck, repent. If you are prideful and think you are right, repent. If you are not sure, repent. It's not going to hurt you. Only bring you closer to God to know and understand Him.

You can be excited and celebrate when you are wrong, because now, you can learn to be right!

*"By this we can be sure that we have come to know Him:
if we keep His commandments.
If anyone says, "I know Him," but does not keep
His commandments,
he is a liar, and the truth is not in him."*
1 John 2:3-4

What if some did not have faith? Will their lack of faith nullify God's faithfulness?

*Certainly not! Let God be true and every man a liar.
As it is written:"So that You (God) may be proved right
when You speak and victorious when You judge."*
Romans 3:3-4

The power of choice for God and His Kingdom rule is a great weapon against the works of darkness.

CHAPTER 12

THE CHARACTERISTICS OF GOD'S SOVEREIGNTY

YEAR OF 2015

I wrote this revelation of Sovereignty in 2015, also in Chapter 1,though it was before the time, as it is the basis of this book. The revelation of His Sovereignty came slowly to me over the course of the dark night. I am emphasizing it in this chapter again, as it is something that is needed to be remembered for the coming days.

Much will be new and brought to the light as the books have been opening (Daniel 12 and Revelation). Revelation, knowledge and understanding are being poured out to those who will receive it.

February 4, 2015

God's Motivation for His Discipline is Love. God's Motivation For Sovereignty is for the Good of Everyone Else. It Is A Major Master Trump Card

Being in the Spirit, I was able to hear how God's Sovereignty Works:

20 CHARACTERISTICS OF SOVEREIGNTY

1. **You Cannot Change SOVEREIGNTY.**

2. **SOVEREIGNTY wipes out your past level of life or experience as you know it.** (i.e. Job, Joseph, David all went through it and came out different on the other side, according to the Will and Plan of God). Total game changer.

3. **SOVEREIGNTY costs a person greater than what they have sufficiency to pay.** Job 13:15 - "Though He slay me,

yet will I serve Him." Reigning and suffering are synonymous. The one is a down payment for what is to come (2 Timothy 2:12: "If we suffer, we shall also reign with *Him*: if we deny *Him*, He also will deny us"). Moses, Joseph, David. Their suffering was not for anything they did wrong. **God allows hardship or evil for a greater plan.**

4. **SOVEREIGNTY is for a specific work.** Is it an ordained structure over a person, place or thing, to change everything around it.

5. **SOVEREIGNTY guarantees Satan's arrival.**

6. **SOVEREIGNTY *does not* have to tell you anything.** It rules. You don't.

7. **SOVEREIGNTY seems very dark.**

8. **SOVEREIGNTY seems like a separation from GOD.**

9. **SOVEREIGNTY is lonely.** No one really understands unless they have been through the same things. No one else can do this with you. It's proof of separation from everything and everyone else. Chosen. Sanctified for His cause and purpose.

10. **SOVEREIGNTY requires you to watch out and pay attention.** Your whole life is being turned upside down and inside out.

11. **SOVEREIGNTY is aligned to a specific cause** (God's trump card).

12. **SOVEREIGNTY will change the course of History *if* you** don't fight it.

13. I hear the Lord say, *"SOVEREIGNTY will shake man to their very core. It will set the course of action to bring to*

divine order."

14. SOVEREIGNTY looks like chaos.

15. SOVEREIGNTY will highly offend you to the point of turning from God, *if* you let it.

16. During SOVEREIGNTY you understand nothing.

17. SOVEREIGNTY sets apart for great change.

18. SOVEREIGNTY will change your point of view, but first it will confuse you because it will not fit in the small box you have put God in. God is Infinite. You are finite.

19. During SOVEREIGNTY you will not understand your life.

20. Allowing the work of SOVEREIGNTY is trusting God without knowing what it looks like through it.

GOD'S RIGHTEOUS JUDGMENT IS NOT A BAD THING

Much like God teaching me about Sovereignty through experience, He taught me first about His righteous judgment. Many people think that the God of the Old Testament is a mean God, not One of Mercy. But the opposite is true.

I ruminate on the extraordinary and supernatural work God had to do, to orchestrate the prophecy about the Messiah (mentioned first in Genesis 3 in the Garden, the seed of the woman to crush the head of the enemy), all the whole 4000 years long to completion. All the while, His rebellious people were always in danger of the enemy wiping them out, before Messiah ever got here! He had to be born of a certain line. If you've ever seen the historical tribal flow charts and kept it in mind while reading the scriptures, you would have a better understanding of God's judgments and why.

God's judgments are a discipline. God chastens (brings correction to) **those whom He loves**. Here, this will make sense:

"In your struggle against sin, you have not yet resisted
to the point of shedding your blood.

You have forgotten the exhortation that addresses you
as sons: "My son, do not take lightly the discipline
of the Lord, and do not lose heart when He rebukes you.

For the Lord disciplines the one He loves,
and He chastises (God sending severe pain
in the best eternal interests of the believer)
every son He receives.

Endure suffering as discipline; God is treating you as sons.
For what son is not disciplined by his father?

If you do not experience discipline like everyone else,
then you are illegitimate children and not true sons."
Hebrews 12:4-8

Father is home! Daddy is in the House! God's discipline should let us know He cares and He is correcting us for the outcome of good in our lives. This is how we remain secure as children. By the balanced love and discipline of a Father.

By the way, the above verses are taken from the New Testament, for those who like to make distinction of the Old and the New. There are actually Seven Covenants and what we call the "New Testament" is literally, the Seventh Covenant that God has made with His people through accepting the Messiah.

If you are unaware of this, it's just another very important detail that has been left out of the church's teachings. There is a real big reason that the Old Testament is still there and not just the "New one". There have been many books removed from the Bible as well as the changing of the Messiah's Name, Yahushua.

Back to my point about God's righteous judgment. God remains the same. He does not change. But He requires change from us. That's why, the discipline. That's why the gift of repentance. He taught me that His judgment it is like putting a period at the end of a sentence. Enough! That's it! Game over! All of our own shenanigans come to an end when God steps in.

Read these scriptures:

Paul wrote: *"Now if we judged ourselves properly,
we would not come under* (God's) *judgment."*
1 Corinthians 11:31

~ and ~

*"... Let God be true and every person a liar, as it is written,
"That you may be justified in your words,
and prevail when you are judged."*
Romans 3:4

The Psalmist writes: *"Righteous are You, O LORD,
and upright are Your judgments."*
Psalm 119:137

~ and ~

*"Against you and you alone, have I sinned;
I have done what is evil in your sight.
You will be proved right in what you say
and your judgment against me is just."*
Psalm 51:4

Isaiah said: *"In the night I search for you; in the morning
I earnestly seek you.*

For only when you come to judge the earth
will people learn what is right."
Isaiah 26:9

And lastly, Ezekiel writes: *'This is what the Sovereign LORD says:*
"'I am against you, Sidon (Modern Lebanon, near Beirut),
and among you I will display my glory.
You will know that I am the LORD, when I inflict punishment on you
and within you am proved to be holy."
Ezekiel 28:22

So judgment is a part of God's Character and His Nature. Just as Mercy, Truth and Salvation are. God could not be Sovereign without Judgment. King Soloman wrote:

"Now all has been heard; here is the conclusion
of the matter:
Fear God and keep his commandments,
for this is the duty of all mankind."
Ecclesiastes 12:13

February 18, 2015

Vision: I looked and saw so many people standing in front of me. They had black coal or something that looked liked tar (about the size of a football) in their heart. It was in the middle of their chest, it was very dark.

"If we sin willfully after that we have received the knowledge
of the truth, there remains no more sacrifice for sins,
But a certain fearful looking for of judgment and fiery indignation,
which shall devour the adversaries.

He that despised Moses' law died without mercy
under two or three witnesses:

Of how much sorer punishment, do you suppose,

shall he be thought worthy, who has trodden under foot
the Son of God, and hath counted the blood of the covenant,
wherewith he was sanctified, an unholy thing,
and has done despite unto the Spirit of grace?

For we know him that has said, Vengeance belongs to me,
I will repay, says the Lord.

And again, The Lord shall judge his people.
It is a fearful thing to fall into the hands of the living God."
Hebrews 10:26-31

To be especially noted, these are people who know. God not only gave to every person a conscience, but to those who accepted His Son, in addition to having a conscience, He gave to them of His Holy Spirit! Why is there not only a breakthrough in conscience, but also not a conviction by the Holy Spirit? Because God revealed that it is willful sin. On purpose.

So, there remains no more sacrifice for sin. They just kept sinning and did not repent. Heartbroken, I have to let go of them, for God's righteous judgment to come forth. It will bring them to the point of making a decision. A firm choice.

February 28, 2015

Once it is written, then spoken, it can happen. Until we get it, God will keep repeating it.

- **Vision:** Something is being set up regarding Israel (in the realm of the Spirit) for an undermining and to take a fall. It's between America and Israel. I see Israel, the golden dome and the Muslim Mosque.

- I hear: *"A great quaking, A great shaking, A voice of thunder"*.

- **Vision:** I see a vertical moving of darkness, billowing thick darkness and I sense it is not good. I sense it is regarding the Anti-Christ setting himself up.

- A changing of the guard is coming in the USA, in the Fall; it is something regarding the USA.

- **Vision:** I see all the people running for office, scurrying to get in place and it has to do with Israel. It is not good.

- I am reminded of scripture about the dragon, beast, Anti-Christ and the false prophet (Book of Revelation). It's coming to mind that the Fallen Council is four (types of entities) also. September is the time frame and it is a solidification of evil. Today it feels like a done deal and it is sealed with evil in the system from that point forward.

March 7, 2015

In the early morning hours, the Lord began to speak to me about the mind being like a computer program and that He wrote the program for it and that is why we need to renew it. He has the code for it. The enemy understands the code. The renewal of our mind (through God's Word, knowledge and understanding), changes the code back to our original DNA.

Humility allows you to see the truth and if you don't have humility, we are left to our own way of thinking, where the knowledge can make one prideful (1 Corinthians 8:1).

Judgment is being put through the fire to see what we are made of; pride, ego, or purity. What is pure will abide the fire.

"If anyone builds on this foundation (of Christ in us) *using gold, silver, precious stones, wood, hay, or straw,*

his workmanship will be evident, because the Day
will bring it to light.
It will be revealed with fire and the fire will prove
the quality of each man's work.
If what he has built survives, he will receive a reward.
If it is burned up, he will suffer loss.
He himself will be saved, but only as if through the flames
(of God's Righteous Judgment).

Do you not know that you yourselves are God's temple
and that God's Spirit dwells in you?
If anyone destroys God's temple, God will destroy him;
*for God's temple is holy and **you are** that temple.*

Let no one deceive himself. If any of you thinks he is wise
in this age, he should become a fool, so that he may become wise.
For the wisdom of this world is foolishness in God's sight.
As it is written: "He catches the wise (wisdom of this world)
in their craftiness." And again, "The Lord knows
that the thoughts of the wise (of this world) *are useless."*
1 Corinthians 3:12-20

I prophesied, calling the things of God in my life, to God's order. Each experience I have, that I am getting stronger and every evil thing that He allows, will bring strength and healing and not my demise. No more plan of Satan or mankind to bring hurt or harm to me, but instead, for the pain, it will bring me healing.

I proclaim that, I match the strength of not giving in to anyone or anything, but the Northern iron and steel (Jeremiah 15:12). My relationship with God is Yes and Amen. Satan, you lose and you are judged to your demise.

God, You alone, have called me and raised me up, but You alone have caused me to suffer. You put your hand on me, buy they cannot touch me. I clear the table where the enemy is sitting and bring the things of God to the table, in the presence of my enemies (Psalm 23 and Esther 5). I will speak a Word to the people and Your conviction, according to your will, will be on the people of God.

I prophesy the day of the rebuke of Your love, that confronts, to come into existence now.

March 17, 2015

I am sensing a strong spirit that opposes You Father. The hearts of many growing cold, a hardening of their hearts.

March 19, 2015

- Vision: I see leaders that have knowledge of Truth. They are guardians of truth who do not follow the system. I see that they are major targets of the enemy.

  We pray for their protection and safety, for these that you will raise up in the earth. They are being seized by the enemy and the enemy wants to get them to come under another power, so they won't follow God. The enemy wants to pull them down so he can get to the masses easier. I see that these people are heads of corporations, high level and low level. They govern over thousands and millions of people. We pray and are thankful for all these that You have chosen, that have not given into the system.

  I don't know if they know the Lord, but they are aware of what is going on. They are singular and alone. We bind the enemy and loose the Spirit of God on them to be saved. We pray for their strength, that it does not fail. We pray for Your strength to enter into them.

I see them at different levels (some are presidents of companies) everywhere scattered here and there. They are elevated in a supernatural strength in the atmosphere.

I heard the Lord say: *"These are receivers from the Lord and receive from Heaven."*

- I see the system and it has a long tail like a dragon. It is so evil and it has inhabited America. So, complete evil is here now. God is in America and will not abandon us.
  The emphasis is on being accessed or penetrated, seduction.

- I see in the Heavenlies and the angels are lined up on 2 sides across from each other. They have trumpets and have them ready to blow.

Just the Beginning of Sorrows

March 26, 2015

- The Spirit of the Lord is reminding me of the scripture, *"So if they tell you, 'There He is in the wilderness,' do not go out; or, 'Here He is in the inner rooms,' do not believe it"* Matthew 24:26. Also of the 10 virgins that don't have their lamps ready when the bridegroom comes (Matthew 25:3).

- There will be a lot of distractions of images, even of Christ's image. He has been talking about identity and image.
- That spirit that has been coming around for about a week, I am sensing that spirit is in the background. It makes everything seem like, "whatever," "Que Sera, sera". It is very passive.

- The love of many growing cold (Matthew 24:12). It's a delusion. It's progressing. I see it affects those who love the Lord and tries to make the things of God of no effect in their lives. It's a type of, "Okay, complacency, a lukewarmness", like a fog that takes over the people.

April 9, 2015

- **Vision:** I see Seven years. A Seven year cycle. And I see a territory, like a body of water. It is like a lasso that comes back around. A territory in the heavenlies. We are outside of the lasso. When I spoke, my sentence was on the outside of it, so we are not in it yet.

April 15, 2015

- The Lord was giving me this consideration: When you hear the word technology, think Fallen Council. When you hear Fallen Council, think technology. It's another realm. We are going to see things in the future we will not believe with our eyes and it is rapidly increasing. Technology, signs, wonders at a rapid rate, we will not be able to believe what we will see.

- **Vision:** I see something coming up: I see a format in the world. It is jealousy, in the structure of the fallen world and I am to pull it down into the judgment zone of God right now. I see the structure of judgment and it is more solidified. What is that about? Jealousies *are a* type of judgment. Considering: They were jealous of Yahushua and in the end, judgment came and it took Him to the cross.

  Father, Take us out of our own mindsets to go forward with You, because we will be healed and delivered as we go. We cannot be hung up on ourselves. The Spirit of the Lord laments, *"The people will be so burdened with problems, it will be hard for them to come out and follow."* The Lord reminded me that in my dark how I have felt. This is how the people will be; they won't be able to get free so easily.

Taking notice that people like to use judgments a lot, like a sport. The late night talk show hosts etc, getting presidents or other political figures on their shows and make "sport" with them. Judgments are increasing. The people will do this in the last days against the witnesses of God (Revelation 11) and the enemy will go after the anointed seed of the woman (Revelation 12).

I am noting that science is advancing. Some of the Fallen Council that are actually our leaders. Hovering things, holograms and magicians making things appear in ways that are not reasonable. The danger is imminent and this is what they want to do. It is intentional.

I am reminded of the dreams I had in the 80's and 90's about camps in the USA where Americans were being held.

- The Lord reminded me: "I told you I was merging the dimensions" (Speeding up the time).

"Through faith we understand
that the worlds were framed by the word of God,
so that things which are seen
were not made of things which do appear."
Hebrews 11:3

This is a bigger mystery than I can receive right now. Lord, open us up for more reception of greater faith.

- I am reminded of the technology that was shut down in Daniel. The Lord says, *"And your Government is one with it."*

- A reminder, that in 2011, God left the Government system. The Lord says, *"This is what they wanted all along, power. They don't want to follow Me, **they want the power.**"*

- Lord, more grace and mercy for us. We break off all agreements with the American Government and the enemy in the Government. We are of the Kingdom of Heaven. We don't want the American mindsets. Only Yours Father.

- Scriptures on *"do not be afraid of sudden fear"* (Proverbs 3:25) and not to believe it. Seal this, Your revelation, to our hearts and minds.

- This has been an agreement with generations, before (Roosevelt in the 40's) like a covenant contract. And they have passed it down to generations. That we have to do it *this* way. And what they think to do, is to bypass our understanding. They have plans beyond our comprehension, that we do not understand and no one will be able to figure it out. Except that God is exposing it to some of His people. The only remedy for what is coming, is to have Your mind - The Mind of Christ.

Remembering also of the divine acquisitions. The Lord had also said: *"The longevity of Moses had to do with Moses emptying himself."*

Intercession: Forgive us of ungodly ties and connections. Cleanse and purge us from those connections. Cleanse our cells and DNA. I call forth right now our original DNA from Heaven that you originally formatted, that we are the fullness of our authentic DNA from You.

All conditioning of soul and fallen nature, we speak destruction to it and break and destroy it now. We don't want to have our own opinions. We don't fight for it. It's against You, God, it is sin.

Lord, I pray that we are in the structure of the Kingdom of Heaven, not this fallen kingdom here. That we are paying attention to Your ways and thinking and putting things together by hope and faith.

- I heard the Word: *"Insignia"* a badge of authority or

honor.

May 20, 2015

On the evening of May 19, the Lord impressed upon my spirit, this scripture, which says:

> *"Likewise also these filthy dreamers defile the flesh, despise dominion, and speak evil of dignities."*
> Jude 1:8.

I also was impressed upon: Revelation 9:19:

> *"For their power is in their mouth, and in their tails: for their tails were like unto serpents and had heads and with them they do hurt."*

The books are being opened. The answer to Jude verse 8 is Jude verse's 20-21:

> *"But you, beloved, **building up yourselves on your most holy faith,** praying in the Holy Ghost.*
> **Keep yourselves in the love of God, looking for the mercy of our Lord** *Yahushua, the Christ, unto eternal life. "*

While I was praying about all this in the spirit, I heard:

Haggai 2:5-9 Verse 6 says:

"Shake the heavens and earth" So I declare and decree according to the word of Haggai:

> *"For the LORD of hosts says; Yet once, in a little while, and I will "shake the heavens, and the earth, and the sea, and the dry land."*

A great shaking in the heavens and the earth! I call it forth now, where God has put the provision

When David came into the Kingdom that was prophesied before hand, it was by the Word of God. He had no right to be a King, Jonathan (King Saul's Son) was next in line after Saul. But David obeyed God and kept His laws and statutes, so the promises came to pass.

The Lord spoke to me saying,

"YOUR OBEDIENCE CREATES YOUR WEALTH"

May 31, 2015

Vision: The Father said to me, *"Look up".* I did and saw a huge wave of "denial" coming in on the earth.

June 5, 2015

The Lord spoke to me saying: *"The merging realms are not merging on their own, I Am bringing it down. Let everything be, don't stress out, just let it be".*

Be responsible without anxiety.

July 5, 2015

- I heard: *"Falling away."*

- Vision: I see the enemy targeting certain people. And they are targeted because they can help other people. The pressure is so hard and harsh on them. If forefront people of the spiritual battle, are taken away, then Satan comes in and hits everyone else. Who then would make it?

Speaking of the times of the end:

*"Those with insight will instruct many, though for a time
they will fall by sword or flame, or be captured or plundered.
Now when they fall, they will be granted a little help,
but many will join them insincerely.*

*Some of the wise **will** fall, so that they may be refined, purified
and made spotless until the time of the end,
for it will still come at the appointed time."*
Daniel 11:33-35

~ and ~

Yahushua said: ".....*When the Son of Man comes* (the second time),
will He find faith on the earth?"
Luke 18:8

July 15, 2015

- I was lamenting for all I had gone through and God said:
*"Seven years of evil....I had to let you go through the
overcoming. I had to teach you to overcome evil, so you
would not rely on your own self, but seek Me."*

- God reminded me, that I laid the foundation in 2008 with
opening and overseeing City Rock Church. A Church that
only says what He is saying and does what He is doing. A
Church led by the Spirit of God.

- I hear the Lord say: *"Turn the page"*

- **Vision:** I see a blank page. I see a City divided in leadership.
(Do I write on this page? I think so)   Lord, what are the
intentions of the Kingdom? (*Authors Note: I have a
prophetic work I do called, "The Intentions of the Kingdom"
for individuals, households, businesses, Cities, and
Countries).

- I was reminded of a dream I had in 2012, where the buildings were all made out of glass. I was doing warfare in the City and the Nephilim emerged out of the structures. It was as if they were a part of the buildings and they were holding them up. When they came out, the buildings crumbled.

- The Lord said to me: *"I've sent you here to bring the division. In judgment division happens. Judgment is a courtesy that helps them make a decision".*

Judgment is God's love. For example, if a leg is infected and you let it go and never treat it, they will have to do something drastic to save your life and so they amputate the leg instead of letting you die.

I think of the scripture where Yahushua said: *"And if your foot causes you to stumble, cut it off. It is better for you to enter life crippled than to have two feet and be thrown into hell."* Mark 9:45

- The Lord declares, *"Come out from among them"* to His people.

July 23, 2015

I was doing warfare and the Lord said to me: *"This battle* (the one specifically, that I had been fighting) *is for your office position".* For Kingship, dominion and authority on the earth, in order that I don't make it up to Judah (re: 2005 Prophetic Word [1 Samuel 30] through leadership and prophets at Glory of Zion, Denton, Texas).

The Old system has passed away (I Samuel), so I do not find comfort in it. 2 Samuel 2 is the closing off of the old system, that was confronted in 2 Samuel 1. So I came out of Ziglag and into Judah and the old system is being confronted. The enemy is trying to prohibit this. So, our resolve is that we keep on practicing "dominion warfare" and take it back from the enemy.

The systems and America are being judged and God is setting up his Kingdom through His people.

July 26, 2015

- I am there at that curve now. Obeying God daily and waiting on him, this is the faith that He was speaking of.

- Eve and the fruit ie. seduction and lies. Satan says, give of this fruit to the woman, ie seduction and lies. Just as the enemy has said, 'Give these 4 Tablets of stone written on to Dawne, (the tablets of stone were lies and seduction - a dream in 2010 that an intercessor had regarding what the Enemy thought to do through others to make me ineffectual).

  Satan's new Method of Operation *is the same as* the old Method of Operation! Corrupt the woman, so the seed cannot come forth! A Deception. Eve was deceived. But Adam sinned willfully: *"For Adam was formed first, and then Eve. And it was not Adam who was deceived, but the woman who was deceived and fell into transgression"* 1 Timothy 2:13-14, Says Paul to Timothy in a letter.

  Yes, but he did not mention there:

  That while Eve was deceived by her own lust, she took the fruit to Adam and he took of the fruit and ate it *willingly, knowing* that he was going against God in willful sin (Genesis 3). It was because of this act, Adams willful sin, that it was passed down through Adam – the first born who had the original instruction of God. That's why we needed the 2nd Adam, Yahushua to redeem us from the curse that came from not obeying God's written law after the Garden fall. 1 Corinthians 15:47.

  There was no law in the Garden. They were made in God's image and carried God and His Word within them. Until the disobedience of the agreement. Ah, and how simple and uncomplicated that agreement was back then!

- Now the tables will be turned.

- To be clear, in a broader sense, the Woman is the Church. The Bride of Christ.

- The Catholic Church appears to crush the head of the enemy, but it actually will set up the Anti-Christ.

- A big lie and delusions are coming. The Pope is to speak to Congress on the 24th and to the United Nations on the 25th. The connection is political. Something very, very evil is coming through the Catholic Church.

- The pathways of God are hidden in earthen vessels (God's people), that's why Satan can't get to them so easily (2 Corinthians 4:7).

July 29, 2015

- The Lord spoke to me, saying, *"Judgment is ruling in the Heavens."* It is coming to the earth. They are making preparation for all this to happen.

> *'And I heard the angel of the waters say:*
> *"Righteous are You, O Holy One,*
> *who is and was,*
> *because You have brought these judgments.*
>
> *For they have spilled the blood of saints*
> *and prophets, and You have given them blood*
> *to drink, as they deserve."*
>
> *And I heard the altar reply:*
> *"Yes, Lord God Almighty,*
> *true and just are Your judgments."*

Revelation 16:5-7

~ and ~

'Then I heard another voice from heaven say:

"Come out of her, My people,
so that you will not share in her sins
or contract any of her plagues.

For her sins are piled up to heaven,
and God has remembered her iniquities.
Give back to her as she has done to others;
pay her back double for what she has done;
mix her a double portion in her own cup.
As much as she has glorified herself
and lived in luxury, give her the same measure
of torment and grief.
In her heart she says, 'I sit as queen;
I am not a widow and will never see grief.'

Therefore her plagues will come in one day—
death and grief and famine—
and she will be consumed by fire,
for mighty is the Lord God who judges her."
Revelation 18:4-8

- **Vision:** I see God's judgment is crystal clean, clear and sharp and powerful. It is so pure. And His judgment is the only thing that puts all of this chaos in order.

"For the earnest expectation of the creature (God's Creation)
waits for the manifestation of the sons of God."
Romans 8:19

Lord, merging of the realms, how do I work it and have access to it?

"Above the roar of many waters—the mighty breakers
of the sea—the LORD on high is majestic.
Your testimonies are fully confirmed; holiness adorns
Your house, O LORD, for all the days to come."
Psalm 93:4-5

- The Lord is speaking to me about letting things go. He says, *"That's what I'm trying to help you do."* When the crowds followed YAHUshua, many turned from Him and He did not go after them.

- I choose submission to the process of God. I need motivation to go through with the writing.

- **Vision:** I saw myself as if I were like Moses and I put everything, appointed by God, in order through my writings. I see the people being brought into order through Your Words and Your Laws, Sovereign Lord.

- God says, *"I let you suffer according to the measure of the people. I have you all measured out."*

- Jude 1:23 *"On some have compassion pulling them from the fire..."* (judgment). God's Law and His prophets will make room for His 2nd Coming.

A Remnant

August 3, 2015

- **Vision:** God is showing me a sharp wedge of division. I see this sharp sword or metal coming down and literally dividing through something solid. It is cutting off a small portion of a whole. It's not even quite a 3rd. It is actually less than 1/4 of the whole.

- What I am hearing is, *"Let that happen."* Do not fight division. You are fighting against God when you are fighting the people. God made sure as long as the people obeyed Him, that they would be protected.
Just like during the times of Jeremiah, the people were in shock that God was handing them over.

  The Republicans are going to be in shock because they have not been in tune and seeking God with their whole heart (though they will fight for their right to be right).

  *On this note: I am not saying *all* Republicans, nor am I leaving out Democrats. But largely, the Church follows the Republican Party and all they say. And God is and has been showing that they (the Church and the Republican Party, at large, have missed the mark widely). Don't be offended. Be reconciled. We all fall short. That's not a secret. What you keep will be your downfall.

- Vision: Father, this division I see cutting off the very small portion of the whole, that we are to accept division when it comes. I feel it is God's protection - the division. The smaller part is the minority and they are to stand strong. Father, as the prophet cried, *"everyone is corrupt from the least to the greatest"*! Jeremiah 6 and 8.

- Vision: I see people dying, young and old, suddenly.

- I hear: "Great changes are ready to take place."

There were such attacks against me last night. I asked if it was because I am learning dominion. But, I sense it is because God is getting ready to separate the false and the remnant. This is so painful and disturbing for me. What time it is.

I hear the following:

- *"California"*

- *"Negotiations underway"*

- *"Tri-state partisanship"*

- *"Congenial liabilities"*

- These words were set over California like a blanket and there was a shaking and breaking loose; a detachment; a slight detachment. The blanket was form fitting, though it was not a blanket of protection.

- *"Concealed".*

- *"Guardianship"*

- *"Successor"*

Partisanship means bias, one sided. It separates you, it is a division. Congenial means of a person, hospitable, pleasant because of a personality. Liabilities means, a state of being responsible to something especially by law. God is saying a breaking away, so something is going to happen with California.

Tri-state means pertaining to a territory made up of 3 adjoining States. I don't know if He means literal States or 3 different states of being, divisions, territories, etc.

Negotiations under way; so something is happening right now. Tri-state partisanship; a division, which is what He talked about earlier. Then congenial liabilities, perhaps, some sort of seduction to bring them to the end of being a liability.

California comes from the Arabic word, "Caliph" which means steward or leader. It also means, land of the female Queen Calafia.

I further hear these Words:

- *"There are great changes in the atmosphere".*

- *"Sightings and Signs".*

- *"Election"*

- *"Chosen few"*

- *"Terminal"* - Has 4 meanings: of, forming, or situated at the end or extremity of something: Of a disease predicted to lead to death, especially slowly; incurable: The end of a railroad or other transport route, or a station at such a point: a point of connection for closing an electric circuit.

- *"Catch 22"* - a dilemma or difficult circumstance from which there is no escape, because of mutually conflicting or dependent conditions.

- *"Situational Occurrences"*

- *"Black Masses"*

- *Target Venues"*

- *"Choice for change"*

- *"Constitutional Law"*

- *"Perpetuum"* - (it means Forever). But when I gooogled it, this came up: "A global leader in vibration energy harvesting".

  The power of vibration, is ancient technology. In ancient times, they used the underground caves and pyramids because they could translate the energy of vibration.

Born from Above

August 9, 2015

- This morning, I awoke to God speaking to me about our money; about the strip that is in the United States currency.

- **Vision:** I saw a magnetic strip in the money. As crazy as this sounds, I saw, as if, there were eyes and energy coming out of them and I had a knowing, there is a communication that the money strip has. God and I were going back and forth talking. I then saw a hand and I saw money in the hands, exchanging.

- I heard the Lord say, *"That is what the mark of the beast is - On the forehead. I said, put My Word there."*

  I asked, why the hands? *"Because they are a sign of what you give your power to and how you get money. Hands give worship and allegiance to; that's why the forehead and the hand"*.

- **Vision:** He showed me that the strip is influencing us. That it has sound that we cannot hear. A type of brain washing (It reminds me of *'the love of money is the root of all evil...*1 Timothy 6:1"*). He showed me that it goes in through our senses. Our eye gates are receptors. I think of the all-seeing eye on the United States currency. That is the mark on our forehead. The people are marked by them, influenced by them.

  Then He showed me the hand. The hand is symbolic of our power. Who you give your labor to. Your hand to, you pledge your allegiance to. They watch who is connected to them and who is not. Who is influenced by them and who is not.

- Then I had another revelation on our DNA. Being born again, by God's Spirit, changes our DNA. The enemy uses our fallen nature DNA and knows how to use it. They (the enemy and the fallen ones) cannot use our born of heaven DNA. And they know who is who. Our DNA (those who have His Holy Spirit) is changed by being in the Word of God. The more you know God, the more different you think than everyone else.

- The revelation God gave me last night was about the woman. How the last shall be first and the first last. He created woman 2nd. Adam sinned willingly. Eve was deceived. It is women who will take the lead back to the (restored) Garden, hence all the reference to women in the book of Revelation (The Church, the Harlot, Jezebel, the Woman who is clothed with Creation, the Bride).

It reminds me of the Prophetic Word that I received from the Lord in February 1996. Here is just a portion of it:

INSTRUMENTS OF SUBMISSION

"For great are My instruments says the Lord, to use in the battle. They are made of hard substances that have already been tried in the fire. The furnace of affliction has perfected and purified them for use. My secret weapons. The weapons of war. My warheads and spears against the day of battle. For the enemy has not regarded just what level they are on.

For I have set them above that they be not beneath. Was the woman not subject to the man through the curse? Is the woman now cursed through the blood of My Righteous Son? Have I redeemed the woman from the curse? I have said, the least shall be the greatest. I have said, that the last shall be first. I have said, that the weaker vessel shall be filled with My strength.

These are women of honor, who know their position in Me!
They are subject to the elements and standards of My Kingdom. They
know what it means to be under authority-that it means to be
demonstrating power! My power. My anointing. My deliverance's.
My salvation's. My life. Me. I. For I Am All in all, and all of these
are of Me, says the Lord God of Hosts.....

And there shall arise many of you for the front line battle.
Some may say, "Women for the front lines?" Have they not read that
in MY Kingdom, there is neither male nor female? Shall these
women not stand where I put them? For they shall be bold and
courageous and confront the battle head on. For the time has come
for all things to be put in their place. This was My design from the
beginning and now it shall be fulfilled in the end. I Am faithful to My
Word and that Word which I send out shall not return to Me void. It
shall accomplish that whereunto it was sent".
Through Dawne D. (Kirkland) Basler February 1996

August 28, 2015

- **Vision:** I see an undercurrent with Donald Trump. I see evil behind him. I pray preparation for us and the country when the tsunami hits.

- I hear the Words: *"Trouble the waters"*

- *"Influx of Evil"*

- **Vision:** I just saw the tsunami and it will have an effect.

- **Vision:** In this vision, I saw penitentiaries and they were being washed out and then I saw an infilling of the penitentiaries, because of the tsunami. There were more people than ever before filling up the penitentiaries to overflowing. In other words, breaking in, for a breakout of evil. Picturing what is in the penitentiary is being pushed out into the land and then I saw more evil in-fluxing in. That is what the tsunami will do.

- **Vision:** I hear it as an unleashing. I see it as all of creation groaning and travailing. Water, tsunami, creation; crying out. God cleanses the land by water (flood) and by fire. That is His method of operation and choice. It proceeds Romans 1 and 2 judgments. His Sovereign judgment <u>will not</u> precede natural disasters. He sends (or allows) the natural disasters so the people will cry out to Him. These are His mercies. God doesn't change his judgments or His Laws. He changes our hearts. For reference, read the entire Bible. Prepare us God. Read this:

"The wrath of God is being revealed from heaven
against all the godlessness and wickedness
(injustices) *of men who suppress* (hold back)
the truth by their wickedness
(violation of God's truth).

For what may be known about God is plain to them,
because God has made it plain to them.

For since the creation of the world,
God's invisible qualities, His eternal power and divine nature,
have been clearly seen, being understood
from His workmanship, so that men are without excuse.

For although they knew God, they neither glorified Him
as God nor gave thanks to Him,
but they became futile (Perverted, Foolish) *in their thinking*
and darkened in their foolish hearts,

Although they claimed to be wise,
they became fools and exchanged the glory
of the immortal God for images (Idols)
of mortal man and birds and animals and reptiles.

Therefore, ***God gave them over***

in the desires of their hearts to impurity
for the dishonoring of their bodies with one another.

They exchanged the truth of God for a lie,
and worshiped and served the creature
rather than the Creator, who is forever worthy of praise! Amen.

For this reason, **God gave them over to**
dishonorable passions.
Even their women exchanged natural relations
for unnatural ones.
Likewise, the men abandoned natural relations
with women and burned with lust for one another.
Men committed indecent acts with other men
and received in themselves the due penalty for their error.

Furthermore, since they did not see fit to acknowledge God,
He gave them up to a depraved mind,
to do what ought not to be done.
They have become filled with every kind of wickedness,
evil, greed, and depravity.
They are full of envy, murder, strife, deceit, and malice.
They are gossips, slanderers, God-haters
(through disobedience to His Word), *insolent*
(delights in hurting others), *arrogant, and boastful.*
They invent new forms of evil; they disobey
their parents. They are senseless,
faithless, heartless, merciless.

Although they know God's righteous decree
that **those who do such things are worthy of death,**
they not only continue to do these things,
but also approve (Agree, Consent, Even by staying silent)
of those who practice them.
Romans 1:18-32

Wait!....There's More:

*"You, therefore, **have no excuse,
you who pass judgment on another.***

*For on **whatever grounds you judge another,
you are condemning yourself;***

Because you who pass judgment, do the same things
(have sin also. We judge another by and through
our own skewed sense of perception through our own sins).

*And we know that **God's judgment against those
who do such things** is based on truth.*

*So when you, O man, pass judgment on others,
yet do the same things* (sinning),
do you think you will escape God's judgment?
*Or do you disregard the riches of His kindness,
tolerance, and patience, not realizing
that it is God's kindness leads you to repentance?
But **because of your hard and unrepentant heart,**
you are **storing up wrath against yourself**
for the day of wrath, when **God's righteous judgment
will be revealed.***
God "will repay each one according to his deeds."

*To those who by perseverance in doing good
seek glory, honor, and immortality,
He will give eternal life.*

*But for those who are **self-seeking
and who reject the truth and follow wickedness***
(which reveal those that are not His sons and daughters)**,**
there will be wrath and anger.

***There will be trouble and distress for every human being
who does evil,** first for the Jew, then for the Greek* (Gentile);
*but glory, honor, and peace for everyone who does good,
first for the Jew, then for the Greek* (Gentile).
For God does not show favoritism.

All who sin apart from the law will also perish apart from the law and all who sin under the law will be judged by the law.

For it is not the hearers of the law who are righteous before God, but it is the doers of the law who will be declared righteous.

Indeed, when Gentiles (those without God), *who do not have the law, do by nature* (their own conscience) *what the law requires* (says to do), *they are a law to themselves, even though they do not have the law, since they show that the work of the law is written on their hearts, their consciences also bearing witness and their thoughts either accusing or defending them.*

*This will come to pass on **that day when God will judge men's secrets through** Christ Yahushua, as proclaimed by my gospel."*
Romans 2:1-16

And these are the things God wants for you to know. So that you can make decisions for your own life. Not based on what you've heard or your opinions formed through various thought processes, but what you personally know. And it all starts with ***knowing Him.*** **And knowing Him, is knowing all the things He has said in His Word and allowing His Holy Spirit to interpret.**

Battles are Won through Obedience

September 3, 2015

- People like the churchy stuff. But they don't like the true wisdom that comes from above (James 3:17). They only like the sound bites that make them feel good. The Lord spoke to me and said, *"My people don't have conviction anymore".*

They don't want to be bothered by God's way of thinking.

They don't <u>live by</u> the conviction of the Holy Spirit.

"When he (the Holy Spirit) *comes, he will convict* (prove to) *the world* (all of creation) *to be in the wrong about sin and righteousness and judgment."*
John 16:8

I protested asking, If they don't want to hear anymore, what do we have left to get through to them?

- The Lord said to me: *"Concede that the battle is too strong on the earth, that you may do the will of Your Father in Heaven."*

- **Vision:** I saw a battle. The people in the battles are on horses and shooting arrows into the heavenlies; as if taking down the strong men in the clouds, where we can't see.

  Horses stand for supernatural strength, because it is beyond human strength. The battle is in the heavenlies where the battle takes place first, but it will take a supernatural strength to do that effectively.
- The Lord said: *"The battle is won through obedience."* He has His hand on my shoulder and saying, *"You cannot win this* (End time) *battle without obedience."*

September 26, 2015

- The Lord started speaking to me at 4:30am. He said, *"Dawne, I have something to tell you."*

- 1st part:

  "Rising Tides"or
  "Rose Tides Rising".

*"From the West, people will fear the name of the LORD,
and from the rising of the sun, they will revere his glory.*

*For he will come like a pent-up flood
that the breath of the LORD drives along."*
Isaiah 59:19.

*"Therefore, this is what the Sovereign LORD says:
I am your enemy, O Tyre, and I will bring many Nations
against you, like the waves of the sea crashing
against your shoreline."*
Ezekiel 26:3

Yahushua said:

*'There will be signs in the sun, moon and stars.
On the earth, Nations will be in anguish and perplexity
at the roaring and tossing of the sea.'*
Luke 21:25.

Interesting to note that the Revelation 12 Woman is clothed with the sun and the moon and the stars.

- 2nd part
  "Monuments Crashing"

It is something erected in the memory of a person, event, etc., as a building, pillar or a statue (*Author note: We have seen this starting in the US in 2019).

- 3rd part
  "America Falling"

- 4th part
  "You will be My Voice"

CHAPTER 13

THE DESCENT INTO SOVEREIGNTY

YEAR OF 2016

January 6, 2016

- The Lord says: *"There must be a change in the system."* Regarding the Government. I feel like God is going to give the people what they want. The Lord says, *"I love them enough to give them what they want. I've tried and tried and they would not* (listen, respond, etc)*"*. Giving them what they want is out of love.

- He wants me to get this, **that this is the time.** *"I want them to know anyway."* I lamented, where are all the prophets at? I do not think there will be many of God's true prophets around. When the truth is revealed, then He will be able to judge them according to His Truth.

January 14, 2016

- Praying for the Nation. I said Lord, Rick Joyner had a lot of understanding. The Lord replied, *"So do you. The dark night sovereignty was to undergird you with strength"*.

- The Lord had told me in January 2014, *'It IS "that time"'.* From January 2014 to January 2016, it has taken for God to convince me that, It's *that* time! Although He has told me since the 1980's.

  It's hard to imagine what you've never seen happen, especially when the events are to be so Catastrophic and Cataclysmic. In Jeremiah God said the same thing. It is that time now. Jeremiah had a hard time believing it as well. I'm not alone.

- The Lord said to cry out for the *"Salvation of Souls and mercy extended, for the people are dull of hearing and they are not going to hear."*

- *"Challenge for change. The muscleman is here."*

- I was praying regarding getting a bigger team together to pray. But God is saying to me: *"I did not have the whole Nation praying in the book of Jeremiah. I had Jeremiah and Baruch to do My will.* He does not need for me to come in and give him good ideas, but be compliant.

- The Lord said to me, *"You can't change this, it is sovereign."*

January 15, 2016

- **Vision:** This is a sovereign time for America.

  I see Donald Trump, as if he were like a dragon.
  (Note. He is of German and Scottish decent. His father's name is Frederick Christ Trump)

January 18, 2016

- This is our 'reasonable service' (Luke 17:10 – doing what God has commanded us). Looking at America and how to pray, this is our reasonable service. What do we do God?

- **Vision:** Last night I saw two realms merging into one. I saw and heard the United States voting who we want to represent us for a global election. It felt like we still had our own Nation, but we had people representing us to go the global summit. It felt like the US going the way of a type of "Hunger Games".

- I see the people are deceived. They look like a shell overtaken by political parties.

Crying Mercy and Salvation

January 26, 2016

- Donald Trump is the first person I have had a witness on with who is running for the election. Not Hillary Clinton, Jeb Bush or President Obama (as others have said he will try to extend his time in the presidency, but it is not constitutional).

- The Lord had instructed for us to pray continually *"Mercy and Salvation"* for America. It means we are in big trouble. Like an ocean liner that is sinking and we are the ones that have to get people into the life boats. It's cold, dark and the water is freezing.

- **Vision:** I see a cold gray room. People are in rows and I am shaking them, but they are mesmerized. I'm looking to see who to shake loose from the mesmerizing. The eyes of the people are blind.

> *"The god of this world has blinded the mind of the unbelieving*
> (any who do not think like or have the mind of the Messiah)
> *so they may not see the light of the Gospel of Messiah."*
> 2 Corinthians 4:4

- I am reminded of Gideon taking men to the water and seeing who drank with a cupped hand or who put their face in the water (Judges 7). It is a choice.

We pulled down the structure of the old, every false structure around us, that they are building, we will not be ruled by the false.

- I hear the Words and see a **Vision**: *"Troubling America"*. I have a box in front of me and I do not know what to do with it.

- **Vision**: I saw Donald Trump perching (like a bird on a branch) singing. And the song he is singing, is the funeral song of America. A dirge.

February 1, 2016

- **Vision**: I see Donald Trump high and lifted up over the United States of America and he is happy. We lift You up over this vision God. Have mercy and salvation on America.

- Romans 1 and 2 is in effect in the US now. God has given us over to what we want. He has nothing to do with the system in America.

- The books of Daniel are being opened to pour out the Truth for us. Prepare us, deliver us, keep our hearts and minds open to You only Lord.

- **Vision**: I see angels attending to deposits left by other angels. There are pockets that go down and an angel is putting things in there. The deposits that the angels are leaving, are for what is needed. They are embedded. We pray (as Daniel did in Daniel 10), for the answer and that the angels to be able to make it to the earth to leave the deposits, as you have shown.

February 16, 2016

- **Vision:** I saw mercy and salvation were like seeds in the ground when we pray for it. I also see something coming up and it is something bad. I see bad and evil *and* revival together, happening at the same time.

March 7, 2016

- This is what the Sovereign Lord is impressing in my spirit:
  "This is what the LORD Almighty says:
  'In a little while I will once more shake the heavens
  and the earth, the sea and the dry land'."
  Haggai 2:6

  ~ and ~

  "See to it that you do not refuse Him who speaks.
  For if the people did not escape when they refused Him
  who warned them on earth,
  how much less will we escape, if we reject Him
  who warns us from heaven?

  At that time, His voice shook the earth,
  but now He has promised,
  "Once more I will shake not only the earth,
  but heaven as well.

  "The words "Once more" signify the removal
  of what can be shaken—that is, created things—
  so that the unshakable may remain.

  Therefore, since we are receiving an unshakable kingdom,
  let us be filled with gratitude, and so worship God acceptably
  with reverence and awe.
  "For our God is a consuming fire."
  Hebrews 12:25-29

Father, the burden on my heart, is that Judge Scalia and Nancy Reagan represented justice and they are both now gone from the earth; justice through them is gone.

The Lord brought to my remembrance that, *"witchcraft will be large in the earth in the last days."* Jezebel and witchcraft are found in the last days spiritual Babylon (Revelation 16-18).

I asked Yahuwah, Can there be repentance from the remnant to change the course of things <u>at this point</u>?

The Lord answered, *"No. During sovereignty it can't.* He will accept repentance from individuals, but not an unrepentant Nation (System). He will use sovereignty for breaking the people (of their hardened heart and wills to do evil). It is to get their attention and to scare the hell (literally) out of them."

March 12, 2016

- Evil will increase in all things.

March 20, 2016

- Vision: I instantly saw Donald Trump and I saw a man understanding 'dark sentences' (Daniel 8:23). He understands the way in which to manipulate dark sentences.

  In other words, they are dark and not brought to light, so people don't know what he is actually doing or saying.

  When he says certain things, people like to make fun of the way he talks, but he knows what he is doing.

  When I was a teenager, my father taught me something regarding marketing and sales: that if there is something you don't like, it gets you to talk about it and you will remember it. It will stick with you, just as much as if you loved it.

It doesn't matter if you love it or hate it. This is what God has shown me regarding soul ties also. Whether you love or hate someone, it is something united to your soul; it ties or binds you to that thing, person or place.

People hate him, so they are tied to him. People love him, so they are tied to him. We cannot afford that. As God showed to us before, those who are in pride - don't be up there! Those with self-pity - don't be down there! It is the same thing, your soul attached or united to things or people through your emotions.

No accusing. No excusing (Romans 2:15). Don't do either one. Both are evil to God. To walk in that place with God, through that straight and narrow gate, it takes sacrifice. Giving up what you like or are accustomed to doing.

- **Vision:** I also saw this strong aggression on Donald Trump, like a fierce aggression.

- God is reminding me, *"I told you thick darkness on the earth. The enemy is here to stop you. There are as many of them, as there are of you. Now what are you going to do?"*

- Lord, it's been an overwhelming battle to get here, this far. The Lord said, *"The enemy is not willingly going to hand everything over to you. You have to take it by force."*

"Yahushua said: *"From the days of John the Baptist until now, the kingdom of heaven has suffered violence and the violent take it by force."*
Matthew 11:12

That's what subduing is, you make them. That's what a King does, make them bow to your authority.

- The people, they want their resemblance. What is in their

241

heart will be reflected through their vote.

- What is in Mr. Trump is going to **grow exponentially and he will get bigger and stronger and he will bring us all under his power and this is what people don't see.**

- I do sense our rights in America will be infringed upon, based on the whim of the President. I don't see it at this very moment, **but I see it coming.** He will think there is nothing he can't do.

Lord, I ask You to intervene because we have to live here. I do realize, You said these are the last days (of this Nation being the same). If you are talking about the last days Father, I am still in this and just really hoping that I am wrong.

March 26, 2016

A prayer of Intercession for the Remnant: Lord, grant your people a spirit of submission and a gift of repentance to respond to the voice of the living God, so when we hear it, we will recognize and respond with submission to it.

- I was reminded of things spoken by the Lord, in the past: Merging the realms and quickening the times.

- **Vision:** I see an apocalyptic dark sky. It's dark orange, gray and ashen, with a mix of other colors. Extremely dark, dark clouds and out of them coming sharp spear like swords. They are around and surrounding a monument. It's made of stone (it looks like a temple) and there is a skull at the top of it. It has a sense of hell coming to the earth. I also see there, chain links, like the huge ones in the ocean.

- Monuments are a place set for a stronghold, where the power of that entity or intention goes out from.

- I asked, where is the monument? Is that important? Or, are they established here now? The Lord answered and said, *"It is the Kingdom* (of God) *within you, that will fight these forces."* Put on the full armor daily.

God's stronghold is His people in this world

- **Vision:** This monument structure (that I saw above) is where the signs and wonders of Egypt are coming from. They will give power to the Anti-Christ to recover from a deadly wound.

- **Vision:** I see armies come out and they are dressed in black fatigue. They have long hair, like women and are dressed in military garb. Amidst them, are blue green beams, that is their protection, they are Nephilim, but they are so covered, that we can't tell. The God of Heaven will take them down with a shout!

- The Lord said, *"You are perfected through the furnace of affliction. Perfection comes through the trials of your faith. It needs to be tried at that extreme. You will not face this battle alone. I Am with you. But I had to raise you up to meet, (greet?); be a formidable foe to the enemy and face off with that kind of power* (power to match). *I had to give you a working knowledge and it comes through experience. If I had not informed you, you would not know what kind of battle this is. Eyes to see, ears to hear and a heart to understand. What I am doing in the days ahead, I have perfected that in you."*

- **Vision:** I see a narrow and dark hallway. There is a door opened at the end. A door or opportunity. It is bright on the other side. I have to do this by my faith because it is so dark. The door is from the Father. He is with me. In the background, I know He is here with me, but I can't see Him.

So I will continue to walk through the dark to the get to the door, as He is with me. It feels like glory is on the other side.

Telling the Kings Business

April 11, 2016

- **Vision:** I see Donald Trump with his eyes narrowed, he is angry and indignant. I see this anger, but it is worse than that, it is a force coming through him. The spirit that is operating through him is like, the sensing of a train on a track gaining speed and coming at you. It would be a formidable (very powerful or strong; deserving serious attention and respect; very difficult to deal with; large or impressive in size or amount) foe. You wouldn't be able to stop that train. It's like that. A force on the inside of him.

  The enemy is using the people on the earth in connection to this election and I am reminded of the book of Daniel and the scripture, Daniel 7:25 *"He thinks to change the laws and time."* He has a penetrating anger and I predict he is personally, going to try to change some things.

- I feel this part, God is not saying it: That the force that I see, is in there working and I feel it is something yet to be.

- I hear the Lord say, *"Continuum" and "For changes that will be"*

- **Vision:** I see again, the train on the track, **it is continuing.** In other words whatever is set in action **will continue.**

  Continuum means 1. a continuous sequence in which adjacent elements are not perceptibly different from each other, although the extremes are quite distinct.
  2. a continuous extent, series, or whole. 3. Mathematics
     A. a set of elements such as that between any
         two of them there is a Third element.

B. The set of all real numbers.
C. Any compact, connected set containing at
   least two elements.

So this says to me, this is all ordained and has been set in place ahead of time. At the bottom of the page of the dictionary that I was looking up the word "continuum", an ad came up that said, "Horn blower". We are sounding the alarm!

The sense that I get regarding the vision of Donald Trumps' narrowed eyes, is that it is a force beyond human and it is going to make sure it will win. Like a train at full speed, it is literally breaking wind.

In Daniel, those that try to rise, are falling left and right. We must keep this at the forefront to be steadfast, fixed and focused on Yahuwah.

- I heard: *"Landslide"* It's like how a dump truck opens up, but this was more forceful. I feel it is connected to this vision of Donald Trump. And in the natural realm, a landslide like a law being changed. (The term is typically used to describe a type of natural disaster, but became popular in the 1800's to define a resounding victory, one in which the opposition is buried in an election.")

- I feel we are to read in Daniel. Starting in Daniel Chapter 8 through Chapter 12, which is the last chapter, because it speaks of the times we are in. We need to set our heart and faces to know and understand God. This is what Daniel did to understand the time he was in by reading Jeremiah (Daniel 9:2). We will seek You Lord, with all our heart.

- **Vision:** I see those that are unfaithful in this dispensation, because of what they want. God will take the authority of what they are doing from them. They are coming low and giving over to the next generation. It is a part of the proving process, testing and trying. The Valley of Decision.

They refuse correction; in pride, they refuse it, so they will have to stumble over it (the Rock of Offense) Isaiah 8:14, Romans 9:33, 1 Peter 2:8. Satan already has them captive (I saw them in cages). They keep their offenses because of unforgiveness. There is No faith in pride or unforgiveness.

I reasoned with the Lord, If they are cut off, they are not covered and the enemy can steal them away. It is not okay! How do we pray? We cry mercy.

- **Vision:** I see a division that wants to divide them from submitting to God. That's what the bottom line is. That they won't enter in to submission and we say "No"! *They will* enter into submission to the living God, because we cry mercy for the salvation of their entire souls; mind, emotion and will, to be subject to God! Work in them both to will and to do of your good pleasure and do whatever it takes to bring them (Your people) to that place.

Remember what I saw in 2014. That anyone who was walking in the flesh, the darkness would strengthen their flesh and I do see them being cut off if they do not repent, so that is why we cry mercy. He has given us to pray mercy and salvation. But now I am seeing this that connects back to 2014 and being covered in the darkness and stronger because of their agreements (in how they think) with the darkness.

I said to the Lord, What we need is signs, wonders and miracles. He answered quickly, *"Those are for the unbelievers. Those that know Me and My Word don't need it, it is not for them."* (Not that we won't operate in them or see them, but it is for those who don't believe).

- **Vision:** What I see, is that angry right fighters are going to get stronger and stronger and stronger. That is how we will know who is who also. You know that fierce anger I saw in Donald Trump? That is a spirit. I see that operating through the people. And what that looks like, is that there will be a rage and anger and they will be operating in right fighting. They think they are right about everything and they have to have their own opinions, their own knowledge and what they think, they will fight you with it. And it will not be God.

- God is telling me, *"Disengage from that battle."* We choose to not be a part of that and we do disengage.

- **Vision:** I see that there is a division and a line drawn in the sand. You stand on that side and we stand on this side. I am reminded that the Lord said, *"if they don't think like Me, don't trust them".* Remember, the scripture says, they would be those of your own household. (Matthew 10:36). They are an enemy, because they don't think like God and they will fight Him, though they say they are for Him.

> *"For the* (carnal) *mind that is set on the flesh is hostile to (is the enemy of) God, for it does not submit to God's law; indeed, it cannot. That's why those who are still under the control of their sinful nature can never please God."*
> Romans 8:7-8

- The Lord says, *"This is why I said, mercy and salvation."* He may have to take people early in order not to lose their salvation. We cry mercy!

- The Lord said, *"They say that they know Me, but in their works they deny Me."* There is a penalty for this according to the word of God.

- I sense your word, *"Be Holy as I Am Holy"* (Leviticus 11:44, 19:2, 20:7, Hebrews 12:14 and I Peter 1:16).
- The next phase is multitudes, multitudes in the valley of decision (division) ~ Joel 3:14. Their decisions lead to the division.

May 16, 2016

- **Vision:** I see the earth turning in its rotation. I see the inside of it and then I heard the word, *"Credibility."* No one is checking Donald Trump's credibility. In this rotation, a shadow of turning and deception and delusion **will increase as time goes on**. We need to question everything we hear and experience. Don't jump into anything! Check with God first, until He verifies and makes credible.

- **Vision:** I see something that looks like a clock. The dial is like on a sun dial. It is going faster than a second hand and this could stand for the quickening of the time, because the days are evil.

- I hear the words: *"Countdown to Armageddon"* and then I saw seven years. There is extreme darkness over the cities, there are only stars in the sky and they are illuminating and getting closer and lower to the city. The stars come close and are bright and giving light. The stars represent angels that come to help and the people that are illuminated, but not all make it, because they are cast down in the warfare - Daniel 11.

- I hear *"Choosing"*. "The little light that we will have is enough to choose the Truth. It's little light because the people have chosen only a little truth. But its little light, is enough.

- I hear the Word: *"Remnant"*. As many that call on His Name, shall be saved (Romans 10:13).

- *"If He does not quicken the time, no flesh will live. And*

- *except those days should be shortened, there should no flesh be saved: but for the elect's sake those days shall be shortened"* Matthew 24:22.

- **Vision:** I see people that have died and are gathered together for Armageddon; the book of Jude:

> *"...Listen! The Lord is coming with countless thousands of his holy ones to execute judgment on the people of the world. He will convict* (expose with evidence to be found guilty) *every person of all the ungodly things they have done and for all the insults that ungodly sinners have spoken against him."*
> Jude 1:14-15

- I am reminded of REM's song "It's the end of the world (as we know it)." That song was released in 1987 and the lyrics point to the time we are living in now. Did they know just how prophetic they were?

  I heard the following Words:

- *"Second Chance"*

- *"Seeing Clearly"*

- People have not repented, so hardship and darkness will put pressure on them to have a second chance to see clearly. A dark night. Sovereignty.

- In the next 7 years all of this will go down.

- Regarding the Jude passage, the Lord reveals that it is to be a progression, them coming back little by little. He says to me that people think He does everything all at once. While in fact, most things are done in progression. The reason we need faith and patience to see the Truth and inherit the promises.

> *"That you will not become spiritually dull and indifferent. Instead, you will follow the example of those who are going to inherit God's promises because of their faith and endurance."*

- I find it interesting that Scientists have found a planet called, Earth 2.0 and it has just come into our solar system. They say it is exactly like planet Earth, only larger. It reminds me of this scripture:

"For as the new heavens and the new earth that I make shall remain before me, says the LORD, so shall your offspring and your name remain".
Isaiah 66:22

'Then I saw "a new heaven and a new earth,"
for the first heaven and the first earth had passed away,
and there was no longer any sea."
Revelation 21:1

To be noted, all this talk of water by the Lord and in the new earth, there is no sea. That is pretty interesting. All this water on the earth has covered a whole lot of things.

- I hear: *"Chosen Ones."*

- **Vision:** He is showing me everywhere, everywhere, everywhere, there are temptations on every side. I see in the atmosphere, above the people, are shiny things dangling down to get their attention; temptations everywhere; a lure; deception and delusion. It's not a little, but heavy and thick. There is no room in between; you can't see through it.

- I hear the Words that Yahushua spoke to Judas: *"That which you do, go do quickly"* (John 13:27). In this case, I see that the Lord is making reference to Revelation 12. The last days reference of the two signs in the Heavenlies. The Woman and the Dragon.

- Check all that we hear for credibility with the Word.

I heard the following Words:

- *"Night rider"*

- *" Things written"*

- *"Things that go bump in the night"*

- **Vision:** People giving in to temptation (but covering it); being fearful, self-preserving, full of anxiety and in confusion.

- There will be a transference of power to get the keys. The house is not yours, even the key is not yours **until** you get the signature (authorization) from the Owner.

"Have nothing to do with the fruitless deeds of darkness, but rather expose them"
Ephesians 5:11

May 24, 2016

- **Vision:** Regarding America: I see land and people on it. And in the atmosphere above them, there is a wind blowing fast carrying electricity. Directly and moving along the top of that, is like black burnt wire.

  On the top of that, is Donald Trump and Hillary Clinton. And I see that the wind is moving across their heads. But they are above the people.

  They had American flags in both hands and are dancing on that darkness at the same time.

  It has the appearance like they are on opposing teams, however, for what is going to happen in America, they are both used of the enemy. All of these visions I have had today are moving, it reminds me of the dial that is continually moving on the clock. Advancing the time.

June 1, 2016

- Vision: I was in prayer worshipping the Father and speaking of His Power and how it was the day of His Power, when I had this Vision: I am in the Heavenlies somewhere and I see a throne and an altar in front of it, like where sacrifices are done. I am there standing at the bottom of the steps, but not really known or seen, I'm not important, but I am privy to what is going on. I am privy to the plans of the enemy.

  Next, I see a ram's head, with horns. Is that the enemy exalting his throne above Yours Lord? It reminds me of a pagan altar.

  It seems like he is seated on the throne waiting. There is only darkness, not light, so the comprehension is that this is not you, Father. But he acts like You and comes across like You and he pretends to be You and he copies everything You do.

  I wonder about Revelation 12:11 that says:

  "And they have (overcome and) *conquered him* (the enemy) *by the blood of the Lamb* (sacrifice) *and by the word of their testimony* (personal test of overcoming), *for they loved not their lives even unto death."*

  And I wondered, has the enemy prepared the sacrifice for all those that made covenant with God, but are now bowing their knee to Satan (through their words not aligning with actions or deeds).

- Vision: Continuing in the vision, the throne and altar are illuminated. It is elaborate and ornate. I am small down by the steps, insignificant, not being seen. I am just watching. The ram's head is coming to the forefront and the background is very dark, pitch black. Is Satan preparing everything. He is on the throne, with fire around the bowls of the altar and it is lit. This says to me that he has made preparation and he is ready.

June 27, 2016

- I heard the Lord say, *"Don't forget, your kindness leads* (others) *to repentance. Kindness is an attitude."*

June 28, 2016

- I sense a shaking on the inside. *"Trouble the waters".* A Word that keeps coming up.

July 11, 2016

- During the night a murderous spirit came in and he was trying to murder me over a key Word God gave me on Saturday morning, regarding "Forgiveness". He was attacking me, trying to make me look like the unforgiver. He was thick and heavy on me for about 2 hours or more. It took me a while to pull myself out of it and overcome.

- When I woke up today and turned on the news, I heard Donald Trump say, "I am the candidate of law and order." It reminded me of what Daniel says the Anti-Christ is about (Daniel 7, 8, 11).

- People think Mr. Trump is good. He literally matches what Daniel says about the Anti-Christ. All people need to do is read. How Daniel knew what time it was, was because he was reading in Jeremiah and did the math to notice it matched the time he was in.

- That spirit changes everything. Why? Because we are in a Nation of chaos and it has nothing to do with the upcoming election. The chaos we have been having is also a sign of the times. It has to do with offenses in our country. This is exactly what God said. The terrorism, the law against the people, people against the law; it is mass chaos. It is a sign of the times. Yahushua said that we would know it, if we were watchful and prayerful (Matthew 16).

- My concern is that the people of God will not be seeking God day and night as His Word says to do and things will go unnoticed, if you are not walking in the Spirit, but the flesh. If you are in the flesh, you are not pressing in and pursuing God for His wisdom and to think like He does. So what is going to happen, is it will take you over and you won't notice. You can't afford to be there.

- We need to pursue after God because it is going to get worse. In this condition, the best case scenario, you are deceived; and that is if you don't seek after God. Worst case scenario, is that all those things that are going to go on in the dark world, will happen to you. It's going to get bad and I am watching innocent people who don't deserve it, with injustices happening to them. I am disturbed just knowing what they go through, with so many that I know and meet. They must be told to get out of the line of fire if they can. Or be equipped to go through it.

- I will watch the news and I see another spirit with them. They have a false sense to them. I see it daily. In the natural, I see that everyone is about themselves. It is happening everywhere. If those that serve God are doing that too…. If you feel God is calling you to 10% of knowing Him and 90% of what you want, then go live that way.
I was reading in Psalms today and David would not let God go. God trusted him to go through hard things because he did nothing but want God. God says, I want people who are willing to talk to Me all day; to open up their Bible and sing

songs to Me. That is what it needs to be. He is Worthy of it all.

- When I see all these things going on with Donald Trump, I am reminded of what God told us to do:

  "Pray for those in authority over you that you may lead a Godly and peaceable life."
  I Timothy 2:1-3.

  It was not a friendly time in the Nation when Paul wrote that verse. We are brainwashed in the times we live in. When Donald Trump said that today about being a 'candidate of law and order', it sent a chill all the way through my being and the newscaster echoed my discomposure and said, "Well certainly, it is a sign of the times"!!!

- Remember, God said after I was finished with the dark night of the soul, the darkness would go on into the Nation. This is all part of it; this is the enemy causing division and offense. Everything is offensive out there and it will get worse. Killing people is offensive, for the color of their skin! It is all offensive. The Bible says, *"The love of many will grow cold."* Matthew 24:12. That's a sure sign.

  "For the hearts of these people are hardened, and their ears cannot hear and they have closed their eyes— so their eyes cannot see and their ears cannot hear, and their hearts cannot understand, and they cannot turn to me and let me heal them."
  Acts 28:27

- We are in big trouble. I don't know anyone that I could call on the phone and ask what do we do. No one I know has answers. Many people who claim to know God are causing the division. They believe what they are doing is the will of God. We have a Nation of "Right Fighters."

- God spoke two things to me on Saturday morning. The first thing He said was, *"All My power will work through forgiveness in the days ahead.*

That is scary to me, because what He is telling us is the answer is forgiveness. If the answer is forgiveness, guess what is coming? Strong offense. So that means we need to pay attention right now and not get caught up in the fight. All of these people are offending and hurting one another, so we can't jump in and agree with them and give our proverbial 'two cents'. We need to be praying. And we need to be speaking love and forgiveness.

- Concerning the second part, *"My laws will be governed through obedience."* God's laws (signs, wonders and miracles work through God's supernatural laws) are going to happen through obedience to Him. That is where His power is, He said to forgive. It is right now we need to experience this and implement it. These are major keys. This is how we will make it in the days ahead.

July 13, 2016

- Regarding Donald Trump. He is strengthening the law (already), so he can use the law.

- Donald Trump will empower the police so that injustices will be done. The people will take the law into their own hands. They will have an attitude of "I can do whatever I want!"

- **Vision:** I see martial law. And I see darkness over the land.

July 15, 2016

- To be clear, **God is not** electing Donald Trump, **the people are**.

- God is giving to the people, what they want (like in 1 Samuel 8 and 9 with King Saul). It will get worse before it gets better. It will get better, but then worse again. My prediction, is that all hell will break loose between now and the election and then after the election. He will rule with an iron fist. He will get a lockdown on it.

- The possibility of America rising up will reflect on Donald Trump. It doesn't matter if or what previous presidents did, it will look like it is Donald Trump. He will make it look that way. He is going to get a lockdown on everything and if the economy comes up, it will look like, (in his own words) everything turns to gold. He is the Trump. Everyone will think he has done it. Then, we are setup to bow down - And then we go down.

July 19, 2016

- **Vision:** I see a clock face again

July 20, 2016

- Today feels like a slight shift. Everything is in it's place. This is what is happening to America - Sovereignty is coming. Now the shift, is the dominion.

- It's a done deal. I can look and see in the spirit, that Donald Trump is the clear winner. I don't see another way for it to happen.

- God has been telling me about America in the darkness,

  Donald Trump being elected and other details as such. You know what is worse than the darkness? That nobody would notice it, because they have become hardened through the deceitfulness of sin (Hebrews 3:13) and so they are so one with it. I think only those that are spiritually in tune will notice it.

July 25, 2016

- **Vision:** Thank you Father, that You have heard all my prayers today. I am going to move on to Donald Trump because that is who is standing before me in the spirit. I see his eyes like stone, with fire coming out. I hear the Words of Your scripture and it says, *"A man who understands with a fierce countenance, who understands dark sayings will rise among the people"* Daniel 8:23.

- I see the word *'intent'* also.

- All the words he speaks are going around in circles. It is a mesmerizing on the people, like manipulation and witchcraft. The people love it. I was watching his eyes and wondering, how not one Christian person cannot see that God is not there. There is no God there.

  There has never been one President who can do all they want to do and that's why people turn against them. So far he has done everything he says he is going to do, that's why people like him. He has undermined everyone that told him he won't and did it anyway. That's what it says about Anti-Christ. Whether he is *the* Anti-Christ or not, I can tell you this, he has an Anti-Christ Spirit.

- **Vision:** You know how under Hitler, the people became brainwashed and to think like him. Not all Germans were Nazis, but many were. I see that coming, not that we would be called a Communist Country, I don't see that. But I see a brainwashing and it will fall on the people. They will be like drones. I see this kind of mesmerizing, if he were to say to "Kill every "<u>fill in the blank</u>" the people would go, "Yes, we will do that." I see them hypnotized and under his power.

I see He thinks that there is nothing that he cannot do. And I see him looking far off and what I perceive that means, is beyond America. If he has conquered America, what else can he do? He is contemplating, like he is strategizing.

- It's as if he stands alone and all bow to him. That is not democracy. We will be under this governing. What do we do?

- I hear, *"This is not a good time for America."* People will think it is good, but it is not. I heard God say, *"I set the times."* And the Lord says, *"He* (Donald Trump) *will betray the Nation and he will govern for himself."*

God told the people the truth regarding Saul too. But they still wanted what they wanted. This is God speaking to Samuel:

*"Now **listen to them; but warn them** solemnly and let them know what the king who will reign over them will claim as his rights."*

'Samuel told all the words of the LORD to the people who were asking him for a king.
He said, "This is what the king who will reign over you will claim as his rights:

He will take your sons and make them serve with his chariots and horses, and they will run in front of his chariots.
Some he will assign to be commanders of thousands and commanders of fifties, and others to plow his ground and reap his harvest, and still others to make weapons of war and equipment for his chariots.

He will take your daughters to be perfumers and cooks and bakers.
He will take the best of your fields and vineyards and olive groves and give them to his attendants.

*He will take a tenth of your grain and of your vintage
and give it to his officials and attendants.*

*Your male and female servants and the best of your cattle
and donkeys he will take for his own use.
He will take a tenth of your flocks, and you yourselves
will become his slaves.*

*When that day comes, you will cry out for relief from the king
you have chosen, but the LORD will not answer you in that day."*
1 Samuel 8:9-18

- What do we pray Father, I feel kind of dropped off in prayer; like, okay you did your work, move on. I feel like any kind of praying for him will be like tiny pebbles, sounding like, 'ping, ping' against a strong hold, a fortified city.

- The Lord says, *"I just want you to see what time it is."* No wonder He said pray mercy and salvation. Pray for the people!

- I also see that the military will be under his command.

- *"I want you to warn the people what is going on."*

  I protested because the people are arduous, but God said, *"You can't get caught up in the fight."*

July 29, 2016

- I hear, *"I didn't come to bring peace, but a sword"* Matthew 10:34.

  I do believe that, *this is that time,* because You have shown me this is the end time. It looks like the Tribulation has started and we have 7 years, but we know one day is as a thousand years with You Lord (2 Peter 3:8 and Psalm 90:4).

I'm more than likely still hoping I'm wrong. It is the time of division for decision.

August 3, 2016

- I hear the Lord saying, *"Daughter, do you see what time it is?"* He is excited. Remember He showed us the clock? It is time. I hear Him say, *"The whole world and creation has been waiting for this climatic hour. The grandstands of Heaven are bursting at the seams, they are so excited."*

  I am reminded of this scripture: *"Therefore **rejoice**, oh heavens and you that dwell in them. Woe to the inhabitants of the earth and of the sea! For the devil is come down unto you, having great wrath, because he knows that he hath but a short time."* Revelation 12:12

- *"Daughter, you have been faithful over the little, so I make you ruler over much. I have chosen you from among them, because I knew you would do My will."* Is it possible the remnant will be blessed even greater? Could we have the resurrection power?

  We will occupy until you come, Father. We will continue to do and be and putting our hands to the plow. Give us guidance and direction, so we don't get caught up in anything to distract us. As we take occupancy, You are in it, all of it.

- All of a sudden, I understood the word, "occupy" as different; I see it as, "Take Ground until I Come". Like, own it. Take dominion. It's the first time I heard it like that. Cover the earth with Your Word and Dominion, as the waters cover the sea. I just heard that differently too – 'as the waters cover the sea' - in other words, create; creation, the waters, create. Let *My* creation be on the earth. Let God's Word take on the form of creation.

August 16, 2016

- **Vision:** I see Hillary Clinton at the feet of Donald Trump. Her hand is around his ankles and she is putting her strength into it. He is not bothered, but stoic. He is looking into the distance and doesn't have a care in the world. It's a look of focusing on the future. From the backside of him, are dark forces.

I hear the words:

- *"Determent"* to cause (someone) to decide not to do something, to prevent (something) from happening.

- *"Captivity"*

- *"Confidence"*

- *"Acceptance"*

- *"Meager"* very small or too small in amount; not having enough of something (such as money or food) for comfort or happiness.

- *"Generational warfare"*

- *"Genocide"* the deliberate and systematic destruction of a racial, political, or cultural group.

(*August 2020 - Authors note: Wow)

August 28, 2016

I think about how judgment starts in the house of God.

"For it is time for judgment to begin with God's household; and if it begins with us, what will the outcome be

*for those who **do not obey the gospel of God?"***
1 Peter 4:17

God is going to judge His people. We are commanded to come out from among them:

*"Therefore **come out from among them
and be separate**, says the Lord.*

Touch (have no participation with)
nothing unclean, and I will receive you."
And: "I will be a Father to you,
and you will be My sons and daughters,
says the Lord Almighty."
2 Corinthians 6:17-18

To come out from any and all things that do not agree with Him, glorify Him, talk like Him, think like Him. This also includes mainstream Christianity, if they do not sound like His Word that He speaks in the Bible, if the can quote His Word, but live the opposed to His Word. This would take each person knowing God for themselves (which was His original plan) instead of allowing another tell you who God is and tell you who you are. Know for yourself!

"No longer will they teach their neighbor or say to one another,
'Know the Lord,' because they will all know me,
from the least of them to the greatest."
Hebrews 8:11

September 3, 2016

If many people agree with you, be careful that you are not being led astray and leading others astray, going in at a wide gate.

Those that are trailblazers and pioneers lead people in a more narrow path where less people follow.

"Enter in at the straight gate:
for wide is the gate and broad is the way,
that leads to destruction, and many there be
which go in there at.
Because straight is the gate and narrow is the way,
*which leads to life and **few there be that find it"***
Matthew 7: 13–14

September 7, 2016

- Dream: I dreamed that it was dark outside. There were wars everywhere. Political wars were outside. There were big political bandwagons, so to speak, with many people on them. And they were under siege and in war. Inside, they were putting us in protection in places everywhere. In some places, they were stacking people in attic type spaces and it was crowded. But, there was danger coming. There were large rabid animals to destroy us. It was going on at large and no one could escape it.

September 3, 2016

A Word to God's Leadership and Servants:

If you are one that labors for God, your labor is never in vain in the Lord. While the workman is worthy of his wages, If you exact payment for your deeds, when you work for God, He very well may profess that "I never knew you ".

"Which of you, whose servant comes in from plowing
or shepherding in the field will say to him,
'Come at once and sit down to eat'?
Instead, won't he tell him, 'Prepare my meal
and dress yourself to serve me
while I eat and drink; and afterward
you may eat and drink'?

Does he thank the servant because he did what he was told?
So you also, when you have done everything commanded of you,
should say, 'We are unworthy servants;
we have only done our duty.'"
Luke 17:7-10

~ and ~

"Not everyone that says to me, Lord, Lord,
shall enter into the kingdom of heaven:
*but he that **does the will** of My father, which is in heaven.*

Many will say to Me in that day, Lord, Lord,
have we not prophesied in your Name?
And in your Name have cast out devils?
And in your Name done many wonderful works?

And then I will profess to them, I never knew you:
depart from Me, you that work iniquity (lawlessness;
the utter disregard for God's law. His written and living Word;
includes the end-impact of law breaking – i.e. its negative influence
on a person's soul and status before God). *"*
Matthew 7:21–23

The Greek word for 'iniquity' here equals the practice of sin,
not a slip up or mistake repented of, but a practice.

When you truly work for God, you are a servant of God, just
like His son, Yahushua. It was written of Him, though He was a
King, He took on no reputation for Himself but took on the form of a
servant.

"Let this mind be in you which was also in Christ Yahushua:
Who, existing in the form of God,
(yet) did not consider equality with God
something to be grasped, but emptied Himself,
taking the form of a servant,
being made in human likeness.

And being found in appearance as a man,

He humbled Himself and became obedient
to death—even death on a cross."
Philippians 2:5-8

We are not greater than our Master. We are to take upon us His yoke, His burden, His likeness as His disciples and even more so, to lay down our lives, if we are called to a greater calling of service. To whom much is given, much is required.

Yahushua said, *"I have set* (for) *you an example,*
so that you should do as I have done for you.
Truly, truly, I tell you, no servant is greater
than his master, nor is a messenger greater
than the one who sent him. If you know these things,
you will be blessed if you do them".
John 13:15-17

He also spoke saying, *"That servant who knows his master's will,*
but does not get ready or follow his instructions will be beaten
with many blows.

But the one who unknowingly does things
worthy of punishment, will be beaten with few blows.

From everyone who has been given much,
much will be required; and from him who has been entrusted with
much, even more will be demanded."
Luke 12:47-48

We are His Servants. These are His Words. They are written in the Bible.

Did we forget these things?

October 3, 2016

- During the dark night on the earth (God's Sovereignty), people will say, "how is God letting this happen?" They will feel the evil, but not understand; where is God? Why did He leave me?

October 29, 2016

- Vision: Today I saw it so clearly; it's the time like the days of Elijah and Jeremiah. The time of confrontation between those who say they know and serve God and those that actually do.

October 31, 2016

- Dream: Donald Trump was over the people and he put people on a 'type of chemotherapy drugs' (treatment). I saw them sitting in chairs with needles in their arms.

December 28, 2016

- Vision: I sense Donald Trump in a dictator roll. He answers to no one. I see he is controlled by another power; he is one with it. There is an unforeseen force upon him; a pressure coming down on his head. Words are coming out and they are law. Remembrance of God saying He was going to "exalt the law in the last days" (Evidently, all Law).

CHAPTER 14

ALL THINGS THAT DWELL IN THE DARK ARE BROUGHT TO LIGHT

YEAR OF 2017

January 15, 2017

- The Lord says, *"This is the day all of creation has been waiting for. This is the day of the Bride. This is the day of the Wedding Feast. America is being brought into judgment."*

January 16, 2017

Wise as Serpents, Harmless as Doves

- I keep hearing the words, water, water, water, water, water.

- Vision: I see a type of prison and the people are being pushed down; it's coming down on them.

- All the ones that voted for Donald Trump will be under his power, unless there is mercy for repentance. I saw them going down to prison, I saw them running and hiding, not many will make it, unless they repent.

- Vision: I see corruption come into America from other Nations. It is not only coming from within, but from without as well. This is part of God's judgment. He is allowing it (picking up from where God delivered us, America, from in the 1940s).

- Vision: I saw the people raging and I heard the scripture, *"Why do the Nations rage and the people plot in vain?"*

"Why do the heathen rage, and the people imagine
a vain thing?
The kings of the earth set themselves,
and the rulers take counsel together,
against the LORD, and against his anointed,
saying, Let us break their bands asunder
and cast away their cords from us."
Psalm 2:1-3

- **Vision:** Regarding the inauguration of Donald Trump: I am seeing, as if it were a lightning bolt, that came out of heaven. It's as if the heavens parted and the heavens parting, **were** the bolt. It parted and shaped a bolt that came down.

  And the Lord God of Heaven said, *"Great division on the earth."* And it struck the earth. People scattered running to and fro. *"Many shall run to and fro and knowledge shall be increased"* Daniel 12:4. Until verse 9, when the power shall be successfully scattered, then all these things shall be the end.

  This is for the power of the Gospel to be preached on the earth.

- This Friday (when Donald Trump is inaugurated) that bolt is coming out of heaven and dividing the earth. It doesn't matter if it's about politics or not, it's what is in the human nature. I don't know what that is going to look like, but the bolt is going to divide.

  In verse 11 he says "and" and that was what the angel left off with when he came in 2008. This July (23rd) will be 9 years since his visitation.

  "And the abomination that makes desolate is set up". I don't know if that has anything to do with Donald Trump and setting up an embassy in Israel. And God showing evil taking place, but also the Word of the Lord is to come to pass. There will have to be some

rules or sanctions in which the Capital City, the street and the wall can be rebuilt.

All these things will be finished. But we go to another time, troublous times, Daniel 9:25. So to summarize, we need to get on board, this is what is happening. We are still to pray Mercy and Souls. It says in Daniel, that he will basically obey his own instruction. And what I saw before, that if people don't agree with him, I see them run for cover and take cover because they do not like what he does.

So Father, mercy. Mercy and souls.

- I'm hearing that scripture about Anti-Christ, a man of fierce countenance and understanding dark sayings. Daniel 8:23. I keep going back to his description - *"And in the latter time of their kingdom, when the transgressors are come to the full, a king of fierce countenance, and understanding dark sentences, shall stand up."*

- **Vision:** I see Donald Trump. He is at the front and he has his arms down to his sides, with his hands open and backward, as if to hold people back. He is brazen, facing everything, like he has all the power and he owns it and everyone else is behind him.

Daniel 8:24 says: *"his power shall be mighty"*. And this is how the people see him, because deception is on them.

"And shall prosper and destroy the holy and mighty people." I saw them going down into prison, I saw them running and hiding; not many will make it in those days.

"and through his policy also he shall cause craft (deceit, treachery, dishonesty) *to prosper at his hand."* This is what he does now with the politicians. *"By peace he shall destroy many. He shall also stand up against the Prince of Princes."*

Well here it is in context:

"At the end of their rule, when their sin is at its height,
a fierce king, a master of intrigue, will rise to power.
He will become very strong, but not by his own power.
*He will cause a **shocking amount of destruction***
and succeed in everything he does.
*He will **destroy powerful leaders and devastate***
the holy people.

*He will be a **master of deception** and will **become arrogant;***
*he will **destroy many without warning.***
*He will **even take on the Prince of princes in battle,***
but he will be broken, though not by human power."
Daniel 8:23-25

Continual Forgiveness

March 6, 2017

The enemy dwells where there is unhealed wounds and rebellion. The enemy will win, except that God's people show mercy and forgiveness to others continually in these days ahead.

So, we have to constantly, constantly forgive. Remember when God was telling us we cannot have offenses as they will be huge in the last days. We that know and hear God, have to be free from offense. The only way to be totally free from offense is to die to self; the only way you can forgive, is if your feelings do not rule you.

Forgiveness *is* submission,
which is the power of God to salvation

March 16, 2017

Spiritually speaking, it is thick with those spirits; there are as many of them as there are of us. That is the darkness in our Nation. It means that they are ruling. The light that has been in the world has grown dim. Scripture tells us that Satan is the ruler of this world (John 12, 14, 16). God needs those that are growing stronger (in submission to Him) and learning more wisdom and dominion to be able to bring the Kingdom of God here.

March 20, 2017

- The Lord said, *"The enemy is not willingly going to hand everything over to you. You have to take it by force."* He brought that up before. He had been talking about that about a year ago. That is what you do if you are a kingdom. You take it by force, because they will not give it up willingly. He is reminding me, this is not going to happen easy, you are going to have to stay on top of this and make them do it. That's what subduing is.

- I hear Him say, *"All of creation is yours, call it into existence."* So, it is as simple as that and I am making a big huge thing out of nothing; it's so easy. Call it into existence!

April 14, 2017

- A Word regarding Canada: I hear this: *"Canada's eyes are dry and their knees weak. Call into them the strength to sustain My movements among them."*

April 16, 2017

- **Vision:** I see that Syria is a pawn in the hand of Putin. I see that Vladimir Putin and Donald Trump have this whole thing set up on purpose to disturb the world to bring everyone under their power. I asked the Lord as I was watching all of this, if there was anything else that was going to happen with all this. He has been speaking to me about Russia since 2014 and mentioning the word "Trump" since 2011. We need to pay attention to this. Remember, He taught me, *"it is everything He says and nothing we think about what He says"*.

May 5, 2017

Haggai means festival, like a party and he was a prophet to Israel, as was Isaiah. And he was prophesying here that God was going to shake everything down and then prosper them after that. I see the correlation with God's house and America.

> *"This is what the LORD Almighty says:*
> *'In a little while I will once more*
> *shake the heavens and the earth,*
> *the sea and the dry land.*
> *I will shake all nations and what is desired*
> *by all nations will come and I will fill this house with glory,*
> *' says the LORD Almighty."*
> Haggai 2:6-7

First is everything negative, then the positive. The glory of the latter, will be greater than the former, verse 9.

> *"It shall come pass, in the last days,*
> *that the mountain of the Lord's house*
> *shall be established in the top of the mountains*
> *and shall be exalted above the hills*
> *and all nations shall flow unto it."*
> Micah 4:1 and Isaiah 2:2

May 12, 2017

- **Vision:** I felt I had to go in deep somewhere, I went down levels deep and when I got there, I didn't know what I would find. I thought maybe revelation somewhere, like buried treasure.

  But then, I saw Donald Trump. He is in a deep, dark place and he opened up a door in the ground, like a big basement door, that was in the ground. I saw men in suits and they are coming up from that area. I see Donald Trump and he is shaking hands with them, as if to say, okay, it is time for you to come out now.
  That they are men in suits in the ground, is very concerning. It also speaks of something hidden. The sense I got about it from the beginning was like an ancient plan that has been underground the whole time. Something from before, held back until now. The sense is that he is doing it right now. It appears that he has help from the underground or a group of people from underground.

- I hear the words, *"A secret plan from ancient times."* Well Father, what I want to say about that is, You have a secret plan as well!

  I am hearing and impressed upon with the following:

- *"Criminal activity and corruption"*, are coming from the White House leaders. It is being loosed out, they are coming, like that vision, they are coming with their agreements with the underworld.

  It is like they have struck a deal and now it is time for them to be on the earth and bring that *crime and corruption* with them. With that corruption and crime there will be no justice in the land. That is why people are going to be more angry and frustrated and also in the darkness, because justice won't prevail.

In scripture, when there is no remedy, no repentance from the injustices, that is when God steps in by His Sovereignty. How sad of a realization for God, that the people not only do not want Him, but they are willing to destroy others for their own gain. Love God and love your neighbor as yourself have been manifestly destroyed. It saddens me to know how God must feel, when He entrusts us to make right decisions and to repent until this point. That His grace is extended out this far to enable us to make right decisions. How hurt and disappointed He must be when it is fully realized what He must do.

- I received a Word - *'Contractual Agreements'* these are agreements that are set in writing.

Father, during the dark night, You have taught me the power of the Written Word and the power of the Spoken Word. They both have their own (law of) power. I'm in consideration, that regarding the 'Contractual Agreements', The contracts that we (America) have with You: The Declaration of Independence and The Constitution of the United States of America. That is where the law of agreement is with You and the people of America.

I perceive You are sharing with me, that they are being changed right now. When I said that, I felt impressed upon that is what Donald Trump is in office for. He is literally, (seemingly) single handedly, changing the laws.

When I brought up the constitution and the declaration and how it was ours, I felt like the Lord was showing me that's what the President is personally doing right now, he's changing everything right under everyone's nose.

- The Lord is saying *"The meeting with the other World leaders are about agreements to bring change to certain things."* It was bothering me. I stopped and stared at the TV when they showed Donald Trump at the Western Wall. I thought, all the Christians are thinking is, what a good man that he is, there at the wailing wall to pray. I thought, he has a whole agenda himself and he is there doing that right now with these world leaders to bring these changes.

I didn't get this part from the Lord, but I see it fitting that he would go to the communist leaders of the world, such as Vladimir Putin (and I do believe they are on the same page). I believe they have a secret agreement, again, that is what I personally believe; God has not told me that. But I have enough information from the Lord, that I could see how it fits. I think they have a secret agreement to bring America under a different power. I think the whole thing is to bring us under subjection. I think it is to establish a new world rule. It's been going that way for a long time.

But I am seeing all of these things right now, agreements are being made.

- I am hearing another announcement in the realm of the Spirit: *"Divide, Separate for the fall is coming."* Is that as in the fall (like the fall) or the fall as in (the season)? How I took it was falling, but it could be in the fall.

- I hear the word *"Disgrace"* so that's what time it is in the realm of the heavenlies. It's like the angels announcing, *"Divide! Separate!"* It means come out from among them, don't be a part of any of that. We have to steer clear of everything that is evil, for the fall is coming.

May 22, 2017

You know why everyone misses it? Because they think Donald Trump is the savior. That's what they thought in Daniel too about the Antichrist. The reason they made a covenant with him (Daniel 9:27). All the Christians believe that he is God's chosen. Similarly, the way that the Roman Emperor Constantine (A.D. 306-337) beguiled Christian victims and led them to deception, by becoming a Christian himself and implementing additional laws that would appease those who followed the Messiah. And it worked.

The connotation to it was, as if everything is set in place. Where does President Trump go after he leaves, because he went to Iran now he's in Israel and he has another stop after that, it's Rome. So why wouldn't he...because he's going to Muslims, Jews and next Catholics. The previous chapter in Daniel says, he becomes mighty with the people of the covenant. Take all the world religions and he's trying to make peace with all of them. Which is what a President should do, there's nothing wrong with that. But when we look at it in light of the scriptures....everything is set in place. It looks right to everyone, that's why he gets away with it. That's the best way to do it, in plain sight, right under our noses. It looks like everything he's doing is good. After all, other Presidents have travelled to all of these places too. So one just cannot tell, can they? Unless they are paying attention.

Mercy Father, mercy on America. Father, is there anything else?

I hear the words:

- *"Changing Times"*

- *"Changing Laws"* This reminds me of the time of Jannes and Jambres in Exodus (Those that opposed Moses with signs and wonders).

- The Lord just said, *"A Unique Ability to change what the people see"*. This reminds me of, *the forecasting his own devices* (Daniel 11:24). That he can project what he wants them to see. Jannes and Jambres could do everything that Moses did. Donald Trump can create what he wants it to look like, he has a unique ability to do it.

- I hear the words, *"Stranger things have happened, but nothing this cataclysmic."* (It's like in history, stranger things have happened, but nothing of this size, because it's the end times).

- **Vision:** And now I see *'that he shall mount or take mount"* - **continue to climb.** He shall mount or take mount *"and shall prosper until the time of the end, until the Lord steps in."*

Write these words down too, because I can't get past them:

- *"Control"*

- *"Consumption"*

- And then I was reminded of the words *"Challenge for Change"*. I saw Moses. That's what he went into Egypt for. He went down there, because he had to challenge Pharaoh, for change to come to God's people. The people needed to come out from among them.

Moses didn't change the Nation, he changed the situation, so the people could come out of there.

Moses didn't go in there to change the mindset of the King; he went in there to 'challenge' for the 'change' to come.

May 23, 2017

- I am to announce that the people of God are to be ready and to prepare for what is coming.

- I think it is around politics in America, but also something about President Trump's Middle East trip.

God was addressing: first Iran receiving a 100 billion dollar deal. Then to Israel, the Jews. I saw Donald Trump at the Wailing Wall with his hand on it. Then thirdly, he is going to the Catholics to the Pope in Rome. God showed me there is something with that.

- He led me yesterday to Daniel 8, in pulling that out and there was four notable ones that came up from the west wing. We are the western world. Gabriel is talking to Daniel saying, this is what will happen in the latter days. It was about the very latter days.

When I read the Word of God, the way God has shown it to me, I see that the Anti-Christ rises from the West, not the East, as Theologians have always said the East. To note, Donald Trump's family does come from East of here (Germany and Scotland). America is the West.

I perceived regarding the vision, where those men were coming out from the ground, I sensed there were four men who came out. I cannot say for sure there were four, it may have been three. But not more than four. There were not many coming out. I thought about Revelation 9 about the four angels released from the river Euphrates to kill and in Revelation 16 about the three frogs being released from the Euphrates; they were false lying spirits and that stands for lying spirits in the mouth of people.

If we don't think God does or allows this, read on:

"Then the messenger who had gone to call Micaiah instructed him, "Listen to us, with one accord: the words of the prophets are favorable to the king. So please let your words be like theirs, and speak favorably."

But Micaiah said, "As surely as the LORD lives, I will speak whatever the LORD tells me."
When Micaiah arrived, the king asked him, "Micaiah, should we go to war against Ramoth-gilead, or should we refrain?"

"Go up and triumph," Micaiah replied, "for the LORD will give it into the hand of the king."

But the king said to him, "How many times must I make you swear not to tell me anything but the truth in the name of the LORD?"

*So Micaiah declared: "I saw all Israel scattered on the hills like sheep without a shepherd.
And the LORD said, 'These people have no master; let each one return home in peace.'"*

Then the king of Israel said to Jehoshaphat (King of Judah), *"Did I not tell you that he never prophesies good for me, but only bad?"*

Micaiah continued, "Therefore hear the word of the LORD: I saw the LORD sitting on His throne, and all the host of heaven standing by Him on His right and on His left.

And the LORD said, 'Who will entice Ahab to march up and fall at Ramoth-gilead?'

*And one suggested this, and another that.
Then **a spirit** came forward, stood before the LORD, and said, 'I will entice him.'*

*'By what means?' asked the LORD.
And he replied, '**I will go out and be a lying spirit in the mouths of all his prophets.'***

*'**You will surely entice him and prevail,**' said the LORD.
'**Go and do it.**'*

So you see, the LORD has put a lying spirit in the mouths of all these prophets of yours and the LORD has pronounced disaster against you."
1 Kings 22:13-23

This is a very insightful look into what goes on in the realms of the Heavenlies and how it looks down here on earth.

June 9, 2017

In this intercession we are literally creating the pathway for God's Kingdom come, His Will be done, on earth as it is in Heaven (Matthew 6:10).

It reminds me of Psalm 18:

"Then the earth shook and quaked and the foundations of the mountains trembled;
they were shaken because He burned with anger.
Smoke rose from His nostrils, and consuming fire came from His mouth; glowing coals blazed forth.

*He parted the heavens and came down with **dark clouds** beneath His feet. He mounted a cherub and flew; He soared on the wings of the wind. **He made darkness His hiding place** and storm clouds a canopy around Him.*

From the brightness of His presence His clouds advanced—hailstones and coals of fire.

The LORD thundered from heaven; the voice of the Most High resounded—hailstones and coals of fire.

He shot His arrows and scattered the foes; He hurled lightning and routed them.

***The channels of the sea appeared** and the foundations of the world were exposed, at Your rebuke, O LORD, at the blast of the breath of Your nostrils."*
Psalm 18:7-15

We know that what happens in Hebrews 12, are things can be

shaken will fall and those that cannot be shaken, those things will remain.

July 6, 2017

Last night I woke up with a distinct sensing of doom and gloom regarding America. I have never felt that before. I turned on the TV and my hearing was in a heightened awareness. It was like everything they said was Alert, Alert, Alert! The News people are conditioning the public to receive and believe that President Trump does not know what he is doing; when in fact he does.

In the middle of the night, I was troubled and I felt that the United States of America would never be the same. I was reminded of the time two years ago, when I was driving down a highway and it felt like I needed to enjoy this freedom while I could, because the freedoms that we are accustomed to will be taken away from us.

July 14, 2017

My worst fear for America, is we go into captivity. Lord, You told me years back that America would go into captivity. You gave me the book of Jeremiah. I didn't know if You meant spiritual captivity only or did You mean the whole Nation would fall and burn and a communist country would come in and take over and make us slaves? I perceive in modern day it would look different. We don't know what it would be like to have war in our cities like other countries have had.

I have had dreams of tornados, floods, tsunami's, etc. They speak of spiritual allegories, as well as the natural disasters and of Your people being overtaken. God taught me, if He shows it to me in the spiritual, it will happen next in the natural. Father, we ask You to prepare us for that.

"IF IT HAPPENS IN THE SPIRITUAL, YOU WILL SEE IT IN THE NATURAL"

July 28, 2017

- The Lord is telling me is, *"What the world is waiting for and what will happen are two different things."*

- **Vision:** Now He is saying the Word, *"Vacancies"* and He is showing me, stars are falling from the heavenlies right now. Everything that can be shaken will be shaken in the last days. There is shaking going on with a spiritual power struggle.

- He is telling me that, it is sort of like Brexit in the heavenlies; there is a split going on and some of the powers that be, are being shaken. Once more I shake the heavens and the earth (Haggai 2:6 and Hebrews 12:26).

- This is a political thing. He is telling me, that it is a set up as what happens in the spiritual then happens in the natural. The spiritual corresponds to the natural also and reacts to what is going on down here.

- He is telling me, Everything that I am discerning, is what is coming on the earth. Because when Satan realizes he has lost the whole thing, it will be worse. As that is when he knows he has a short time Revelation 12:12.

- I brought before the Lord, the disrespect, the lack of love and kindness that is out there in the world.

  He is saying to me: *"Well did you think about the time they said to me, Lord, Lord?"* He said, *"That is what I am showing you, everything appears to be opposite."* He is showing me what is really in the people. I need more grace. I can feel their lies, but it is none of my business, unless You make it my business.

- Lord, You gave me a word in 2009 about California when I was flying into Orange County. It wasn't good. And Kim Clement gave a word about a man coming out of California and it was tied to the word gold and here is the word I hear: *"California treason"*. It's only been **my theory** according to Kim Clements's prophecy, that someone will rise up in President Trumps place (at the time appointed). It would be interesting if anything comes up about "gold" because of Kim's word. (*Author note: I have known and followed Kim's Ministry and prophetic work since the early 90's. I love Kim and I believe He is a man of God and a true prophet. However, I do not subscribe to every prophecy that Kim has had, especially if they include politics. I am very careful about what I receive and who I am hearing it from. I test everything by the Word and the Spirit of Truth. As so you should).

- The only other thing I recall the Lord speaking to me about California from 2009, was there was something being done in secret.

- The Father is just telling me that this is the order He has given these Words to me: choices for change, challenge for change, create change. Your choices will bring you to challenge for change. Then if you pass the challenges, you can create.

- He is telling me, *"The only thing that can sustain these things is* (proven, tested, tried) *character."* Your character is changed by choice. Your character has to be built. Like in Exodus, they could not sustain leaving Egypt, going in to Canaan to take over the land, *until they grew* to that level (Exodus 23:29-30). Growing character comes from the challenge. God will not trust just anyone to handle the things He can share with them, unless they have proven strong character. Every choice we make will take us there. Whenever a stronghold comes up (the things in our lives that have kept us back) doing things God's way and choosing against the stronghold or sin, that choice will bring us to the challenge.

And that isn't even really the big challenge.

The larger challenge is when Satan is standing in front of you to stop you and making it difficult. We have to get our own lives under control before God will trust us with the larger works of His Kingdom.

- God always speaks in advance with what He is going to do, so it does not happen when we want it. Most of the things He says don't, but I was waiting for it none the less.

- With the Brexit and the vacancies and the falling away and the power struggle, it is not the very moment I am supposed to be getting more information. Everything is just a little busy with them falling away right now.

- An Intercessor brought to remembrance that God told us, *that in Malachi, the tables will turn.*

In Malachi they were calling evil good and good evil. Saying, "God, we did this and this and this for You". And He is saying, "no you did not". He is calling them out on it. You did it for you. It was all selfish and He brought them through everything. He brought them through Assyria, Babylon and Persian rule. And finally, some 400 years later, before they even get to Greece and Rome, He could not trust them. He could not trust them being in their own land alone. He had to bring them into where they were at and have Greece and Rome over them, because they were not trustworthy and obeying Him, but calling good evil and evil good. And He was calling them out on it.

"He who has an ear, let him hear
what the Spirit says to the churches"
Revelation 2:29

July 31, 2017

I awoke this morning with an urgency and this Word in my spirit and in my hearing:

The Word of YAHUWAH
spoken by His servant, Dawne D. Basler

Letter To God's Leaders

"I have said that I will stand at the door and knock and if anyone will answer, I will come in and make My abode with them.

Instead, My people have not opened when I have knocked. I have stood outside, knocking and waiting. Your formalities in your open meetings are repulsive to Me. I Am not there. I Am not there because you did not invite Me.

How, you say, did we not invite Him? You did not invite Me because you did not keep My (first) Word to you. Do you think I would be in your golden assemblies that you honor and placate in place of Me?

My requirement is for you to keep My Word. I have said, Love the Lord your God with all your honor and strength. I have said; love your neighbor as yourself. You say, but we have.

I say, you have not. How so? You have judged your neighbor. Who is your neighbor. Anyone around you. Do you want to play semantics with Me? Fine. Then love your enemies!

You have judged your neighbor; you have judged your enemies. You have spoken ill of those around you and have had evil thoughts about others. All the while thinking that I do not notice. I have been knocking and not one of you have opened the door!

If I were inside of your assemblies, you would keep My Word. Your hearts are now exposed. You should have examined your own selves to see if you were in the faith, but your hearts have become hardened by the deceitfulness of your own sin. Faith keeps My Word. But you did not even notice.

So, I send My messenger to say, Repent. Repent of your lack of faith in not keeping My Word. You have estranged Me from yourselves in your acts of judging. I Am the Righteous Judge. Not one of you are qualified to judge righteously, because you have your own judgments in the way. At what time I would raise you leaders among you to lead an army of powerful warriors, you are still basking in your own glory, calling it My presence.

What shall I say to these things? This is the Word of the Lord to you: That you repent for your sins. For your separations from Me. For departing from My Word and calling evil good. And this is the sign that will follow if you do not repent. The very unrighteous judgment you mete out, will be measured back to you again swiftly. The sign to you will be your own sin overtaking you. And I will not be there to help you in that day. Unless you repent.

I Am coming back with power and vengeance the second time. Be ready."

****

"And I saw heaven opened, and behold a white horse;
and he that sat upon him was called Faithful and True
and in righteousness he does judge and make war.

His eyes were as a flame of fire and on his head were many crowns;
and he had a name written, that no man knew, but he himself.
And he was clothed with a vesture dipped in blood:
*and his name is called **The Word of God.***

And the armies which were in heaven followed him
upon white horses, clothed in fine linen, white and clean.
And out of his mouth goes a sharp sword, that with it
he should smite the nations: and he shall rule them
with a rod of iron: and he treads the winepress of the fierceness
and wrath of Almighty God.

And he hath on his vesture and on his thigh a name written,
KING OF KINGS, AND LORD OF LORDS".
Revelation 19:11-16

August 7, 2017

- **Vision:** I am seeing a battlefield, bomb shells (an explosive bomb or artillery shell, a surprise or jolt, a jaw dropper). I perceive God was showing me there is a battle for the truth; like being in a war. I see that He is sharing this with me because of the hardness of hearts, it has to be explosive, shocking because the people are hard of hearing, hard of seeing their own hearts.

August 7, 2017

- A couple of nights ago I had a golf ball size orange ball hovering over me. The Prophets Handbook says: The color orange means one who is tried and proven. It is the color of fire.

August 11, 2017

- This scripture is in my spirit: *"For every battle of the warrior is with confused noise, and garments rolled in blood; but this shall be with burning and fuel of fire"* Isaiah 9:5.

August 21, 2017

- **Vision:** I see that President Trump will **continue** to do something outrageous. We will be with our mouths wide open. It won't be good. God is showing me that he glories in getting away with doing things. Other Presidents would have been impeached for the things he does, but he will continue to push the envelope.

- I feel Yahuwah is telling us to stay focused on Him. He said that on Friday and was talking to us about praising Him and through all that is ahead, we have to focus on him. It's as if the whole world in increasing into darkness. But as we focus on Him, it is a small narrow shaft of light. The focus on Him will keep us in that very straight and narrow path that He requires.

- **Vision:** God is showing me across the globe, mass suffering and people crying out. As if in agony.

August 25, 2017

- **Vision:** I see Heads of households, Heads of Churches and Heads of Government, will all be affected, because God left the Government system, now the enemy has come in (Luke 11:21-26).

In Thessalonians, he who now stops everything from happening will now let go and then evil can take over - 2 Thessalonians 2:7 .

"Let no one deceive you in any way,
for it (The Anti-Christ, the Anti-Christ System) *will not come*
until the rebellion occurs and the man of lawlessness—
the son of destruction—is revealed.
He will oppose and exalt himself above every so-called god
or object of worship.

So he will seat himself in the temple of God,
proclaiming himself to be God.
Do you not remember that I told you these things
while I was still with you? And you know **what is now restraining**
him*, so that he may be* **revealed at the proper time***.*

For the mystery of lawlessness (Anti-Christ Spirit) *is already at work,*
but the one (The Holy Spirit of God) *who now restrains it,*
will **continue until** *he is taken out of the way.*

And then *the lawless one* **will be** *revealed, whom the Lord*
Yahushua will slay with the breath of His mouth
(Prophetic Messengers Words) *and*
annihilate by the majesty of His arrival.

The coming of the lawless one (Anti-Christ) *will be accompanied by*
the working of Satan, with every kind of power, sign,
and false wonder, and with **every wicked deception**
directed against those who are perishing,
because *they refused the love of the truth*
that **would have** *saved them.*

For this reason God will send them a powerful delusion
so that they believe the lie, in order that judgment
may come upon all who have disbelieved the truth
and delighted in wickedness."
1 Thessalonians 2:3-12

Listen, God is talking to those who call themselves Believers, who prove that they do not believe HIM *by their actions*. Not only unbelievers of God and His Son in general.

If God didn't care you wouldn't be reading this. These Words are what is in His Holy Scriptures. Shocking to those that do not read all of God's Word. Or read at all, I know. It's alarming to me too. But it's supposed to be.

"So too, faith by itself, if it does not result in action, is dead.

But someone will say, "You have faith and I have deeds."
Show me your faith without deeds, and I will show you my faith
by my deeds.

You believe that God is one. Good for you! Even the demons
believe that—and tremble" James 2:17-19.

God's Word will divide between soul and spirit (Hebrews 4:12). Or break like a hammer. Whatever it takes. Because He loves us.

"Is not my word like fire," declares the Lord,"
and like a hammer that breaks a rock in pieces?"
Jeremiah 23:29

The Sheep hear His Voice and follow Him (do what He says). The goats, who are mixed up around the sheep, do what they want to do, but **look like** followers of the Shepherd, according to the Word of God.

The bottom line is, if we do not do what the Word of God *actually says* and allow His Holy Spirit to convict us of sin and righteousness, *we actually do not know God.* That's a scary reality that people that say they know God need to wake up to! I did not write the Bible, I am just a messenger.

Anytime the presence of God is in a place and He leaves that area, the enemy will come in strong (Matthew 12:43-45). It has (spirit of Anti-Christ) already been in our world, it has infiltrated in our American Government system and now it is intrinsically making its way through to every Head of every-single-thing.

Food for thought: If the people of God were truly the preserving 'salt and the light' to the degree we needed to be in this world, this would not be happening. There is no condemnation though through repentance. Besides, it's all written and the time is set. Father, we ask for Your forgiveness of sins and spare Your people and draw them to You.

September 13, 2017

- **Vision:** The Lord is showing me to walk the straight and narrow path. The time is now to walk this straight and narrow. The sheep and goats will be divided and will fall, to the right and left. But those that are chosen and anointed to stand on His behalf are going to be walking that straight and narrow path.

- I hear the Lord say, *"The system is broken and failing"*. He is raising up a brand new system <u>within His people</u>. Don't look out there for any assistance. The assistance will be with Him. He is saying:

- *"Among this system you will have everything you have need of and it will work"*. That is what we have been doing, calling down the kingdoms of this world and the systems of this world and submitting them to Him. And now He is saying, *"**I will** give it to you, this* (new) *system and this* (new) *way."*

- The Lord says, *"Again, everything in the* (**Kingdom**) *system, everything you have need of will flow and will work according to its original format, the original way it is supposed to work from the beginning."*

The book of Acts was a system that worked like an underground networking. We pray for the furtherance and knowledge of development and how to bring it about. We call in development to divine networking among your people.

The Lord was so happy about what I was praying. He says, *"I Am the Bread of Life. I can sustain everybody that comes to Me."*

September 20, 2017

The mark of a true servant, is you are willing to do whatever it is God says to do. The more you want the power of God to flow through you; and what you say to have meaning, the more obedient to God and His Word you must be. Remember, we are vessels and containers so what is ever on the inside of us will come out, that is why God's character in us, is so important.

- I hear the Lord saying, *"The creations and the heavenlies and all the things I Am doing, are all signs for those that don't believe. All those that come into My presence will not have an excuse."*

  He said *"My people believe I Am coming back. Those that know Me, have the earnest of My Spirit on the inside".*

  He said, these signs are Romans 1 and 2. So, He can accurately judge them.

Father, we renounce playing church and being about the "affairs of this life" (2 Timothy 2:4) and all things that are not of You, like You and from You. We renounce getting entangled with things and all ungodly soul ties; the things that bind us to something in this world.

October 9, 2017

- I heard the Words: *"FEMA"* and *"Control"*. The Lord brought this up before.

- There is a spirit out there that wants to reduce people to nothing. To make them feel they are nothing. The people are fighting for their rights and fighting for their identity, because it is in them to know that they *are* somebody. But that spirit says, 'Shut up and sit down.' It makes me angry. But it is affecting the people this way.

- What came to me was 2 Thessalonians 2:3: *"Let no man deceive you by any means: for that day shall not come, except there comes a falling away first, and that man of sin be revealed, the son of perdition;"* The Lord is saying, *"It's not very much longer."*

Father, it feels like we are entering into a different time, that is why I had to go to the book of Revelation. To study the seals, the trumpets and the candlesticks and these that have numerical values; the fours and the sevens and all that I need to put it all together, because I need to know what is going on. I feel it is a revelation being unveiled in the earth.

- **Vision:** I heard the Words, *"Season of triumph"* and I saw under that, the word *"Trump".* And I saw Donald Trump emerge from all this "collusion mess". I saw a rising up of shininess; and he rose above it.

October 18, 2017

The Lord is saying: Each person is likened to an open vessel, a glass and He wants to pour into us. We each are set apart to be poured into (2 Corinthians 4:7).

- The Lord says, *"I am raising up a people that will go where I say go and do what I say do."* They are so in sync with Him. I am sensing He is choosing those whom will choose Him back. That is this discipline and training. To grow with Him and have His nature, means spending more time with Him. Our being who we are, as we spend more time in His Presence. In essence, "Wherever I go, I will bring His Presence in a powerful way. I bring change without saying anything, I am the example without words". *That is* intercession. Because of the time spent in His presence and His Word, just by being there, it is intercession and change. A righteous person of God's presence in people's lives is like a preservation, ie like Abraham was with Lot. It is protecting people by being there.

- God is into longevity; He wants us to stick in there, that way He can trust us. He says, *"All the signs, wonders and miracles work through laws."* Know The Law Giver and you will get to see His ways and how they work. For example, gravity works to keep us grounded. That is a natural law. But *knowing* Him, means we will know the supernatural works.

"He revealed *his ways* to Moses,
his *deeds* to the people of Israel."
Psalm 103:7

In other words, to those that will do it God's way, God will reveal how it works.

October 23, 2017

- I hear the Words:

- *"Technicality"*

- *"Technically"*

- *"Dis-robed authority"*

- *"Candid re-enactments"*

- *"Poised positioning"*

- *"Catch 22"*

- *"Strong warning"*

- *"Challenging the people"*

- *"Way of escape"*

- *"Straight and narrow"*

- *"Shakedown, shake it down"*

October 30, 2017

- I am hearing right now, *"That the whole world will believe him* (President Trump)." I lift this before You. **This is going to continue.**

- **Vision:** What I am seeing is President Trump, actually *is in* the collusion, but he emerges out of it and looking shiny. What this says to me is, he is going to get away with it.

- I am hearing the Words *"diplomacy"* and the word *"diagnostics"*.

- **Vision:** I am seeing arrows pointing opposite directions from each other and hearing *"oppositional defense"*. It's like changing directions or something. It appears to be rather confusing, because the arrows are opposite of each other, like parallel up and down and the arrows are facing different directions.

- I'm hearing the words *"chosen elimination."* And also, *"Selection deterioration."*

November 6, 2017

- An insight God is giving, is when the Godly are afflicted, it will bring unity between them and God (Psalm 119:67). And when the Godly are afflicted, they will recognize one another. But those that say they are godly, but it is just an outward form or appearance of godliness, when they are afflicted, it will bring an offense to the point of division.

Great peace have they which love your law:
and nothing shall offend them."
Psalm 119:165

That is how it will take place. That is the division between the sheep and the goats. The truly godly, when put in that position, it will strengthen their resolve to hang onto God. Those that are offended by the calamity, it will bring that division in their lives. And that will be the Lord, to do that. The Valley of Decision for division.

Destroy mediocrity in us Lord. Any little seed, root, tree, anything in us, whatever level it is, that does not bring You glory; destroy it in the Name of Yahushua.

November 7, 2017

Adam was made from the soil of the ground. He was given a job to till the soil, as a mist came upward from beneath and watered the soil. When he had to leave the garden and was outside of the original provision, the soil was hardened.

God's Word is seed, faith is a seed. He planted it in us when we were born again of His Spirit. He planted it deep in the soil of our hearts.

"Whoever believes in me, as the Scripture has said,
'Out of his heart will flow rivers of living water."
John 7:38

The ground (soil of our hearts) is dry and hard. We need to continue to plow or till, until we reach the depths, where the water is. That water then, can reach the seed and it creates greater faith. Like the mist or water that came up from under ground in the Garden of

God, it will water the soil of our hearts.

I saw this scripture, *"But we have this treasure in earthen vessels, so that the surpassing greatness of the power will be of God and not from ourselves"* (2 Corinthians 4:7). It's a secret. Buried treasure within us. "Out of your hearts shall flow…."

And then I saw where the seed of a man is planted in the depths of a woman. Just like God's seed in the ground. A secret place. And the seed connects with the egg in moisture, and grows within that soil of the woman's womb. It's all encased in water. In a sexual context: The husbands' "authority", enters into the "holy place" (of the woman/wife). And this is separated to God, what is created in the womb, in secret, in the dark.

Then I saw that this is why pornography is against God. The man is giving his body part (penis) rod (his authority) over to 'strange flesh'. Like the fallen angels did and they taught mankind to do as well. It was an abomination to God and He judged them for it. Genesis 6 and Jude 1:6-7, also book of Enoch.

November 13, 2017

- I hear the Lord saying, *"Sound the alarm for the next generation, because they will usher in the Second Coming."*

- The Lord says, *"There is only One way to Me and it's the hard way, dying to the flesh."*

- Like the thief on the cross, who did not have the time to come to know Him. He recognized Him while dying. God said, *"He was also dying to his flesh."* It's an allegory. He is telling a story.

- Vision: While watching the news, I saw a split screen on the TV between the Philippines (where the President is now) and

America. I saw either a shaking or explosion (or both) in the vision.

- The Lord is showing me an inner working of His Kingdom

and it is in Satan's face. The church has learned to function in their flesh and they go to the Lord with mixture (of carnal mind flesh and spirit).

The Kingdom works separately. It works on God's laws, rules and principles (spiritual) and because it does, it operates perfectly. God is showing me, that the people who receive from the Lord and work it down here, that it is so strong, the enemy can't figure it out. That is why at the end (of the book) the two witnesses are not asking the Lord what to do; **they know what to do,** because it is Kingdom and they are One with Him. To be noted, they are not asking God to spare their lives in the midst of chaos either. They do not love their life more than God and doing what He has called them to do.

What God was showing me, that in this Kingdom, Satan can't stand that there are people that believe God to that degree, to have that much power (faith), because they *know* they are one with God. We come into the maturity of sons and daughters at the point that we *think like Him.* The entire battle is just that. Satan's endeavor is to stop souls from believing the Truth of God, in an effort that they should not become God's sons and daughters, for a powerful (full of faith) relationship with God on the earth.

- God has taught me to tell the devil about his shame. But, God is telling me, *"What will shame him, is My kingdom on this earth, right where he thought it was his domain."* Now that is to His shame! Like the impaling pole Haman set up for Mordecai and the gallows that were for the Jews, the tables turned at the dinner party.

When God grows you to the level that you can be seated with your enemies at your table, do not fret...
It is for the tables to be turned and to wipe the enemies of your life out once and for all.

Even Yahushua did it, calling Judas, friend.

David understood this. He said to God, *"You prepare a table before me in the presence of my enemies..."*. This is where we have grown to the level of disciplined dominion. Because Satan has said to the Lord it will never happen, You will never establish Your Kingdom here, because he *thinks this is* his domain.

When Yahushua was questioned on setting up a kingdom on earth when He was here the first time, he clearly taught that His Kingdom was not of this world (John 18:36).

But He also made it clear: *"When asked by the Pharisees when the kingdom of God would come, Yahushua replied, "The kingdom of God will not come with observable signs. Nor will people say, 'Look, here it is,' or 'There it is.' For you see, the kingdom of God is in your midst"* (Luke 17:20-21).

So, it's a coordinated and disciplined aligned Kingdom. One that lives within you. God's Kingdom (hidden earthen vessels) on this Earth.

- The Lord is reminding me of the teaching that He gave me in the dark night of the soul, that there was creation there. He was showing in darkness, is when creation was happening. It turned dark suddenly with Yahushua on the cross and then His death (darkness) was when the work was finished, so new life could begin.
  Before He ascended, He went down into hell, in the dark, to

bring new life to those who were locked in prison (Ephesians 4:9).

- God is saying *"It can't be a kingdom without rules and laws."* He is showing in Heaven, that His domain has rules and laws. If you have carnality – flesh, leaking out all over the place, you can't enter in beyond the gates (Revelation 22:14-15).

- This is exciting: *"The seventh angel sounded his trumpet, and there were loud voices in heaven, which said: "The kingdom of the world **has become** the kingdom of our Lord and of his Messiah, and he will reign forever and ever"* (Revelation 11:15).

Why this is exciting is because God is establishing His kingdom here through us and we are making the way straight, so He can come back the second time. In other words, **we are establishing His Kingdom through our faith** (the kind of faith that has proof with works, like Abraham), so He is coming to His kingdom that we are establishing.

- I hear God say, *"Well you finally turned the page."* He is talking about all things being new where you can write your faith. That's what Kings do, they write on pages (reference Chronicles of the Kings and the book of the Kings). There is something about the kingdom of God on that. Kingdom clarity we call in. He is showing me the only way to get there, be there and stay there, is to love not your life to the death.

- I am hearing this again, *"Trouble the Waters".*

- I hear the word: *"Torrid".* It was in this sense: full of difficulty or tribulation. For example: "Wall Street is in for a torrid time in the next few weeks".

November 15, 2017

I hear this following:

- *"When I bring a sword, what remedy do you have?"*

- *"What is the chaff to the wheat?"*

- *"Shall I challenge you for this change?"*

- *"Should I rely on one of you?"*

- *"Who among you thinks like Me?"*

- *"What shall I find you doing?"*

Then He tells us, what He is going to do. God is serious. His judgment is simply this. It is much like when He wants us to seek Him with our whole heart and He will hide Himself away so we will say, 'Hey, where are you?' He wants us to talk to Him like that…'I show up here every day, where are you?' Like Jacob when he wrestled with the angel of the Lord (Genesis 32), he was so serious engaging in battle with a celestial being. How did he think he was going to win? But he prevailed and that day, changed his trajectory and the history of His Israel. And that's what God wants of us; to be interactive with Him for change, not only for ourselves, though it starts there, but for future generations.

- **Vision:** When God is talking about *"quickening the times"*, He is talking about merging the (parallel) realms. You know in Jude 1, how He talks about coming back with 10,000's (myriad) of His saints.

  He showed me simultaneously, that when Yahushua had risen from the dead and all those that were dead and walking around on the earth, that there was a merging of Heaven and earth going on at that time; it is spiritual.

That is why all the signs, wonders and miracles were happening simultaneously. The end result was converging and conversion. That is the end game, salvation of souls. It becomes effortless when we walk in that merging.

I sense that is what He is showing me, that it is getting ready to happen. Judgment is eminent when you bring the kingdom of God down here. That merging the realms, will be like spirit and natural. It is going to be awesome. He is telling me right now, *"Those of the Kingdom will bring it here."* We are instrumental in bringing down God's Kingdom.

He is showing me now those in Heaven, the 10,000's of His saints, that are coming with Him are excited too. They are rooting us on like the Hebrews 11 and 12 saints, because they want us to bring down the Kingdom of God, so they can do their part. They will be executing judgment (Jude 1).

'Enoch, the seventh from Adam, also prophesied about them:

"Behold, the Lord is coming
with myriads of His holy ones
(different and unlike others. Having "likeness
of nature with the Lord". Different from the world)
to execute judgment (krísis - to separate, distinguish,
judge") *on everyone and to convict*
(to expose, reprove, rebuke, discipline,
show to be guilty, to convince with solid,
compelling evidence, especially to expose and prove
wrong) *all the ungodly* (lack of reverence, "without
due respect", i.e. failing to honor what is sacred)
of every ungodly act of wickedness
and every harsh (hard - because dried out.
Figuratively - stiff, stubborn unyielding;
describing people who "won't budge")
word spoken against Him by ungodly sinners,
(to forfeit by missing the mark" – loss from falling
short of what God approves)."
Jude 1:14-15

Did you catch the meaning of "Holy ones"? I will repeat it here for significance: (*different and unlike*), *others, holy; (hágios) means "likeness of nature with the Lord" because "different from the world).* These are the ones that are with the Lord. The ones with His likeness and His nature. The others, that are like the world, are being judged.

Christians that practice sin like to say, "Well, we all sin and we all fall short"! That scripture is a *part* of Romans 3:23. That passage in context is *not* justifying sin, it's saying that God is giving you a chance to overcome! And no, we should not be practicing sin because the Word of God has said that we all have sinned. It is for our overcoming, that we would want to be holy as He is holy.

If one reads the whole Bible, it also says in there, *"**Strive** for peace with everyone, and for **holiness**, <u>without which no one will see the Lord"</u>* (Hebrews 12:14).

And it says: *"But now that you **have been set free from sin** and have become slaves to God, the fruit you reap leads to holiness, and the outcome is eternal life"* (Romans 6:22). And, *"But just as He who called you is holy, so **be holy in all you do**, for it is written: "**Be holy, because I am holy**."* 1 Peter 1:15-16. For those who don't think the "New Testament" has laws, that is a command.

Why would one rather quote such convenient scriptures that allows their sin to continue? That is not why the Messiah came to the earth the first time. Ok look, Bible 101:

*"Whoever makes a **practice** of sinning **is of the devil**, for the devil has been sinning from the beginning. The **reason** the Son of God appeared was to **destroy** the works of the devil."*
1 John 3:8

We are not to be like the Devil. We are to be like the One we have the Nature of! Unless you really do not have the Spirit of God? Test yourself! This is totally do-able and the whole reason Yahushua came to earth the first time, to make the way.

So, let's quit using our excuses to sin and step up to the plate to stand before the One who called us.

But don't you think God knows the benefit of your convenient denials? Listen to Isaiah the Prophet:

> *"Woe* (warning) *to those who dig* (seek) *deep*
> *to hide their plans from the LORD.*
> *In darkness they do their works and say,*
> *"Who sees us, and who will know?"*
> *You have turned things upside down,*
> ***as if*** *the potter were regarded as clay.*
> *Shall what is formed say to him who formed it,*
> *"He did not make me"?*
> *Can the pottery say of the potter,*
> *"He has no understanding"?*
> Isaiah 29:15-16

December 20, 2017

Last night I was praying for more of God's love, because I think it will take that to get through to people (not necessarily the external outward affection, but the love of God within that is immoveable).

That proof of love is kindness and respect in the face of all adversity. A laying down one's life through reasoning with them. I felt as I was praying, that the darkness will push against the light of God's love, kindness and respect.

And I heard the Lord say, *"The enemy will start crowding love out."* He was talking about the enemy coming, as if to snatch away immediately the plan to 'conquer by love'.

Something that God taught me many years ago, you cannot prevail against witchcraft (a rule of carnality, that which operates through control and manipulation) except through love. You can do warfare against the spirit of witchcraft, but with the people, who are controlled by the spirits, God's love is the way to conquer.

You can only do this, if in fact, you have been conquered by God's own love in the first place. Otherwise, you cannot do it. It is impossible to love in a conquering way without God on the inside. You must first be conquered by Him and His love.

As a reminder of what God's love looks like on the outside, coming from the inside, Paul the Apostle, wrote:

"If I speak in the tongues of men or of angels,
but do not have love, I am only a resounding gong
or a clanging cymbal.

If I have the gift of prophecy and can fathom all mysteries
and all knowledge, and if I have a faith that can move
mountains, but do not have love, I am nothing.

If I give all I possess to the poor and give over my body
to hardship that I may boast, but do not have love,
I gain nothing.

Love is patient, love is kind. It does not envy, it does not boast,
it is not proud. It does not dishonor others, it is not self-seeking,
it is not easily angered, it keeps no record of wrongs.

Love does not delight in evil but rejoices with the truth.
It always protects, always trusts, always hopes,
always perseveres.

Love never fails. But where there are prophecies,
they will cease; where there are tongues, they will be stilled;
where there is knowledge, it will pass away.

For we know in part and we prophesy in part, but when
completeness comes, what is in part disappears.

When I was a child, I talked like a child, I thought like a child,

I reasoned like a child. When I became a man, I put the ways
of childhood behind me.
For now we see only a reflection as in a mirror;
then we shall see face to face. Now I know in part;
then I shall know fully, even as I am fully known.

And now these three remain: faith, hope and love.
But the greatest of these is love."
1 Corinthians 13:1-13

- **Vision**: I see people in the world with sin. Their unrepentant sin, will get thicker and darker and the (spirit of) darkness will push against us.

IN MY NAME, YOU WILL CAST OUT DEVILS

I learned of God's Son's Name, Yahushua (YHVH) early, as I studied Hebrew. If you read the Hebrew, it's not hard, it's right in front of you. However, I started calling Him by His given Name in 2004 when I heard a Dr. of Theology break it down for me.

I have worked in spiritual warfare since the 1980's and I have always been accustomed to calling on the name of Jesus and casting out devils in this name.

However, during the dark night of the soul, when the warfare was overwhelming and there were those beings and spirits that showed up that did not bow to the name of Jesus, it was then that God taught me a new level of spiritual warfare. He didn't teach it to me fast. It was a 'crash course' of sorts, but it was over a course of time. At that time, I believe that God told me that the name of "Jesus" would "work" in spiritual warfare for a time period, but in the future, it will not work as, "*In the past God overlooked such ignorance, but now he commands all people everywhere to repent*" (Acts 17:30).

It is not a hard thing today to find out for ourselves the Truth.

"No longer will they teach their neighbor, or say to one another,

'Know the Lord,' because they will all know me, from the least of them to the greatest" (Hebrews 8:11).

If at that time, you are being ganged up on in the spirit realm and need some assistance and the name of Jesus does not have the power of God as it once did in your life, remember His true given Name. As God has shown me, in the darkness those spirits will overtake and what God has allowed before, will not work any longer.

I believe that this is one of the ways that God will prove to His people that His Sons Name is, Yahushua.

I have put this to the test in my own life. I do not doubt that He has grown accustomed to the name of Jesus at all. And He knows who His people are talking about. He has had great mercy on us all.

"Who but God goes up to heaven and comes back down?
Who holds the wind in his fists?
Who wraps up the oceans in his cloak?
Who has created the whole wide world?
What is his name—and his son's name?

Tell me if you know!"
Proverbs 30:4

TESTING THE SPIRITS

"Beloved, do not believe every spirit, but test the spirits
to see whether they are from God. For many false prophets
have gone out into the world.

By this you will know the Spirit of God:
Every spirit that confesses that Yahushua, Christ
has come in the flesh is from God, and every spirit

that does not confess Yahushua, is not from God.

*This is the spirit of the antichrist, which you have heard
is coming and which is already in the world at this time.*

*You, little children, are from God and have overcome them,
because greater is He who is in you than he who is in the world.
They are of the world. That is why they speak from the world's
perspective, and the world listens to them. We are from God.
Whoever knows God listens to us; whoever is not from God,
does not listen to us.*

That is how we know the Spirit of truth and the spirit of deception"
1 John 4:1-6

This is the same Author that writes 4 books of the love of
God and keeping His commands. Can you see why the importance of
the Name of God's Son?

Here is what God taught me early on to help me to steer clear
from deception:

1. Keep myself in the Word and in the love of God.

2. DO NOT have my own opinion or come up with my own
   conclusions about things – ask Him.

3. Stay Repentant for a pure heart. Not keeping unforgiveness
   and not judging others. Let God search my heart and
   try it as David said:

   *"Search me, O God, and know my heart;
   test me and know my concerns.*
   See if there is any offensive (wicked) **way in me;**
   lead me in the way everlasting."
   Psalm 139:23-24

But for most people that won't work. Because they like to

have their own opinion and they like to do things their own way. **You must be willing to give up your own ideas to learn the way that God thinks.** And it all starts by being in His Word day and night.

> *"Keep this Book of the Law always on your lips;*
> *meditate on it day and night,*
> *so that you may be careful to do everything written in it.*
> ***Then** you will be prosperous and successful."*
> Joshua 1:8

> *Blessed is the man who does not walk in the counsel*
> *of the wicked, or set foot on the path of sinners,*
> *or sit in the seat of mockers.*

> *But his delight is in the Law of the LORD,*
> *and on His law he meditates day and night.*

> *He is like a tree planted by streams of water,*
> *yielding its fruit in season, whose leaf does not*
> *wither and who prospers in all he does."*
> Psalm 1:1-4

Those are great promises in covenant with Him, when we keep God's instruction.

CHAPTER 15

FAITH UNFEIGNED

YEAR OF 2018

January 3, 2018

What I am gathering is, this thick darkness is permeating and what we are doing because we have the Spirit of God in us, we can get through it. I feel that, it is to be going forward in the presence of our enemies. When Jeremiah spoke, his Word went in the direction he sent it. Even the Centurion Soldier said to Yahushua, No need to come to my home, speak the Word only and my servant will be healed (Matthew 8:8). Yahushua replied, that he had never seen such great faith in all of Israel (Matthew 8:10). This is the way to impress God.

January 9, 2018

Below is the revelation knowledge that God gave to me:

- Vision: I saw the enemy's presence in the earth now being very large and permeating. The enemy owns the world (system) and everything in it. He rules it.

- The <u>level of faith</u> that God's people have currently, does not rise to the level to win the battle against these forces of darkness.

- Vision: I saw "giants of faith" (so to speak, like people in Hebrews 11) rise, but there were only very few. However, it is what is absolutely necessary to be able to do warfare against the enemy, especially at the level that he will challenge our faith. God needs our faith size to match the enemy's wicked schemes and advances of warfare. To be wise as (the) serpents and harmless as doves (Matthew 10:16).

- **Vision:** I saw God's people grow discouraged and angry. They began to turn against God because there seemed to be no help anywhere. The feeling of the absence of God was very strong on the earth. The people were tormented and angry. It is only our faith in God and the work that He has done through His Son that is going to save us from this time to come. Now is the time to **grow in greater faith** than ever before, so that our lives are not in danger of the enemies' tactics and plans for mankind.

- The ways in which the enemy will fight your faith are:

  1. A block of faith – no breakthrough
  2. Being exhausted – for no good reason
  3. Having sickness (or sicknesses)
  4. Being discouraged
  5. A feeling of God is not with you or for you
  6. Your faith not working like it used to
  7. A lack of empathy or caring; a feeling of que sera sera. Whatever will be, will be.

- **Vision:** I saw, *"When the son of man comes, will He find faith on the earth?"* (Luke 18:8) and *"The love of many growing cold"* (Matthew 24:12).

- I saw a time on the earth such as never has been (Daniel 12).

Honestly, when I think about this, it is entirely overwhelming and disturbing. That God's people will fall into this pit and the enemy will over power them to the point of giving up or turning from the One true living God, is really overwhelming to my heart. That they either won't care or won't notice is even more distressing.

The prophets of old write about these things happening. It's why God gave to us prophets at all. To let the people know what

God is thinking about and saying. In Jeremiah, the people were so tired of doing it God's way, that they literally turned to another spirit, called, "the Queen of Heaven" and tried to persuade Jeremiah that they were doing the right thing! That when they prayed to YHVH, He did nothing for them. But when they prayed to the Queen of Heaven, she poured out blessing and provision (Jeremiah 44).

Listen, if God is not 'doing things for you your way', *that is the TEST!*

Do you love Him for His promises and for blessing you? Or do you love Him for Him and what He has done for you through His Son? If God sending His Son to the Cross to take our place of judgment is the ONLY thing He ever did for us, it is everything. For that alone, He is worthy of our time, our attention and our worship. He is God. He is Sovereign. *And* He wants a living, walking, talking relationship with us. Ask yourself, why is this too much for Him to ask for?

January 9, 2018

- Dream: Last night's dreams and warfare was nothing like I have ever experienced to date. I first woke to see a "blueprint" on the hallway wall that was so detailed, the only way I could explain it is, it is like the Pentagon. It appeared to be perhaps 12 layers thick; it was multidimensional (It reminded me of Revelation 11).

I couldn't sleep after that. I tossed and turned. And then the room began to feel crowded. I would go in and out of sleep, but each time, I was being dragged into a dream, within a dream, within a dream. There were so many dreams, probably 20 or more in all.

In each dream, there was warfare. But I could never really fight it fairly because it would go into another realm. There was much detail, but the biggest part was that the enemy was so absolutely evil, when he was revealed in every section. The evil was so insidious, that the fear was palpable. So much torment in and out of sleep.

When I awoke, I thought of the scripture about wearing out the saints (Daniel 7:25) and this is his plan. For those that know warfare well, Satan will use God's merging of the realms; (quickening of the times) so that those that know the answers in warfare, have a tougher time fighting.

When I tried to wake myself up to be able to fight fairly, I was held captive within the realms and the dreams. I kept trying to speak, but it felt like the air was collapsing in my lungs and it would not come out. It was as if I had plunged under deep water and the weight was on me, where I could not get up or out. I kept fighting for hours and I finally was able to speak a prayer and fight. But it would drag me back in. This literally went on for perhaps 4-5 hours.

This is a spiritual allegory of what the enemy is doing in the lives of those who have the audacity to believe God to get to the breakthrough!

January 13, 2018

- Dream: The last two nights in a row I dreamed that we all lived in community type living.

The first night, it was very dangerous, as if there was a designated destruction that was going to happen and people were taking cover together. It seemed to be a holiday. The next day on the grounds, there was much death everywhere and many people did not make it.

- Dream: I dreamed that there were people living in communities everywhere. We were all gathered together, but people didn't seem to care, they just only wanted to party. I had purchased a couple of apartments for safety and protection. But there were very few that were serious about what was happening.

January 17, 2018

Wait for it

Covenant relationship is obedience to the Word of God, the Call of God and the plan and purpose of God in your life; ie. your time with God in prayer, meditating in the Word and in giving of your finances. Development of all is a process, through being in the Word of God.

If you want to know something from God and you're thinking, He is not telling me; you keep going. He will (eventually) tell you, keep asking (Matthew 7:7, 21:22, Mark 11:24, Luke 11:9, James 1:6). Sometimes, it could be that the block is with you or the enemy or maybe God is just not talking. It is *your responsibility* to find out what it is and to wait patiently on God.

This is how to always know if you have an idol in your way: Anything you want with God and you are not receiving it in life; lay down your life and what you think. Get rid of it, cut it off get it out of your way completely (It's an abomination to God) and then; wait on hearing God's Word. Keep covenant with God (be faithful) on those three things (Prayer, the Word and Finances) or you will not go to the next level.

Any conflict, whether internal or external, submit it to God; Whatever is chaos, He will turn it to order when it is submitted (accept or yield to a superior force or to the authority or will of another person) to Him. He will call order into the chaos. If you feel it is an area of separation or darkness, call God into it; bring order out of this chaos. Bring His light into your darkness.

"For God is not a God of disorder, but of peace..."
1 Corinthians 14:33

January 22, 2018

- From 1am until sun up, God let me experience the intensity of the evil coming to the earth.

- It will permeate and take over everything that does not belong to God. I have to say, they carry the feeling that, there is no God and He cannot help you. The anxiety of separation is penetrable. Their ultimate goal is to drag you down deeper into Hell, the place where there is no God for eternity. Those that are not spiritually in tune will fall to their devices. A reminder, that if you begin to feel this way, it is a spirit. **Don't let it** dull your senses. Use God's Words and fight!

January 24, 2018

- God spoke the words: *"Composition and completion".* The meaning of <u>composition</u> is: the nature of something's ingredients or its
  constituents, the way in which a whole or mixture is made up. Synonyms are: anatomy, framework, formation, makeup, structure.

February 11, 2018

I woke this morning with the feeling of my cells being stripped of life and purpose again. It was an all familiar torturous feeling. And I remembered that the Lord told me to *"Tell My people"* when I woke with the feeling and knowing that Hell was real and everything with it was present. Though it's happened many times, this has not happened since July, when He let me experience this with the Words when I woke, *"Tell My people."*

I'm thinking He is letting me continue to experience this absolute terror feeling, until I write this last Word Letter. I'm writing it today. It's the only *"Tell My people"* that I haven't written yet, that He has told me to do. (*Author note: these prophetic publications are for leaders and are available upon request).

February 12, 2018

- The Lord says that, *"tenacity, longevity, long suffering and patience is a really big deal. Without it you won't finish the battle".* It is a bigger deal than what I think. He said, *"You can have all My knowledge, every anointing or gifting possible, but if you don't have long suffering, longevity, patience or tenacity, you won't finish the race."*

- Vision: He is showing me patience, tenacity, endurance, long suffering, longevity and faithfulness to Him. We need these things to finish the race set before us (Hebrews 12:1 and 1 Corinthians 9:24). Without this, the saints won't make it.

  "This calls for patient endurance on the part of the people of God who keep his commands and remain faithful to Yahushua" Revelation 14:12.

- I keep hearing these two words throughout prayer. *"Date"* as in a calendar and *"Frame".*

March 6, 2018

- Today I had a check in my spirit regarding Benjamin Netanyahu.

- Sovereignty is coming on America for repentance. God is calling it sovereignty; it is His trump card and that is what President Trump being in office is about; to bring about change. The religious swallow camels. They accept everything about this President and believe a lie. They see and hear what He does and they excuse it through sound bites of scripture and "prophecy". Though the prophecy is true, that Donald Trump would be President, I also prophesied it a year or more in advance. But King Cyrus, or a savior he is not! Anyone who reads scripture in the light can see that.

April 2, 2018

- The Lord showed me in scripture last night some things and it was alarming. He gave me 1 Chronicles and then Jeremiah 44. It shook me when I read it. It is simply coming down to making a choice. I thought it was so simple for the people to make this choice. But their sin, over all these years, led them so far away, that they did not realize why God had a problem with them. I saw the church in all of this and this is where they are today.

- He gave the answer in those scriptures above. The answer is: Turn back to My Laws, My Precepts and My Statutes. Keep My Word. As I read that, the simplicity is just astounding to me. Just do whatever it is that God says to do. And why is that so hard, except the Word of God says, the flesh is that wicked and Satan is real and he will continue to entice us and blind our minds so that we are ever sinning and never coming to the knowledge of the truth, to actually live it.

- I can literally feel that our Nation now is being sucked out from underneath us and is being handed over to the enemy. The Christian institutions at large, have made a covenant (agreement) with another spirit for success that is NOT the spirit of God. That agreement has given the power to the enemy to be able to turn things his direction.

- The Lord said to me, *"Solidarity."* It means: unity or agreement of feeling or action with common interest, mutual support in a group.

April 4, 2018

- My room was crowded again last night with every size and shape of entity in the realm of the spirit. I just decided to preach the gospel to them. I don't know who they are. If it's the enemy, it will torment him. Which I am always up for.

April 5, 2018

- Dream: I was in a housing area where whole families were and helping them. Afterward, I was at a facility full of treasures. There, people were helping me hand out things to others. I prophesied to those that did not know the Lord and it brought change to them.

May 10, 2018

- Anubis, The god of death, came and stood at my door way late last night.

- Three women witches astral projecting into my home this last week.

- Heavy attacks, spiritually, emotionally, physically and financially.

- Betrayal by a friend.

- I laid there and prayed and did as much warfare as I could. The room began to fill with other presences. I think there was an Angel there with his sword drawn. It was late and I was inundated.

(*Authors note: There are gaps of time between entries. I did not think that I would make it any further, after I had done the will of God. It was then that there was all out warfare like I had not seen to that point. Slowly, I emerged to the next battle).

July 9, 2018

- This past week, I felt a shift in the spirit realm. The time of the Lord's return is near.

July 2018

- During President Trumps travel (July 10-16 to Belgium, United Kingdom, Finland) the Lord said, that *"the stage was set and now everything will follow. There is no intercession that can change it. Pray for the people, Mercy & Salvation."*

July 22, 2018

- Dream: In this dream, I had understanding and knowledge from heaven that it would take 10-15 years for the New World Order to **completely manifest** over the USA. It was as if that was the time that it would be *completely different* in everything we do here. Everything would evolve until we get there and would be slowly taking us there.

  What I saw, was truly terrifying; the USA never being a democracy again. I looked up and was instructed and saw that there was the enemy all surrounding us. They had infiltrated and *they looked just like us*. They were there not only to spy on us, but also to influence us to make wrong decisions by being a part of our lives and families.

  But God put me and others strategically everywhere interceding and praying for the people. These things would continue to happen, but God would still be with His people.

August 13, 2018

- I was receiving these Words, *"Language"* and *"Agreement"*. It is as if, behind the scenes there is another language spoken, that came into agreement with someone here that knows their language.

- Our Nation has been sold out from underneath us to someone higher up. Satan is involved, as if he is the head of the agreement.

September 18, 2018

- I asked the Lord, for the sake of all of my conspiracy theory friends, once and for all, "is the earth round or is it flat?"

  He immediately responded with, *"The two ends… Meet."*

October 6, 2018

- **Vision:** The Lord is showing me that He is *letting* Satan set the stage on the earth. The enemy is taking center stage and setting everything up the way he wants it. It's as if they had this discussion a long time ago and God is saying, 'Okay, go ahead." Again it reminds me of the plan of God with Esther regarding Haman and him wanting to kill all of God's people. Nevertheless, the tables were turned at the last minute.

  As Mario Murillo says, "God is NEVER late! However, He has missed several golden opportunities to be early."

- I hear the Lord say, *"There is going to come a time that I will raise you and others to confront him* (the enemy). *Right now you are not to interrupt. If I raised you and others up right now, you would be interrupting what Satan would do."* God wants him left alone per their agreement.

"It's what the world doesn't see; it's what His people don't see." No one sees it. Those that know the strategies of God and hear the Lord, per His instruction will know and perform *God's acts, His way.* They will tell God's people the truth and not comfort them with lies, saying to them "peace peace", when there is no peace.

"They (the false prophets) *offer superficial treatments*
for my people's mortal wound.
They give assurances of peace when there is no peace"
Jeremiah 6:14 and 8:11.

But the scripture tells us:

'While people are saying, "Peace and security," destruction
will come upon them suddenly, like labor pains on a
pregnant woman, and they will not escape.'
1 Thessalonians 5:3

- The Lord is showing, "The reason Satan will be successful in the setup is because, God's people are on board with it. ***They think it is God!*** That's how much the enemy has infiltrated the church. It's because they love their own images and they have made God like unto themselves, bringing him down to their level. Thinking that He thinks like them. That is why it doesn't even occur to them that they are sinning.

"You have done these things, and I kept silent;
you thought I was just like you.
But now I rebuke you and accuse you to your face."
Psalm 50:21

I have a healthy respectful fear of God. If I did not always ask God to infiltrate me and my ways, convict me and show me truth about myself, this verse would scare any and all living hell right out of me! This one too:

"For although they (God's people, said they) *knew God,*

they neither glorified Him as God
nor gave thanks to Him, but they became futile
(vain or foolish, perverted) *in their thinking and darkened*
in their foolish hearts.

Although they claimed to be wise, they became fools,
and exchanged the glory of the immortal God
for images of mortal man and birds and animals and reptiles."
Romans 1:21-23

October 27, 2018

- Vision: I asked the Lord, what do I do regarding the spirit that is in the church? And then, I saw the Revelation 12 woman confront the dragon; face to face. The Lord said, *"It's another spirit. The battle is on for souls."*

November 15, 2018

- Today, I saw a resolute evil in Donald Trump's face now. There is something going on.

CHAPTER 16

COME OUT FROM AMONG THEM

YEAR OF 2019

February 20, 2019

- Dream: I dreamt that myself and others were all inside this very large structure. It was like housing and shopping all put together in one place. Like a home and a mall. There were fires that broke out, outside of the building. It was as if it had overtaken everywhere. I was with people and had a little boy with me.

  Everyone was panicked and very concerned. But then the fire spread to the building we were in. There were firefighters outside trying to get the fires put out before it over took our building. We were all afraid and hoping that the fires would be put out. But they weren't and our building started to catch fire. People were running everywhere seeking cover. I remember thinking that I put all of my belongings in various places and I hoped that I had garments to cover us with. I was protecting the little boy that was with me.

  The embers began to fall from the ceilings and fall onto people and they were being burned. It grew rapidly. The fire fell on the little boy that was with me and it killed him. It was awful and surreal. They were urging us to seek shelter so we moved from place to place.

  Everyone around me, the fire fell on and they were burned. Many people did not make it. I made it out without being burned. But I was very alone and looking for the hotel that someone urged me to go to for protection and safety. I was walking around alone and on the phone with the other people who survived, to find them.

(*Author note: Whether this dream is natural or spiritual, it is always concerning to us when children are the casualties. That said, I believe God will show us the truth of the horrors to come, where even the most innocent among us will be affected).

April 4, 2019

- I see in the spirit, a press coming from the right side and pressing down hard where President Trump is standing, but it will make him stronger.

May 2, 2019

Telling the Enemies Secrets

- I have continued to pray exposure on our Government. I still see Donald Trump coming out of everything looking good.

- I have concerns about our Government with North Korea. This is historical, but I don't trust it.

- The French President Macron is talking about a One World Order.

- We need to watch Russia and Iran, something is going on with them. There are big money deals going on with Russia and Iran.

- Also important to note: President Trump is setting up the US Embassy in Jerusalem. Who's seat is this anyway?

May 13, 2019

- Regarding our Government, I am sensing eminent, eminent danger. Once it is locked in, the Government is definitely, definitely over us.

Father, Everything You have said to us since 2013 about the last days, about Russia, all the Words we have heard from You, it is here, it is active. Yet, Father if they vote one more time for this man, Donald Trump, it is the end; it is that time of the end. There is nothing he won't be able to do. He is doing everything in plain sight and no one is doing anything about it; he is getting away with it all. He is twisting it up in our faces and the people are eating it like fodder. He is turning our Nation into a one man show. The Republicans and the Christians are bowing down to him.

God has told us from way back that division is coming and in 2014 He told us not to be a part of it.

May 29, 2019

- I hear the word: *"California"* (The Lord spoke this Word before in 2009, 2014, 2015 and 2017).

- Also, I hear: *"Governor, Government."* I see something in California breaking off and away; it's like the whole becomes a part. I don't know what it pertains to.

- **Vision:** I hear *"Elected Government Officials"*. I see someone walking with their hand in the air and they have this red, white and blue thing around their neck. It looks like a medallion or a ribbon. They are walking like they won. I heard the word *"Celebrated."* It is interesting because a lot of Revelation talks about what goes on in the West and that is where the Anti-Christ comes from. I believe the Lord has shown me, according to scripture in Daniel, he comes from the West. Somehow the Catholic Church and the Anti-Christ are connected together.

- The Lord said to me *"Magnetism was on the rise."* (This word "Magnetism" was given in 2011)

  The meaning is: a physical phenomenon produced by the motion of electric charge, resulting in attractive and repulsive forces between objects. The ability to attract and charm people: synonyms are allure, attraction, fascination, enchantment, magic spell charisma, animal magnetism.

  The Anti-Christ has this ability. That is what is on the earth right now; And God says it is on the rise! We need to be more aware.

  We saw the depths that Donald Trump went down into (May 12, 2017). Now we are seeing magnetism is rising up. People are not going to notice, it because you can't see it, it just draws you to it. The people will go by how it *feels*.

- I heard the words *"Destruction of the people."* When I heard these words, it is like an agreement they have to reduce the population by destruction. They want to reduce us because it would make us more manageable.

- *"Promotion of programming."* I've heard "rise of magnetism" and now, "promotion of programming". It is like the same thing. Programming is where they are brainwashing us. No wonder God said to us before, *"change the channel",* we do not want to be part of that programming.

- I hear, *"Dispose" and "Criminal".* <u>Dispose</u> means: 1. Get rid of by throwing away or giving or selling to someone else: discard or abandon, kill and destroy, eliminate, dispatch, execute, put to death. Another word is consume; quickly or enthusiastically food or drink. 2. Bring (someone) into a particular frame of mind. 3. Arrange in a particular position. Determine the course of events.

- That is what the handshakes underground (May 12, 2017) were all about; they were disposing at that point and the Word of the Lord, *"destruction of the people"* goes with it.

- I heard President Trump accusing certain people of treason in this Country. I believe he will bring his rage out on anyone who has offended him.

- **Vision:** The Lord is showing me in an instant, life out of the darkness. He says, *"Creation takes place and life comes out of the depth."* He is reminding me that the reason He created mankind on the earth was to be like Him. He has called us to be creators and it has not happened because of lies and religion being in the way. So creation groans and travails (natural disasters) to get the people's attention. The sons and daughters of God are to become Co-Creators. The original plan was to be a creator with Him. He has restored that to us through His Son.

July 8, 2019

The Lord spoke to me saying, *"The American church mindset is about careers, gifts, callings. And they have a lot of pride in that."* He has not had many people out there that have not made their calling an idol.

July 28, 2019

- **Vision:** I was parked in a parking area while I was vacationing in Texas and I saw a light beaming, shining up and onto a tall American flag. As I watched the flag blowing in the breeze, in an open vision, the flag changed in front of me. It looked similar to the one we have now, but some things were changed on it.

  Instantly, I knew this was the "New America" much like

Hitler's regime in his day; the New Germany. I knew it clearly as I sat there, that this day is coming. Also with the New flag, the New America would be against the Old America and the New will persecute the Old and they will want to kill them off. The Old America would have to go underground to survive, much like the believers did in the early church. It appears to be the opposite. Usually it is the old persecuting the new. But not in this case.

- **Vision:** I don't know these words. I think they might be military terms. I see a map of America. I see the states sectioned off and divided. Inside of each state there are little square boxes and different sections and divisions of everything. I hear the words:

- *"Squadrons"*

- *"Battleground"*

- *"Embattlement"*

This has something to do with the flag change; it all goes together. This could be division like divided or division like the sectioned off areas.

- He is warning of a lure, *"Watch out for the lure."* (Definition of lure: an inducement to pleasure or gain; artificial bait used for catching fish; appeal, attraction, enticement, temptation, turn on, betray or beguile**).**

- All these things changing in America, it's time for the prophets to rise and address the church. There are the black whales and their connection to Russian prisons, the worst criminals. Then my dream of the authorities being on the side of the enemy. I believe that is what is happening in America. We are going to go into a brand new type of America. Those that stood for 'America is great' not the ones that say, 'make America great'. Those that loved

America, will be the ones persecuted because the new regime will want to kill them off.

August 5, 2019

- **Vision:** I saw a door open in 2020 and the Russians walked right in, strolling in without any problem.

  God told us in 2014 to keep our eye on the Russians. I see the doors opening for them to come right into our country; just welcoming them in and they are not being fought against. I remember in July 2018 when the President was traveling abroad, the Lord said that everything was set from that point forward. Everything God has been talking about is already set in stone. I perceive it is a done deal.

- And these are some of the changes: the American Flag and our money. And everything that it belongs to these. What they represent in our Country.

- What I am hearing is, *"The people are ready for it."* They have been being conditioned.

- After this next election (2020) everything will be changed, blatantly.

August 18, 2019

- **Vision:** The Lord wants to talk about the Nations. *"Peace, peace when there is no peace."* I saw a giant dark shroud over the people. This is a big wave coming in and it has to do with a big lie and cover-up and it will look like one thing, which goes with the peace, peace and the prosperity. They will make it look like something is prosperous, but it is the exact opposite.

Under that darkness, behind it, was total poverty. What I am seeing from the Lord, is that the lie in this Nation is already here, but the event has not come as of yet. It is a huge lie and a cover-up. It's worse than communism. Last July, I said it was set.

- Now I hear Him say: *"The time of trouble as the world has never seen."* I hear the scripture: *"For the eyes of the LORD run to and fro throughout the whole earth, to show himself strong in the behalf of them whose heart is perfect toward him. Herein you have done foolishly: therefore from henceforth you shall have wars"* 2 Chronicles 16:9.

- The "middle of the road" (luke warm) people who are "Christianity", not committed to Him, will suffer affliction.

> *"I know your deeds; you are neither cold nor hot.*
> *How I wish you were one or the other! So because*
> *you are lukewarm, and neither hot nor cold,*
> *I am about to spit you out of My mouth."*
> Revelation 3:15-16

Even this is in order to give them a chance for repentance, because of God's mercy. *"For judgment without mercy will be shown to anyone who has not been merciful. Mercy triumphs over judgment"* James 2:13.

- **Vision:** God is showing me, people with their eyes wide, like mesmerized from shock, it is a brain washing, like witchcraft and under a spell, because the people are in agreement with it. Their flesh is so given over to the enemy, that this spirit of witchcraft has no problem using them as hosts, because the people are in agreement with it.

- The Lord says, *"Don't be shocked when they fight you. Don't be shocked when they disagree with you. Don't be shocked when they don't receive. This has settled on them heavily; they are one with it."*

- I hear: "Heavenly challenges ahead." It is like a warning sign. *"No man has seen* (this) *neither ear* (has) *heard."* I believe what He is saying is this has never been done before or seen before, what He is getting ready to do and what is happening on the earth. This is what it says in Revelation and in Daniel.

- I just heard the Lord say, *"You can understand them* (the people) *all the way to Hell, because that is where they are going, if they don't repent."*

- He says, *"I'm the only One that can change their hearts of stone."* He said, *"Love lays down its life for its friends."*

Sometimes God shocks me by what He says. His Words are strong. But they have to be to get through sometimes. Love always wins against witchcraft. Love is the answer and is shown through kindness and respect, which is a superpower. Seal this to our hearts Father.

- I perceive in my spirit that the extreme deception will take place within a year (not this year) for it to grow. It won't be made manifest, by the caveat of it being deception. It is more of an un-manifest, if you will. The only ones that will know will be the ones hearing from God. So, the manifestation will be somewhat, 'to be revealed', otherwise no one will know, because they will be under this deceptive power.

- When the kings rise, that is when Jezebel shows up. But so do the prophets (false and true). Keep us attentive and alert Father so we know what is going on.

August 19, 2019

Remember last July God said it's finished and so it will now begin. I have been warning a lot this year that it is happening and it will happen right in front of us. There is nothing we can do about it, except pray for ourselves to be ready by listening to God and for other's salvation.

August 26, 2019

- **Vision:** I ask You Father, regarding the candidates that are running for President in this country in 2020. Is Donald Trump going to win or another?

  Just then, I saw a vision of a stage. On it, there was an atmosphere and Donald Trump was alone on the stage to the left of center. He gets reduced into the atmosphere. He becomes very small, but no one else is on the stage. The atmosphere *is* the Anti-Christ spirit and he takes over President Trump and operates through him.

September 13, 2019

- The Lord spoke to me saying the following Words: He said, *"Hebrews 12,* it is upon us all now.

- *"Quit speaking the problem."*

- *"Giants are in the land, so you need giant leaps of faith."*

- *"Many people's "faith" will not enable them to make it* (their faith falls short). *I am requiring more of these who say they believe in Me, that they take ahold of My strength in this hour."* The only power is God's strength, which is His Word Only.

- I hear a sound in the background, *"Sound the alarm."*

- *"The choices are for all of mankind on the earth; how you choose will be your affliction."* It's Revelation 8 and Hebrews 12; It's all about choices our own choices how it will turn out for us. Matthew 24, the beginning of sorrows. *"Enter in at the narrow, the strait gate. Wide is the path that leads to destruction."*

- *"Many people will be cut off* (cut short) *during this time. These are afflicted people and they will not understand."* Psalm 34:19 says, *'Many are the afflictions of the righteous but the Lord delivers them out of them all.'* That is the distinction between those that belong to God and those that do not. There will be affliction, but the Lord delivers out of the affliction, if you belong to Him. We must be choosing God's way no matter what. It is coming on the whole earth and the enemy is here to implement it.

- **Vision:** *"The enemy has given them* (the church – carnal Christians) *enough truth to bait them* (I saw a hook in their mouths) *and go in the wrong direction, so that they all believe the lie."*

September 17, 2019

- Dream: The Bride is in Trouble. Next I was on ground level with many, many, many women. It appears that the Church service was over and we were all walking outside. The ocean was across the street. Suddenly, you could see a huge wave coming right at us. We all started to run back to the church. But many of the women were caught up in the wave and many others of us were soaking wet, but we recovered and kept running toward the huge mega church for safety. I was encouraging other women who were exhausted, but needed to get to safety.

  When suddenly I turned back to look and I saw that there was another huge wave coming. I began to warn and help the women. The pastor was out there too and was seemingly trying to help. The wave did hit and only some recovered and made it.

- I've had many other dreams about title waves and tsunami's and the remnant bride over the years.

- A revelation I had was about the least offenders to the greatest offenders. The least are the ones that don't see clearly because of their own wounds. They are acting out their wounds. The greatest are those that choose to demean, defile, control, be jealous etc. It is about their choices.

- Dream: I also had a dream earlier in the year about India being involved with the political arena in the United States. (*Author Note: Kamala Harris is part Indian).

September 20, 2019

- Vision: The Lord is showing me the Words, *"Traitors in the camp".* I saw it like a military and they are catching people and marching them to their sentencing. In addition, it also reminds me of how the prophet, Balaam was a traitor to God's people.
- I heard: *"Coroner's report."* That is basically a death report.

- Texas is under a lot of warning from God. They are in the center of the United States. What kind of covenants did they make and break?

- I heard the Lord saying: *"The experiment is almost over."* I then I saw great changes taking place in the earth, and I see leaves going through changes so fast; changing as quick as spring, summer, fall and winter; very quickly. I think of the scriptures, *"redeeming* (rescue, seize up, purchase) *the times for the days are evil"* (Ephesians 5:16). And, *"Except those days are cut short, no one will survive, but for the elects sake, they will be cut short"* (Matthew 24:22 and Mark 13:20).

Then I hear the Words:

- *"Original plan"*

- *"Releasing agent"*

- *"Conflict"*

- *"Source code".*

- *"DNA"*

- *"Human suffering"*

It's already here and going to be worse in the days ahead. God is saying, this is what is now - the quickening of the time. Bar codes are coming to mind.

- *"Chosen few"*

- *"Straight is the gate and narrow is the path that leads to life and few that be there find it"* Matthew 7:14. And He gives us instruction: *"Enter in at the straight gate."* Matthew 7:13. Where is it? His Word.

- *"Come out from among them and do not be a participator with other men's sins"* 2 Corinthians 6:17.

- *"Relinquish"*

- *"Anguish"* Such as the world has never seen. *"For there will be greater anguish than at any time since the world began. And it will never be so great again"* Matthew 24:21.

- I hear a proclaiming, *"there is no change on the earth".* No matter what God is doing, there is not enough change to stop, that this is the last days.

  I hear it as if someone is telling God, I'm looking around down there and there is no change, no change in human behavior. He can't let us continue this way; He has to put a stop to it. It is perhaps an angel I am hearing, crying out in the Heavenlies, that there is no change here or anywhere.

- *"Scourged"*. It means to whip someone as a punishment. It is what I am hearing about, *"repeat offenders"*, that they will be scourged. I took that as the enemy getting ahold of them. It will be a cycle of condemnation, never getting over it, because they hide their sin instead of denouncing it. We need to keep in the light, everything we do.

September 23, 2019

- **Vision:** When I see Donald Trump's face, I see evil on him. Lord, You said in July of last year (2018) that all is set. I see something not right in him. Mercy and salvation on America, Father.

- We know that You said that, You removed Yourself from the politics of this Nation and yet the Christian and Republican politicians are saying, Donald Trump has cast out Jezebel (witchcraft) out of the White House and being likened as King Cyrus. If he is, we are going backwards (Persia, Babylon and then Assyria) and yes we know according to the Word, Babylon is to come. That is what the book of Revelation and Daniel says.

It will get way, way worse after Donald Trump is voted in again. Whatever happens is going to be worse. We are at the crossroads right now. If it is not Donald Trump who is in office, there is a vacancy and what will take its place is worse. I don't know how it is possible. But I do consider Kim Clements's word about gold and California. I don't know if that is someone taking his place or something joined together to him. We will see. But God has taught me to listen to Him first and foremost, not to assume or presume.

- The President has been saying, "if the Democrats are successful in removing him from office, "that it will cause a civil war, a fracture in this Nation from which our country will never heal". We are living in the days of the love of many turning extremely cold (Matthew 24:12). Everything now is political.

- This is where I think we are right now: in Revelation 12:10-12:

> *'Then I heard a loud voice saying in heaven,*
> *"Now salvation, and strength, and the kingdom*
> *of our God, and the power of His Christ have come,*
> *for the accuser of our brethren, who accused them*
> *(Gods people) before our God day and night,*
> *has been cast down.*
>
> *And they (God's people) overcame him (the accuser, the devil,*
> *Satan)by the blood of the Lamb and by the word of their testimony,*
> *and they did not love their lives to the death.*
>
> *Therefore rejoice, O heavens, and you who dwell in them!*
> *Woe to the inhabitants of the earth and the sea!*
> *For the devil has come down to you, having great wrath,*
> *because he knows that he has a short time.'*

This is what time it is. All that I am seeing and sensing that God is saying; "Woe to those who are on the earth." This is where we are at. This is when the love of many grows cold. I am encouraged that heaven is rejoicing at this, as God's Kingdom of Heaven dwells within all those who believe (trust, hope and have faith) in Him. Our hope is in Him.

All of the false information and the accusations of one another, will cause betrayal and rob our hearts of the love of God. Being able to stand through this adversity is God's main objective of this book.

The Words of Yahushua speaking of the times we are in now:

"At that time many will fall away and will betray and hate one another and many false prophets will arise and mislead many.

Because of the multiplication of wickedness, the love of most will grow cold. But the one who perseveres to the end will be saved.

And this gospel of the kingdom will be preached in all the world as a testimony to all nations, and then the end will come."
Matthew 24:10-14

September 27, 2019

I am hearing the following Words:

- *"Transaction and Detail"*

- *"Negated and Negotiated"*

- *"Divided and Division"* I see something split down the center.

- *"Catch 22"* Like an impression or a technicality. Something small. (This has been brought up twice before).

- *"Speak the Word, not the problem".*

October 20, 2019

- **Vision:** January 2021 will be a New Year and new President (for the election in November 2020), but I see the same President. Back in November 2015, it was clear he was the people's choice and I found myself depressed. It was what the people could not see and it is still what the people cannot see and that is what the scripture says too. That is why You have raised up Prophets, because they can see and they can announce what God shows them, whether the people like it or not.

- I hear a Word in the spirit, *"Dual heresy."* Heresy means a belief or opinion contrary to orthodox religious (especially Christian) doctrine. Dual; like a double whammy.

- **Vision**: I saw and heard, *"The church is split between division and delusion."* (*that is* dual heresy). Both are deceptive. Out of them, God has a remnant. I hear a report from Heaven: I call Your people out from among them. That they come into the unity of faith and not the unity of the doctrines. I call Your people, that hear Your Voice, out from among them to the unity of the faith! That is how we will know who belongs to God. That is the only thing that can please God. If they can't prove to you their faith, don't believe them, because they don't think like God.

  The proof of faith is what you actually do, not (only) what you talk about. Otherwise, you are a liar. Let our light shine so brightly, that people can see the difference between talking faith and doing faith. Let it be so pronounced, to see the difference. We agree with You Lord, to be conformed to You.

- The Lord says on the dual heresy: *"it is dual doctrine"* and He says, *"Don't agree with either one of them."*

- **Vision:** What I see coming is chaos and confusion, that is why I think it will be Donald Trump who wins the 2020 Election. The people agree with him. We can't afford to have anything in us against him or for him; we must be led by the Spirit.

  I see the people agree to such a degree, then that is where the President says, "I have so much power, I can do anything I want. I have said from the get-go I could stand in the middle of 5th Avenue and shoot someone and get away with it."

He has bragged about the things that he can do and has gotten away with them. That is what Daniel says about Anti-Christ. Donald Trump is not like anyone else and doesn't think like anyone else. And we know this also from all his advisors; that he does only what he wants to do. This is the only person I know that matches the scripture in our time in America. I believe that is what God was saying last year (July 2018). If he is voted in again, it is not only an Anti-Christ system, but a man; that's what I believe. I had a controversy in my spirit last year and God had to get me to understand it is a system now, so don't look at one person; it is bigger than one man. But, I see him getting the whole world to do what he wants.

December 10, 2019

- I have been praying and asking the Lord for the next step on this with President Trump. What I feel I have received from the Lord, is that he will get away with it (all he is doing against America and the American people that they do not know about). I saw him prevail and stand.

- If this is that time then I have to consider the scripture in Daniel about the deadly wound and he could recover. Impeachment would be a deadly wound. Or to recover would be to be voted back in, in 2020. In Daniel, 8:23, it says a man who understands dark sayings will stand up and rise. The people close to President Trump says, he speaks in code. When I hear him speak, I hear purposeful confusion (which is not confusing at all if you are really listening, then you can hear and understand what he is doing). (*Authors Note: Donald Trump did overcome the impeachment trials, February 2020).

"And in the latter time (Final end) *of their kingdoms(s),*

when the transgressors (rebellion, rebels, revolt) *are come to the full (have been completed), a king of fierce* (strong, mighty, insolent – showing a rude and arrogant lack of respect – greedy) *countenance and understanding* (discerns, considers carefully) *dark sentences* (sinister schemes, riddles, mysterious, perplexing), *shall stand up. And his power* (a kind of lizard, in a list of unclean creeping things. A chameleon) *shall be mighty* (consecutive), *but not by his own power* (a kind of lizard, in list of unclean creeping things. A chameleon)*: and he shall destroy* (act corruptly, bring to ruin) *wonderfully* (to be surpassing or extraordinary, fulfill things hard to do, show power) *and shall prosper* (advance) *and practice* (construct, **consecutive**), *and shall destroy* (jeopardize, corrupt, devastate, ruin) *the mighty* (a Nation, numerous) *and the holy* (Sacred, Saints) *people* (of God)."
Daniel 8:23-24

Are we listening?! Are we paying attention?!

December 16, 2019

- If President Trump stays President, we are getting ready to go into hard, hard times.

December 21, 2019

- Vision: When I woke up this morning, I saw in a vision, a bear just casually walking on all fours, moseying along. And it reminded me of the vision I had in 1998.

December 27, 2019

- Vision: I saw another bear paw with claws and it was striking its claws into the ground.

December 30, 2019

- **Vision:** I see giants everywhere. I am recalling the Word where the Lord said on September 3, 2019, that giants were in the land. They are like a hierarchy over these other unseen realms. That they are dictating what to happen, because they are building their structures and doing what they want to do, to create the world that they want to create in the unseen, for it to line up in the everyday world that we live in. The strongholds are set and they will crush us, unless we are stronger than them.

  Greater is He that is in us than He who is in the world – 1 John 4:4. We must let Him demonstrate it through us by His Spirit. It is not by our own might, nor by our own strength, but by His Spirit! Zechariah 4:6.

- Lord, we have to become stronger (through Your strength) and that is why You wrote the book of Daniel and Revelation, to let people know how bad it will be. If we are not that strong, we will not make it. We will fall away and not notice or go through very hard times. It will be whatever way Satan can get us.

- **Dream:** I fell asleep finally and I had asked the Lord to minister to me through dreams. I dreamed that there was chaos at the border. I was waking up in-between and wondering, which border was this. I saw it was the Mexico border. I felt that the Mexican authorities were going to retaliate when this wall goes up completely. There was tension on both sides; especially on theirs. When Americans were on their side of the border, they made it difficult for us to get back. On that side of the border, the Americans were being fined heavy, unaffordable fines to be able to get out of prison and they were stuck over there.

CHAPTER 17

GOD'S MERCY AND SALVATION

YEAR OF 2020

February 20, 2020

- I heard the Words: *"California rising".*

May 4, 2020

- Upon waking, I heard that the envelope was sealed on the election and that Donald Trump's Candidacy was sealed. I saw the envelope being handed over. I heard confirming words that he was the man chosen to lead Anti-Christ (System, movement). I saw some thing, that was more in the future, that showed that he was proud of a deadly wound that he had taken and had overcome it and was bragging about it (Revelation 13:3).

May 10, 2020

- Dream: Last night, through dreams, I saw windows of time, in which, each was perfected through suffering (Romans 8:17).
  There were 9 windows. And each one was meticulously paid attention to by the Lord and had suffering (assigned to it) over the course of time.
  By the time the suffering was complete, each window was pure and was able to bring healing to others just by its virtue, whether by one looking at it or touching it.
  When I woke, there was more insight, but I concluded that these 9 Windows were all the fruit of the spirit:

Love
Joy
Peace
Patience
Kindness
Goodness
Faith
Gentleness
Self control

Galatians 5:22-23.

May God be glorified through the cup of suffering that he has chosen for us, who choose to follow Him, according to His purpose in our lives (Matthew 20:22-23).

"If we suffer, we shall also reign with him:
if we deny him, he also will deny us."
2 Timothy 2:12

June 17, 2020

While praying for the rally in Tulsa, OK. On June 20, I heard the Lord say:

- *"Triggered Decision".*

- **Vision:** I see President Trump with his fists up. He grabbed ahold of something that was up in the air and his face was twisted with it. As he grabbed ahold of this thing in the air (I can't see what it is, as it appears to be invisible), he twists it so hard, that his face was contorted. As he is doing this, he has a vengeance. A vengeance to twist everything and I heard the Lord say, *"He will rule with an iron fist."*

- *"The days of him looking submitted to anything is over."* I saw, that at times, he would show that part of his personality and he looked cordial and gentlemanly. I heard that those days are over. I don't know if that is now or after the election. Father, is there anything we can do as we are here to pray Your will. I hear the Lord saying, *"Warn My people."*

- **Vision:** I see a warning. The parable of the virgins. In the vision, they are waiting for the Lord. They are all very excited that the Bridegroom is coming. But then, there are others that are dressed as brides. They come and say, 'give us *your* oil, because we don't have enough'. Don't be robbed by them. Those that truly follow the Lord, know what time it is. He is serious, telling us, *"keep your lamps trimmed and full of oil"*. We are to warn the others, to go get their own oil from the Lord (Matthew 25).

- **Vision:** I saw a weaving, a tapestry of sorts and He is trying to walk through it. He can barely get through.

- The Lord says, *"The way of the cross has been woven so tightly, like a game, with My people, that I can barely make it through the midst of them."*

- Some other Words I hear in the spirit are, *"Trade agreement", "Negotiation".*

- Father, what else can we do? He tells me, *"Strengthen the Saints."*

- He says, *"Stay in His Presence and be pure."*

All Words of the Lord in this book were written before they had come to pass. While obviously, some of the Words written are yet still to come to pass.

A reminder for all of us: *"But watch yourselves, or your hearts will be weighed down by dissipation* (recreation, entertainment, self indulgence, party life), *drunkenness, and the worries of life—and that day will spring upon you suddenly like a snare. For it will come upon **all** who dwell on the face of all the earth.* **So keep watch at all times and pray that you may have the strength to escape all that is about to happen and to stand before the Son of Man"** Luke 21:34-36.

A PRAYER FOR MERCY

Father in Heaven, I come to You in the Name of Your Son, Yahushua. I ask You for forgiveness of sins, of unrighteousness and iniquities. I ask that You would pardon the separations of Your people, to give them time to consider the Truth and Intentions of Your Written Word. And that they would take time to consider what your servant has written in this book. I pray for their understanding and breakthrough in their spirit.

Holy Father, for the blindness that has covered Your people's minds and the hardness of heart, that comes through the deception of their sins and separations from You, I ask you for your forgiveness and I take authority over the enemy, binding up his work and his evil intent in and over lives, that blinds them to the knowledge of the Truth of Your Word and the leading of Your Holy Spirit. I cut asunder any and all alignment of their thoughts that are in congruence with the power of the enemies of God, in the Name of Yahushua.

It is time now, to come out from among them, to hear the sound of Your voice and to respond to the prompting of Your Spirit. I ask You Father, to help them let go of the things they have clung to, to be good receivers of Your Truth and to come out of agreement with the enemy in every way, no matter what or who stands in the way, no matter what the cost. That they would love You more than they love their own opinions and more than their own doctrines and traditions. That You are their hearts desire once again. Their first love.

Lastly, but foremost, I pray for Your gift of repentance to be granted to them. It is godly sorrow that leads us to repentance. That as they let go of and renounce the things that have been brought to light, that greatly offend You, that they would repent, turn entirely from the life that is not in agreement with You and turn to You with their whole heart. That you would grant them Your heart and Your mind and lead them by Your Holy Spirit, as You promised for those who love You and agree with You and Your Word.

Father, I pray mercy for Your people. And that as You shed light to reveal Yourself to them, that You would grant them grace to grow in the knowledge of *Your* Truth daily. Washing their minds, not with the world or the things they thought they knew or with the agreements of others, but with sincerity, not loving their life more than You.

I ask this in the Name of the Savior, the Messiah, the Shepherd of Your flock, Yahushua, on the behalf of those whom You have foreknown from the foundation of the World, Your Sons and Daughters. Amen ~

"For you were once darkness,
but now you are light in the Lord.
Live as children of light (for the fruit of the light
consists in all goodness, righteousness and truth)
and find out what pleases the Lord.

Have nothing to do with the fruitless deeds of darkness,
but rather expose (to *convince* with solid, compelling *evidence,*
prove wrong, correct) *them.*

It is shameful even to mention what the disobedient do
in secret. But everything exposed by the light becomes
visible—and everything that is illuminated becomes a light.

This is why it is said: "Wake up, sleeper,
rise from the dead, and Christ will shine on you."

Be very careful, then, how you live—not as unwise
but as wise, making the most of every opportunity,
because the days are evil.

*Therefore do not be foolish, **but understand***
what the will of the Lord is."
Ephesians 5:8-17

~

"He reveals the deep things of darkness
and brings deep shadows into light."
Job 12:22

~

"For God will bring every deed into judgment,
along with every hidden thing, whether good or evil."
Ecclesiastes 12:14

~

"My conscience is clear, but that does not make me innocent.
It is the Lord who judges me. Therefore judge nothing
before the appointed time; wait until the Lord comes.

He will bring to light what is hidden in darkness
and will expose the motives of the heart.
At that time each will receive their praise from God."
1 Corinthians 4:4-5

~

"For My eyes are on all their ways. They are not hidden from My
face, and their guilt is not concealed from My eyes."
Jeremiah 16:17

~

"Remember therefore how you have received and heard.
Keep it, and repent.
If therefore you won't watch,
I will come as a thief, and you won't know
what hour I will come upon you."
Revelation 3:3

~

"Humble yourselves, therefore, under God's mighty hand, that he
may lift you up in due time."
1 Peter 5:6

"Be humble before God,

because you have not been workers together with
him, but have received much of his grace in vain."
(Unknown)

May God's Mercy and Salvation be with you and your house.
Acts 16:31

Made in the USA
Coppell, TX
20 December 2020